Shared Wisdom

use of the self in pastoral care and counseling

Pamela Cooper-White

Fortress Press
Minneapolis

2004

For my family

All biblical quotations are from Victor Roland Gold, Thomas L. Hoyt Jr., Sharon H. Ringe, Susan Brooks Thistlethwaite, Burton H. Throckmorton Jr., and Barbara A. Withers, eds., *The New Testament and Psalms: An Inclusive Version* (New York: Oxford University Press, 1995).

Cover image: © Philippe Lardy. Used by permission.
Cover design: Kevin van der Leek Design Inc.
Book design: Allan S. Johnson
Typesetting: Phoenix Type, Inc.

ISBN: 0-8006-3454-3

The paper used in this publication meets the minimum requirements of American National Standard for Information Sciences—Permanence of Paper for Printed Library Materials, ANSI Z329.48-1984.

Manufactured in the U.S.A.
08 07   4 5 6 7 8 9 10

Contents

Preface

AWARENESS IS GROWING in the fields of pastoral care and counseling that our own subjectivity as pastors, chaplains, and psychotherapists is central to our ability to be present and respond empathically to those who come to us for care and support. Classical training in recognizing our "own stuff" prepared us to examine the unfinished business of our own lives, so that our unresolved issues would not distort or interfere with the healing potential of our pastoral relationships. Most of us, however, have known at least subliminally that more is going on in the pastoral relationship and in our own subjective experience of those who come to us for help than just a polarity of "their stuff" and "my stuff." The pastoral relationship involves intersubjectivity, a sharing of understandings and meanings that arises in the "potential space" of exploration between us.[1]

There is a *shared wisdom* that grows and is held between helper and helpee in the pastoral relationship, and this shared wisdom exists in both conscious and unconscious dimensions of "I," "Thou," and "We." As we engage deeply and compassionately with the other, we find that we draw wisdom about that individual's perspective and experience from the shared exploration of meanings that arise between us and are cocreated uniquely in this pastoral relationship. How do we come to discern this shared wisdom?

The purpose of this book is to show that by delving into our own subjective experience of the counseling relationship, our "countertransference," we will come to a deeper, more empathic appreciation of the other and be more open to the other's own thoughts, feelings, insights, and hopes for growth and healing. The book will lead the reader through a method for pastoral assessment and theological reflection that makes use of the pastoral caregiver's own self as a primary tool for discernment and praxis. This method will involve several dimensions: prayerful contemplation; an examination of what is happening in one's own thoughts, feelings, impulses, and experiences; and theological reflection, leading to a deeper assessment of the needs of the other and ultimately a pastoral praxis that is based on the shared wisdom of both partners in the pastoral relationship. In addition, the book will help readers to become clearer about their own boundaries as helping professionals, recognizing that the ethics of care become at the same time more important and more comprehensible when professionals understand the intersubjective nature of the caring relationship.

The book consists of three main sections. The introduction and first three chapters trace the pastoral relationship and in particular an understanding of the idea of countertransference through its historic context. These chapters place this relationship within a larger framework of postmodern understandings of how we come to know another person.

The larger portion of the book, chapters 4 through 6, presents a method of pastoral assessment and theological reflection based on this use of the pastoral self in parish-based pastoral care, in chaplaincy, and in pastoral counseling and psychotherapy. This method is illustrated in four case studies. These are fictional composites, based on numerous pastoral situations and dilemmas in real life but fictionalized so that they do not represent any actual single person.

The final chapter offers the reader a relational theology that attempts to bridge new understandings of human relationships with our understanding of the relationality of God. The chapter suggests implications of this theology for pastoral praxis.

There are many ways to use this book. You may choose to read it from cover to cover. This will give you the most in-depth historical, theoretical, and theological grounding, as well as an overview of how countertransference and the use of the self may be applied specifically in the different disciplines of parish pastoral care and brief counseling, chaplaincy, and pastoral psychotherapy. You may, however, prefer to turn first to a chapter that most immediately addresses your particular pastoral focus or profession and then read other chapters for the background you find most relevant to your work. Especially if you are involved in continuing education, a seminary class, or training workshop, you may also choose to follow one or more of the vignettes in the introduction and chapters 4, 5, and 6 through the book, one at a time, to stimulate focused case study discussion.[2] These chapters are intended for practitioners at all levels of training and experience, since the need for self-reflection follows us throughout our professional lives.

Finally, every reader is encouraged to read the final chapter, including theological reflection on a more multiple and relational understanding of God, and on deepening our own practices of prayer and contemplation. We cannot access our awareness of our own self-experience and the life of feelings unless we also nurture our own selves emotionally, physically, intellectually, and spiritually.

From this commitment to our own ongoing spiritual formation, the nurture of our desire for God, flows the love of both self and neighbor that is at the heart of this book.

Acknowledgments

I have been moved by the generosity and wisdom of a great number of colleagues who read all or part of earlier versions. Thanks go to Phillip Bennett, Wally Fletcher, Sister Helena Marie, John Hoffmeyer, Pamela Holliman, and Robin Steinke, whose feedback was invaluable to this work in progress. Thanks also go to Sara Calderón, Florence Gelo, Carla Harris, Iris LaRiviere-Mestre, Charles Lindholm, Melissa Ramirez, Nelson Rivera, Eloise Scott, and Margaret Tyson for their close readings of case studies. Thanks also go to my daughter, Macrina Cooper-White, to Ann Delgehausen at Fortress Press, and to Constance Goldberg, John Kahler, Gordon Lathrop, Anna Mercedes, Marda Messick, Walter Zev Raine, and Gail Ramshaw for their helpful consultations, and to Paul Hansen for assistance with graphing "Gary's" genogram. I am particularly indebted to my editor at Fortress Press, Michael West, for his perceptive readings, dedication, and enthusiastic support of this project.

Deep thanks are also due to the Episcopal Church Foundation for providing me with a three-year fellowship to pursue the research summarized in chapter 6, and for ongoing support of the Fellows' Forum. I am also grateful for the ongoing intellectual stimulation and support of my many colleagues and students at the Lutheran Theological Seminary at Philadelphia. The treasure we have in the rich, multicultural, and warmly collegial seminary community provided an exceptionally fertile ground in which this project could grow! I also greatly appreciate the support and academic rigor of my colleagues in the Person/Culture/Religion Group of the American Academy of Religion and the Society for Pastoral Theology. Warm thanks also go to my clergy and lay colleagues at St. Martin-in-the-Fields Episcopal Church, Philadelphia, my spiritual companion and mentor Sharline Fulton, and my bishop, Charles Bennison, for providing the spiritual "holding environment" for my continued vocational discernment as a teacher, pastor, and writer. Most of all, I am grateful to my spouse, Michael Cooper-White, whose thoughtful and detailed reading of multiple versions of the book was invaluable. I am grateful beyond words for his patient listening, insightful questions, Saturday talks over decaf lattes, and always loving encouragement!

Permissions

"I Want Jesus to Walk with Me," African-American spiritual, quoted in chapter 4, from *This Far by Faith: An African American Resource for Worship* (Minneapolis: Augsburg Fortress, 1999), hymn 66.

Cesareo Gabarain, "Pescador de Hombres," in chapter 6, from Ediciones Paulinas, OCP Publications, 5536 NE Hassalo, Portland, OR 97213; translation by Madeleine Forell Marshall, Editorial Avance Luterano, from *With One Voice: A Lutheran Resource for Worship* (Minneapolis: Augsburg Fortress, 1995), hymn 784.

Figure 3, "Flow of Stress through the Family" in chapter 4, from Betty Carter and Monica McGoldrick, *The Expanded Family Life Cycle,* 3d ed. (Boston: Allyn and Bacon, 1999), 6.

Figure 5, "The Vertical Split" in chapter 5, from Heinz Kohut's "The Two Analyses of Mr. Z," *International Journal of Psycho-Analysis* 60 (1979): 11. Used by permission of Thomas Kohut.

Photo of the labyrinth and font at Grace Cathedral (Episcopal), San Francisco in chapter 7. Photograph by Cindy Pavlinac, Sacred Land Photography, San Rafael, California. Used by permission.

Earlier versions of portions of chapters 6 and 7 appeared as "The Use of the Self in Pastoral Care and Counseling," *The American Journal of Pastoral Counseling* (Haworth Press), and in chapter 7, "Higher Powers and Infernal Regions: Models of Mind in Freud's *Interpretation of Dreams* and Contemporary Psychoanalysis, and Their Implications for Pastoral Theology," in *Pastoral Psychology* (Kluwer Academic/Plenum Publishers, 233 Spring Street, New York, NY 10013), 50, no. 5 (2002): 319–43, adapted with permission.

Introduction

Linda

LINDA FELT LIGHT-HEADED as she sat in the church council meeting, attempting to project an attitude of calm that she did not feel. In her first year as pastor, Linda had introduced a practice of opening every church council meeting with "check-ins," during which each member shared something important about what was going on in his or her life. Following the check-ins, the council prayed for each member and for the parish and the community. At this meeting, Yvonne, the oldest member of the council, had quietly announced that she had been diagnosed with a recurrence of breast cancer and that this time it had metastasized to her liver. She had been given six months to a year to live. She planned to resign from the council after this meeting but had wanted to come and deliver the news in person. She seemed wan and tired but wanted to stay for the meeting and just be with the group for a while.

The council members at first received this news with shocked silence. Yvonne had seemed to be doing so well, and her cancer had been in remission so long that no one thought of her anymore as a "cancer victim." During prayer, a few members began to weep. The sense of dignity and self-containment Yvonne projected seemed to preclude hugging, but Linda did reach out and quickly squeeze Yvonne's hand. The group slowly found its way toward the evening's agenda. Although Yvonne herself was interested in "getting down to business," Linda felt tearful and distracted from the work at hand. As her eyes wandered to the old grandfather clock in the corner of the meeting room, she kept thinking of her grandmother Eleanor, who had died of cancer a few years before. Linda's mind filled with thoughts of how much she missed her, and how many times in recent years she had wished her grandmother could have been with her, to witness her graduation from seminary, her ordination, and the birth of her first child.

Gary

Gary threw on his blue chaplain's coat and looked over the call list for the morning. He was relieved that this was a day off for his Clinical Pastoral Education (CPE) students, so he could simply do pastoral visits and quietly catch up on work at his desk. Two volatile, angry students, Amanda and Jake, had gotten into it with each other in group supervision the day before, and after twelve years of supervising, Gary was feeling more than a little burned out on facilitating intense group processes.

Gary took the elevator to the seventh floor, the "peds" ward, and knocked on the door of room 716, where an eight-year-old boy named Daniel had just been moved from intensive care. Gary had learned from the nurses that Daniel was recovering from injuries sustained in a severe car accident, in which his mother's new boyfriend, Stan, had been driving drunk. Daniel's mother was also in the hospital, recovering from chest and facial injuries. Stan had been discharged after brief treatment in the ER and had not been heard from since. Daniel's father had been contacted where he lived out of state but had declined to come see him.

In the room, Gary found Daniel propped up in the hospital bed, surrounded by Nintendo game cartridges and one well-loved, scruffy stuffed elephant, a relic from earlier childhood. Daniel was watching cartoons on TV. Gary felt his heart lurch as he saw how thin and pale Daniel looked under the light hospital blanket. In spite of years of experience, Gary always felt awkward talking with children. Nevertheless, he somehow managed to initiate a connection with Daniel that seemed to open the door for further conversation about his loneliness, his feelings of abandonment by both his parents, and how God often felt very far away, too. Gary left the room after promising to return the next day, thinking how he might make contact with Daniel's parents.

As he headed for the elevator, Cora, the hospital social worker, approached him and said, "Daniel will be ready for discharge soon, but his mother won't, and there is no one to look after him. I was wondering, do you know any church people who could take care of Daniel for just a week or two?" Gary was surprised at how much he wanted to blurt out, "Daniel can come stay at my house! It's just me and my two cats, and there's plenty of room!" He bit his tongue and simply said, "Hmm, what a good idea; let me think about that." But Daniel's face haunted him as he continued to make his rounds the rest of the day.

Terence

Terence stormed out of the rectory, got into his Lexus, and slammed the car door, shutting out the last angry words his wife, Jane, was shouting at him from the front steps. "Dammit," he thought, "she knows how much pressure I'm already under. She knows I'm on the short list for bishop of Central Florida, and God only knows, I'm the right man for the job! And now she has to make a mountain out of a molehill about Susan—on whom I have not laid a finger, not once!" His tires screeched as he turned out of the driveway and drove the mile and a half to St. George's, the large, prestigious suburban church he had served as rector for three years.

The occasion for his wife's angry accusations was this morning's appointment: a meeting with Susan, the church treasurer. He was irritated that his day had already started badly. He admitted to himself that he looked forward to seeing Susan, whose shy smiles and light touches on his arm had become restorative for him these last few months. Susan's cool, light manner had been a welcome relief from the demands of home, with three teenage children and a wife who seemed perpetually frazzled and wanting more of his time. Susan never seemed to demand anything, and her efficient work with the church's financial accounts had in fact lightened his load considerably.

When Terence arrived at his office, his secretary, Betty, informed him in her usual gruff, matter-of-fact tone that she had had to squeeze in a pastoral appointment first thing that morning. Terence inwardly groaned but then brightened as Betty told him, "I thought you'd want to see this one right away. It's Elaine Bartles, and she wants to talk to you again about some marital issues." At that moment, Elaine came into the office and said, "I'm sorry to take up your time when you're so busy, but I really do need to talk to you, and your sermon on Sunday was just so inspiring to me about taking hold and changing what's wrong in my life." "No problem at all," Terence murmured in a soothing voice. Elaine's eyes welled up with tears as Terence ushered her into his office, his hand lightly touching her back. As his office door closed, Betty caught the scent of lilac perfume and pursed her mouth in what was becoming a habitual feeling of cynicism and dislike toward "our glad-handing priest."

Sara

Sara practiced pastoral psychotherapy out of a pleasant, sunny parish office that had been lovingly decorated by members of her local church community. Together, they had furnished the office with beautiful plants, a favorite watercolor painting, matching rocking chairs for her and her clients, and a basket of teddy bears and rag dolls. Her first appointment this afternoon was with Miranda, a thirty-one-year-old bank officer with a history of migraine headaches and panic attacks. Sara contemplated Miranda's name in her calendar with a mixture of affection and worry. Miranda had been seeing Sara for over two years and, after a long while, had confided several stories of sexual abuse at the hands of her uncle and one older brother.

Miranda recently had begun speaking to Sara in a small, baby voice, sitting on the floor close to Sara's knees, and clutching one of the teddy bears to her chest. Miranda would sometimes curl up there on the floor and sob with wordless grief and terror, and Sara had, just once during Miranda's last session, reached down and touched Sara's hair in a gesture of nurture and support. Miranda had looked up and smiled through her tears, and suddenly grabbed Sara's knees and hugged her legs. They had stayed in that position until the session ended ten minutes later, when without prompting Miranda slowly stood up, resumed her usual rather stiff adult posture, and wordlessly left the office. Miranda was now ten minutes late. Sara began to pace the office, wondering if the memories Miranda had accessed in the last session were overwhelming her. She began to consider that perhaps she should call Miranda to offer her an appointment at her own house, where Miranda might feel even more nurtured and safe.

~ ~ ~ ~

These four vignettes have something in common. Each of the clergy professionals in these case stories[1] is at a critical crossroads in his or her ministry. Linda, Gary, Terence, and Sara, each in his or her own way, is faced with a challenge that seems to be from an external source but actually is more internal and rooted deeply in each one's intimate history.

Linda is at risk for drifting off into a preoccupation with unresolved grief over a beloved grandmother's death. This preoccupation is distracting her from tasks that need her attention and, perhaps more perilously, drawing her into an over-close relationship of needy nurturing of Yvonne, which Yvonne has not requested.

Gary is lonely and experiencing some symptoms of burnout in some areas of his work. He feels awkward around children but able to make an unusually strong connection with the child Daniel. His heart goes out to Daniel, and he finds himself attracted to the role of the better parent for this child, who strikes him as a fragile, sensitive waif.

Terence is feeling the burdens and pressures of his own success, defined in terms of a ladder of achievement that he has been climbing rapidly his entire life. He is preoccupied with living up to a self-image of importance and accomplishment and often feels thwarted in his ambitions by the time demands of his wife and children. He enjoys the attentions of women in the parish who alternately idealize, soothe, and stimulate him in ways he does not experience at home. He is at risk for crossing a boundary, perhaps sexual, perhaps simply inappropriately intimate, as his parishioners begin to serve him emotionally on his meteoric climb toward being a bishop.

Sara already found herself at least two paces down one fork in the road when her patient[2] Miranda fell out of words into a profoundly emotional enactment and Sara stayed with her in a long moment of silent physical closeness. Sara now is at risk for continuing down that path of nonverbal care and nurture, because she finds herself so deeply moved by Miranda's vulnerability and trust, and also is enjoying how good it feels to be so needed.

These four clergy professionals are at crossroads but not necessarily at precipices. There is no need to assume that any of these four will automatically fall into dangerous or unconsidered enactments with the individuals in their care. In each case, there is an alternative path, which because of the very heightened degree of personal feeling and potential for affective involvement, could be a particularly powerful moment of healing and grace for those in their care. The key to each of these clergy professionals' choices and actions is the subject of this book: countertransference, or the use of the self in pastoral care and counseling.

For the purpose of this book, the term *countertransference* will refer to the sum total of thoughts, feelings, fantasies, impulses, and bodily sensations, conscious and unconscious, that may arise in the pastoral caregiver in relation to any person who has come for help. This represents a departure from classical psychoanalytic definition of countertransference, in which many generations of pastoral caregivers were trained. Based on the work of Sigmund Freud,[3] this classical definition viewed countertransference as unconscious distortions in the helper's perception due to unresolved internal issues usually rooted in early childhood. The concept originated as the counterpart to the "transference," Freud's term for the patient's projections, or transferring of experiences of parents and other authority figures from childhood onto the person of the therapist (or helping professional, or authority figure). From a classical point of view, the work of a caregiver around countertransference was to analyze and thereby neutralize any neurotic "baggage" that might hinder the work of therapy or care.

A newer view,[4] sometimes termed "totalist,"[5] encompasses this classical understanding but also expands beyond it. In the totalist definition, countertransference does include preconditioned patterns of relating developed in the helping professional's own childhood but may also be strongly influenced or even evoked by the *transference* of the helpee.[6] Transference, similarly, is defined as the sum total of the helpee's thoughts, feelings, fantasies, impulses, and bodily sensations, conscious and unconscious, toward the helping professional and may include, but again is not limited to, preconditioned patterns of relating developed in childhood.

In this understanding, transference and countertransference operate together to form a complex interrelation, referred to by some writers as "intersubjectivity,"[7] which operates at both conscious and unconscious levels. "Self" and "other" become intertwined in this relational matrix. Aspects of both "selfness" and "otherness" may be discovered in numerous places: internally in one's own thoughts, fantasies, and memories; externally in relation to the actual other; and in the "between" of the relationship itself—the interstices of the relationship as it is continually being coconstructed. This complex relation informs and generates patterns of meaning-making, which may be enacted or not enacted nonverbally, and also affects the quality of the healing (positive or negative) that evolves in the helping relationship over time.

Countertransference in this construction becomes a valuable tool. It is important to understand one's own neurotic vulnerabilities (from which no one is immune) and to become sensitized to one's own "buttons" or tender places within ourselves that are vulnerable to being pushed by others.

This is the classical contribution to the understanding of countertransference, which has been fruitfully taught in CPE and pastoral care curricula for generations. However, in the understanding of this book, countertransference is not only a hindrance to be worked through or analyzed away. It is also a valuable instrument for listening to the other, because in the unconscious relationship that grows between helper and helpee, our own thoughts, feelings, and fantasies literally absorb the thought life of the other, as we soak together in the intimacy of the helpee's shared confidences. By listening for the music of our own inner world as we sit with another, we listen to the other's music as well, through the counterpoint (both harmonious and dissonant) of shared wisdom that springs up between us. This is how the use of the self becomes a treasure for helping another.

My own interest in the topic of countertransference and the use of the self, like all good research topics, was "overdetermined" by both personal and clinical experience as a pastoral psychotherapist. My psychoanalytically informed clinical training began at a time when the totalist understanding of countertransference was becoming an increasingly strong focus of attention in the field of psychotherapy. This was a strong subjective fit for my own personal development, which fostered a high degree of interpersonal sensitivity and attunement. These factors, combined with my subsequent clinical experience, particularly with survivors of severe trauma and abuse, have resulted in a style of therapeutic practice that relies heavily on my own inner felt experiences of the patient from moment to moment, across all levels of awareness: cognitive, affective, and somatic. I do, of course, sift these experiences for aspects that relate more to my own subjectivity and biases. But I regard them, and have come increasingly to trust them, as an important and reliable channel of information about the inner world of the patient. I often feel as if I have "caught" something from this other person from across the room. I have come to trust that the more vivid this experience is in me, the more unmetabolized the experience is likely to be in the patient's own psyche, and therefore the more in need of being held—initially in my own awareness, until it can be handed back to the patient in words. This in turn initiates an important therapeutic sequence: (1) bringing the unmetabolized and unnamed mental contents up to a level of conscious awareness (however inchoate); (2) symbolizing this material via words or images that can be given words; and finally (3) facilitating an integrative process of meaning-making and working through.[8] This psychoanalytic approach to healing is further explored in chapter 6 on the use of the self in pastoral psychotherapy.

My work in the 1990s[9] in the area of abuse prevention and, in particular, the subject of clergy professional boundaries and sexual ethics also has heightened my interest in countertransference as it relates to the need for clergy self-awareness. In my most recent research, I have sought to explore further the area of pastoral counselors' own self-experience and self-care within the therapeutic relationship, this time from a more psychodynamic perspective. There is already a sizable body of literature on professional sexual ethics,[10] and it is not the purpose of this book to duplicate this work. I have been broadening my own research beyond situations where sexual or other ethical boundaries are violated, to explore sexual feelings in the countertransference where there are no inappropriate enactments. These efforts are aimed at investigating not only the negative and/or ethical aspects of countertransference, but also the positive and constructive psychodynamic aspects of countertransference as a useful tool in understanding a patient's reality.[11]

Readings in object relations and relational theory have further convinced me that it is artificial to attempt to isolate sexual or sexualized aspects of countertransference from aggressive aspects, narcissistic and other characterological structures in the personality, and other unconscious influences that may be at work in the intersubjective field between helper and helpee. I have increasingly come to suspect that isolating the sexual dimension from other aspects of the countertransference may inadvertently collude with the splitting off of sexual feelings from other dimensions of the helper's self-experience. Paradoxically, this can result in an increased risk for ethical violations via harmful enactments of what is dissociated. As one writer on clergy boundary violations, Carrie Doehring, suggests, it is often the aggressive component and not the sexual that is suppressed from conscious awareness. In her discussion of John Updike's novel *A Month of Sundays,* the aggressive component of the offending minister's countertransference is enacted sexually and then disguised under the rubric of "sex addiction."[12]

Therefore self-awareness is key, both in preventing ineffective or even unethical interventions and, importantly, in understanding the complex layers of communication, both conscious and unconscious, between helper and helpee. The thesis of this book is that the more thoughtfully these layers of conscious and unconscious communication are explored, especially by the helper through self-examination and consultation, the more effective the pastoral care or counseling will be. The understanding gained by introspection will enable a reduction in impulsive actions and unethical interventions and the potential for a much richer, safer, and more genuinely helping relationship.

~   ~   ~   ~

What one actually does with this deeper awareness of self and other will differ, depending on whether the specific relationship is one of parish-based pastoral care, chaplaincy, or longer-term, depth-oriented pastoral psychotherapy. For example, in parish-based pastoral care, it would be inadvisable to delve deliberately into unconscious material with a parishioner who has come for help. In long-term pastoral psychotherapy, however, this would likely be the primary focus of therapeutic conversation. But in either case, the self-awareness is the same and can be cultivated in a wide range of pastoral professions.

Our self-understanding, then, will be put to different uses depending on the type of helping we are doing. But the basic concept is the same: The more we are able to tune in to our own inner perceptions and to reflect on these in a thoughtful way, the more sensitively we will also be able to tune in to the nuances of the helpee's own feelings, wishes, and experiences. Then, in turn, we can use these insights to choose responses and interventions that are most appropriate to our role as helpers and to the helpee's needs.

CHAPTER ONE
Countertransference
A History of the Concept

THE THEORY OF INTERSUBJECTIVITY and the concept of an unconscious relationship were fully developed only in the latter part of the twentieth century. The notion of a relationship as a truly two-person coconstruction of reality, as opposed to two isolated subjects each regarding the other as an object, has been most fully developed in tandem with certain concepts relating to postmodernism, in particular, the concept of social constructivism. More will be said about the evolution of this idea in the history of countertransference in a later section of this chapter, and the topic will be fully explored in chapter 3.

The idea that one's thoughts and feelings could penetrate and thereby communicate with the psyche of another is not new, however. From its birth as an idea, countertransference has been understood to some degree as an arena in which the unconscious of the helpee touches the unconscious of the helper in a deep way. This chapter traces the history of the concept, with particular attention to the idea of unconscious relationship and the helper's use of self in the healing process.

Freud

Sigmund Freud referred to the countertransference in only two published papers.[1] In the first paper, "The Future Prospects of Psychoanalytic Therapy," written in 1910, he introduced the term almost as an aside, but in admonitory tones: "We have become aware of the 'counter-transference,' which arises in him [the physician] as a result of the patient's influence on his unconscious feelings, and we are almost inclined to insist that he shall recognize this counter-transference in himself and overcome it."[2] In 1915 in "Observations on Transference-Love," he continued in this cautionary mood: "Our control over ourselves is not so complete that we may not suddenly one day go further than we intended. In my opinion, therefore, we ought not to give up the neutrality toward the patient, which we have acquired through keeping the counter-transference in check."[3] In both papers, the tone is one of vigilance against seduction by a patient's conscious and unconscious erotic pulls on his affections. The only safeguard is an ever-attentive maintenance of emotional neutrality. It was during this same period that Freud wrote the following well-known statement likening the attitude of the analyst to the "emotional coldness" of a surgeon:

> I cannot advise my colleagues too urgently to model themselves during psychoanalytic treatment on the surgeon, who puts aside all his feelings, even his human sympathy, and concentrates his mental forces on the single aim of performing the operation as skillfully as possible . . . The justification for requiring this emotional coldness is that it creates the most advantageous conditions for both parties: for the doctor a desirable protection for his own emotional life and for the patient the largest amount of help we can give him to-day. A surgeon of earlier times took as his motto the words: "*Je le pensai, Dieu le guerit.*" ("I dressed his wounds, God cured him.") The analyst should be content with something similar.[4]

The discovery of countertransference was linked to a crisis, as was the idea of transference itself a decade before. Just as Freud's discovery of the concept of transference can be traced back to his rigorous scrutiny of his own failed treatment with "Dora" in the late 1890s,[5] the discovery of countertransference grew out of a Freud's dismay over a complex and destructive sexual relationship between C. G. Jung and Jung's patient Sabina Spielrein.[6] Freud's first-known use of the term *countertransference* appears in a letter to Jung, urging the younger man to keep his sexual urges in check. The avuncular and reassuring tone of the letter belies Freud's fear about the wider implications of the problem for psychoanalysis as a profession, as well as the potential damage to their friendship:

> Such experiences, though painful, are necessary and hard to avoid. Without them we cannot really know life and what we are dealing with. I myself have never been taken in quite so badly, but I have come very close to it a number of times and had a narrow escape. I believe that only grim necessities weighing on my work, and the fact that I was ten years older than yourself when I came to psychoanalysis have saved me from such experiences. But no lasting harm is done. They help us to develop the thick skin we need and to dominate the 'countertransference,' which is after all a permanent problem for us; they teach us to displace our own affects to best advantage. They are a blessing in disguise. The way these women manage to charm us with every conceivable psychic perfection until they have attained their purpose is one of nature's greatest spectacles.[7]

Freud saw countertransference as a threat, not only to individuals in treatment, but also to the reputation of psychoanalysis as a profession. His ensuing public silence on the topic reflected a growing sense of alarm. Freud wrote privately to Jung shortly before the breakup of their friendship, "I believe an article on 'countertransference' is sorely needed; of course we could not publish it, we should have to circulate it among ourselves."[8] In a thinly veiled reference to Jung himself, Freud also wrote this in his paper on "transference-love":

> For the doctor, ethical motives unite with technical ones to restrain him from giving the patient his love. Younger men especially, who are not yet bound by a permanent tie may succumb to the danger of forgetting the rules of technique and the physician's task for the sake of a wonderful experience . . . And yet it is quite out of the question for the analyst to give way. However highly he may prize love he must prize even more highly the opportunity for helping his patient over a decisive stage in her life.[9]

(Freud's view of the transference itself was one of pitched battle against the unconscious forces in the patient that threatened both patient and analyst.) Freud concluded that Dora's therapy had failed because he had not seen Dora's erotic transference to him.[10] In the decade that followed, Freud gained a great deal from clinical experience. In the case of the "Rat Man," Freud actually prevented this patient from bolting, as Dora had done, by naming and interpreting his hostile transference.[11]

Freud's classic definition of transference, stated most clearly in "The Dynamics of the Transference,"[12] can be summarized as follows: (An individual's patterns of relating develop early in childhood, particularly patterns of loving (including conditions for loving, impulses, gratifications, and aims). These become habitual and reproduce themselves in other relationships throughout life. Some of these patterns are conscious, and some undergo modifications later in life. However, libidinal impulses (that is, those having to do with sexual or aggressive urges) may get held up in development and go underground, where they can be expressed only in fantasy or buried in the unconscious. These unconscious impulses, Freud said, are most likely to be aroused in someone whose need for love is not being satisfactorily gratified in reality in his or her external life.)

Freud likened these habitual patterns to stereotypes, clichés, or, citing Jung's term, *imagoes*. Transference revives and re-enacts primitive father- and mother-imagoes, as well as experiences with siblings and other important figures from early in childhood. Transference manifests itself in extreme reactions or distortions in the patient's perception of the analyst (or other helping figure). This is how transference may be recognized for what it is in the analytic situation—it is characterized in particular by its excess, in both character and degree, over

what is rational and justifiable. The unconscious erotic component of the transference and the hostile or aggressive component would also manifest themselves
as the arena in which the patient would exhibit resistance to the interpretive
process. This resistance was what Freud would then analyze, eventually helping
the patient understand the unconscious origins of the intensity of his or her
feelings toward the person of the analyst, thereby reducing the likelihood of
similar irrational and potentially destructive distortions occurring in other relationships in the patient's life.

Freud concluded "The Dynamics of the Transference" in the language of a
heroic military struggle. The level of distortion in transference resulting from
withdrawal of the libido from consciousness bears similarities to the way dreams
work. The struggle must be engaged to draw the relationship back to reality. The
conflict occurs between three pairs of opposites: doctor versus patient, intellect
versus instinct, and recognition (insight) versus striving for discharge (what in
later terminology we might refer to as "acting out"). The transference is the
battleground on which "the victory must be won."[13] Victory will mean nothing
less than recovery from neurosis. The transference can never be forgotten or
ignored. Nothing else brings the patient's inner conflict more directly into the
analytic container, and the immediacy of the libido manifesting itself in the
here and now moment is what makes the struggle so powerful and so curative.
Freud granted the libido a strong measure of autonomy and even will, anthropo-
morphizing it by investing it with the quality of a worthy adversary. In his last
sentence, he stated, "It is impossible to destroy anyone in absentia or *in effigie*."[14]
Through transference, the libido shows itself in the here-and-now analytic
moment where it can be vanquished.

The heroic, military tone of this paper may reflect a consciousness of the
gathering political tensions in Austria, which erupted in the Great War two
years later. But the heroic tone also reflects the forces of opposition with which
Freud was contending personally and professionally in the years leading up to
the war. Freud's concern whether psychoanalysis elicited transference dynamics
more intensely than other therapies, and his references to Jung in this period,
have an increasingly defensive quality.

In the midst of an atmosphere of growing tension, the situation with Sabina
Spielrein exploded.[15] Freud had become involved with Spielrein as a consultant
to repair the damage caused by what Jung himself later called his "piece of knavery."[16] Spielrein had been a student in Freud's psychoanalytic circle and now
was a doctor publishing innovative psychoanalytic papers herself.[17] It was in
the very year (1911–12) that Freud was writing "The Dynamics of the Transference" that Spielrein contracted with him for a new analysis, to help her get
over the feeling that her life had been "smashed" by Jung.

Freud's recommendation to emulate the surgeon's "emotional coldness" was a reactive, not fully rational one. From case reports, it seems to have been a recommendation he himself honored more in the breach. However, in the years leading into the war, no one needed a thoroughgoing understanding of countertransference more than he did himself, together with Jung and Spielrein, with whom his own ambition, love, and disappointment were so entangled. After his break with Jung and his publication of "Observations on Transference Love" in 1915, which was in some sense his effort to put closure on that painful period, Freud never wrote about the subject again.

Ferenczi and His Circle

The disturbing and personal origins of the discovery of countertransference generated an air of secrecy about the subject similar to the incest taboo itself (which Jung's transgression with Spielrein had actually replicated). This infusion of the concept from the beginning with secrecy and shame was perpetuated through the decades like a "phobic dread"[18] suppressing open discussion about it among analysts, and even much introspection on the subject. Analysts in Freud's close circle did not take up the subject, with two notable exceptions: Sandor Ferenczi and Otto Rank. The eventual ruptures between Freud and Ferenczi and Rank were also due, then, in part, to the taboo surrounding countertransference.

Ferenczi and Rank are generally credited with being the first to introduce the practice of discussing with the patient the immediate experience of what was happening between them in the room.[19] In addition, Ferenczi's "active technique" involved close scrutiny of the countertransference, stemming from Ferenczi's belief that the patient was intuitively aware of the therapist's real feelings, biases, blind spots, and areas of unanalyzed neurosis. Ferenczi believed that the analyst, far from being a "blank screen," was an individual whose emotional responses had a direct impact on the analysis for good or for ill. Ferenczi even advocated occasional disclosure of the analyst's feelings to the patient.[20] This was considered by Freud and most of his followers as a radical departure from accepted technique, and it contributed to the eventual rupture between Freud and Ferenczi in the 1920s.[21]

Ferenczi, as the founder of his own Hungarian Psycho-analytical Society, was painfully marginalized from the mainstream of Freud's circle, but this also freed him to develop his own methods. Most influential among Ferenczi's students were his translator and literary executor, Michael Balint, and Balint's wife, Alice. A paper the Balints wrote in 1939 anticipates by five decades many ideas that are now current concerning the inevitability of mutual influence between patient and analyst.[22] The Balints' main interest was the treatment of extremely troubled patients, in whom they identified the notion of a "basic fault" arising from very early parental emotional neglect or abuse.[23] The intensification of feelings arising in the helper from severely abused and anguished helpees has, in fact, been the major impetus for theoretical investigation of the countertransference in every professional generation—perhaps even going back to Sabina Spielrein herself.

The following statement of the Balints highlights their increasing recognition of the mutuality of feelings in the therapeutic process, which became both controversial and ultimately influential: "[T]he analytical situation is the result of an interplay between the patient's transference and the analyst's countertransference, complicated by the reactions released in each other by the other's transference to him."[24]

Beyond these contributions, there was a virtual silence on the subject of countertransference.[25] This would change, but not in Freud's own lifetime.

The Late 1940s and 1950s: A New Surge of Interest

A resurgence of interest in countertransference occurred in Great Britain and the United States in the late 1940s and early 1950s, in two parallel but quite different psychoanalytic movements. In postwar Britain, psychoanalysis was in a state of heated conflict between the followers of Anna Freud and those of Melanie Klein. The Kleinians were more preoccupied with very early emotional neglect and damage, so they tended to see more severely disturbed and regressive patients. As a result, these analysts were confronted with much more intense countertransference reactions. Their need to understand and make use of these strong feelings toward their patients eventually resulted in the newer "totalist" conceptualization of countertransference as the sum of the helper's responses toward the helpee.

Klein herself had little or no interest in countertransference, since her own focus was almost entirely on the inner fantasy life of her patients. But Klein introduced a concept that soon became central to the evolution of the concept of countertransference by mid-century—the concept of *projective identification*. Two terms become important here. (*Projection* itself is the unconscious process whereby one individual "projects" or throws an image (usually of a person or experience from early in life) onto another, as a movie is projected onto a screen. The individual then sees the other person through this projected image, which may bear much or only a little resemblance to the real other person behind the screen. The first individual may then find him- or herself reacting in irrational or disproportionate ways toward the person on the receiving end of the projection, based on what he or she perceives in the projection on the "screen," not what the other is actually thinking, feeling, or doing.)

(*Projective identification*) takes this projective process one step further. In projective identification, it is as if the projected image is no longer simply projected *onto* the other individual, as if onto a screen, but *into* the other, where it is actually taken inside and identified with by the other person. The person on the receiving end of such an intense projective process actually begins to feel and to behave in the ways the first individual expected, because he or she has unconsciously identified with the projection and begun to live out of it.

In reflecting upon this situation, the receiving individual often can recognize that it feels as if something alien had been put into him or her, and that he or she is behaving in ways that are atypical. Some forms of projective identification will, however, be more congenial or "ego syntonic" to the recipient than others. The greatest danger lies in a projective identification that is so closely linked to the receiving individual's own unprocessed inner tendencies that it goes unrecognized as stimulation from the other. The resulting interlocking pattern of unconscious actions and reactions can create an intense and mutually destructive pattern of habitual relating between the two individuals involved.

This is why self-reflection is so important whenever a particularly intense feeling arises in relationship to another person. Such introspection is not innate but is learned, probably most effectively through personal psychotherapy. It can also be learned or reinforced in personal situations by getting "reality checks" from friends and family, or in professional situations, from professional training, individual or group supervision (as in CPE), and/or confidential consultation from colleagues. When the person on the receiving end is a helping professional, it is in fact incumbent upon him or her to engage in this type of introspection. But such reflection is almost always helpful in all intimate relationships and can be especially valuable in couples' work.

In Klein's own usage, the term *projective identification* was reserved for the effect of split-off archaic inner objects on the analyst in the patient's *fantasy* only. Projective identification, according to Klein, is a process stemming from a developmental phase she called the "paranoid schizoid position," most prominent during the first three months of life.[26] The "schizoid" aspect of this position refers to the process of psychological "splitting" as a primitive means of protecting inner good objects and keeping them isolated from bad experiences. Internal objects are split into good and bad, and negative feelings are thus walled off from the good, preserving an omnipotent sense of keeping one's objects, one's world, safe and good. (Projective identification therefore refers to the mental process from early childhood in which intolerable feelings and experiences are split off and then projected or expelled in fantasy into the mother, where the baby then identifies with them. Feelings thus evacuated into an object are experienced as persecutory if they are bad, resulting in the "paranoid" character of this developmental position, or idealized (and at times unattainable) if they are good.

In normal development, according to Klein, this position gradually gives way to a reintegration of one's own aggressive impulses, guilt, a desire to make reparation, and a pervasive sadness born of the recognition that perfect goodness is impossible. This more mature position Klein called "the depressive position," and she regarded it as the prerequisite for adult mental health. Klein recognized that much pathology resulted in cases where patients remained stuck in the paranoid schizoid position throughout their life. She recognized the mechanisms of splitting and projective identification at work in her adult patients who exhibited primitive psychological structures.

Klein viewed these processes as entirely internal and had little interest in either the impact of external reality on the child's development or the impact of the child on his or her real "objects"—parents, siblings, and caretakers. She was similarly uninterested in the impact of projective identification on the therapist in the analytic dyad. However, Klein's followers soon appropriated this concept in connection with the intense *real-life* effect patients have on their analysts. These clinicians were driven to find a broader understanding of countertransference through their own experiences of projective identification, having been affected at a deep personal level by some of their patients' most archaic, raw, and traumatic mental contents.

Two papers can be considered landmarks in the movement toward an expanding definition of countertransference in the late 1940s and early 1950s: Paula Heimann's "On Countertransference" (1950)[27] and D. W. Winnicott's "Hate in the Countertransference" (1949).[28] After 1949, these two papers were widely known in psychoanalytic circles and generated much discussion.[29]

Paula Heimann

Heimann was a student and analysand of Melanie Klein, and more. As the stage play *Mrs. Klein*[30] vividly brought to life, Heimann was also in some sense Klein's surrogate daughter, at a time when Klein's relations with her own daughter, the analyst Melitta Schmideberg, were deeply strained both personally and professionally.[31] Heimann's experiences, both as an analyst in her own right and as Klein's analysand, no doubt shaped both her interest and her sensitive investigation into countertransference as a phenomenon.

Heimann's work shows her to have been acutely aware of experiences in the countertransference that stretched the prevailing classical understanding of countertransference beyond its limits. She was the first to contradict publicly Freud's idea of "emotional coldness" and to insist that not only were analysts not neutral observers, but that they experienced a wide range of emotional responses. She wrote:

> I have been struck by the widespread belief amongst candidates that the counter-transference is nothing but a source of trouble. Many candidates are afraid and feel guilty when they become aware of feelings towards their patients and consequently aim at avoiding any emotional response and at becoming completely unfeeling and "detached." When I tried to trace the origin of this idea of the "detached" analyst, I found that our literature does indeed contain descriptions of the analytic work which can give rise to the notion that a good analyst does not feel anything beyond a uniform and mild benevolence towards his patients, and that any ripple of emotional waves on this smooth surface represents a disturbance to be overcome.[32]

Heimann went on to say that she believed this was a misreading of Freud's statements on keeping a surgeon-like mentality or being a mirror. At the same time, she quickly added that she believed Ferenczi went too far in advocating for disclosing his feelings toward patients.

Heimann then made the landmark statement that inaugurated what is now called the totalist definition of countertransference: "For the purposes of this paper I am using the term 'countertransference' to cover *all the feelings which the analyst experiences towards his patient*"[33] (emphasis added). She went on to state her thesis:

> The analyst's emotional response to his patient within the analytic situation represents one of the most important tools for his work. The analyst's countertransference is an instrument of research into the patient's unconscious.[34]

In a further statement that anticipated by several decades the thrust of contemporary writers, she wrote, "The analytic situation has been investigated and described from many angles, and there is general agreement about its unique character. But it is my impression that it has not been sufficiently stressed that it is a *relationship* between two persons"[35] (italics in the original). She used the colorful term *mechanical brain* to critique prevailing views of the neutral analyst, and stated unequivocally, "If an analyst tries to work without consulting his feelings, his interpretations are poor."[36] She further proposed a parallel process to Freud's "evenly hovering" or "free-floating" attention, which she termed "a freely roused emotional sensibility," in order to "follow the patient's emotional movements and unconscious phantasies."[37]

Heimann also boldly lifted up the phenomenon of unconscious communication: "Our basic assumption is that the analyst's unconscious understands that of his patient. This rapport on the deep level comes to the surface in the form of feelings which the analyst notices in response to his patient, in his 'counter-transference.' This is the most dynamic way in which his patient's voice reaches him."[38]

Heimann tempered her recommendations with a caution against the dangers of using this "freely roused emotional sensibility" to act impulsively. She cautioned that this approach to countertransference was not to be used as a "screen for the analyst's shortcomings"[39] and continued with a firm prohibition of disclosing countertransference feelings to the patient. She reframed Freud's demand that analysts must "recognize and master the countertransference" as a demand for introspection and insight into the feelings stirred by the patient, in order to "protect him from entering as a co-actor on the scene which the patient re-enacts in the analytic relationship and from exploiting it for his own needs."[40] She similarly viewed self-disclosure as "more in the nature of a confession and a burden to the patient."[41] In the wake of current controversies about therapist-patient sexual exploitation, Heimann's warnings about the therapist's potential use of the patient to gratify his or her own needs sound prescient.

D. W. Winnicott and Further Developments

Another milestone in the history of the concept of countertransference was Winnicott's 1949 paper entitled "Hate in the Countertransference."[42] Although Winnicott later demurred that the paper was "chiefly about hate" and not about countertransference,[43] his effort to classify types of countertransference was influential. Winnicott concurred with emerging contemporary views that the analyst was not merely a blank screen, but made a unique impact on the therapy based on his or her own character, temperament, and personality. Winnicott wrote, "If the patient seeks objective or justified hate he must be able to reach it else he cannot feel he can reach objective love."[44]

Winnicott's courageous acknowledgment of the universality of aggression, baldly stated as hate, in the countertransference no doubt added to the notoriety of the paper. But, as is often the case with Winnicott's writing, the explicit focus of the paper, hate, was arrived at through lengthy discourses on other, related subjects. Winnicott's statement "Countertransference phenomena will at times be the important things in the analysis"[45] became influential in part because it came at a time when the concept was being revived and vigorously debated.

Like other Kleinians' work on countertransference, Winnicott's formulations on the topic derived from his own personal struggles with severely disturbed patients, in particular those who were psychotic or antisocial. In several papers, he enumerated those patients for whom a broadened definition of counter-transference would be indicated—borderline/psychotic diagnoses and two specific types that were of particular interest to Winnicott himself: antisocial personalities[46] and "False Self" personalities,[47] for whom Winnicott's treatment of choice was a planned therapeutic regression to dependence.[48]

In this context, Winnicott gave a famous example of being hit by a patient:

> I find it difficult to miss this opportunity for discussing all kinds of things that I have experienced and which link up with ideas put forward by Dr. Ford-ham. For instance, I got hit by a patient. What I said is not for publication. It was not an interpretation but a reaction to an event. The patient came across the professional white line and got a little bit of the real me, and I think it felt real to her.[49]

This statement foreshadows a notion that became important in Winnicott's late work. Winnicott increasingly came to regard the "real me" as having significant therapeutic value, when the patient's experience of the real person of the thera-pist could occasionally penetrate the patient's projective experience of the ther-apist as an archaic fantasy object. Such a momentary breakthrough could provide a mutative experience of bridging the gap or "potential space" between fantasy and reality. The conceptualization of this process, detailed in Winnicott's late paper on the "use of the object,"[50] is one of his most important contributions.

Winnicott's contributions on the topic of uses of regression strongly influ-enced the work of his colleague and analysand Margaret Little. Where Heimann and Winnicott explored in the area of countertransference, Margaret Little set up camp. In detailing her work with primitive psychotic and regressed states and the importance of judiciously interrupting patients' fantasied relations with moments of contradictory reality within the larger context of allowing a pro-found regression to dependence, Little drew on her work with patients and her own analysis with Winnicott.[51] Transference/countertransference phenomena and the treatment of psychotic and borderline patients became Little's central project, the subject of numerous thoughtful papers.[52] Little considered the countertransference to be an essential component of the central task of moving regressed patients from unconscious enactment to symbolization and finally conscious verbalization of primitive material.

Two other Kleinians should be mentioned for their further contributions to the development of countertransference theory: Heinrich Racker and Wil-fred Bion.

Racker was an Argentinian analyst strongly influenced by Klein. He undertook to classify countertransference reactions, which he regarded as predictable in various types of cases and in combination with certain predispositions in the therapist—the therapist's "personal equation."[53] He believed a "countertransference neurosis" would naturally develop in the therapist in tandem with the transference neurosis in the patient. He also coined the term *counterresistance* to refer to unconscious defensive operations in the therapist, which could cause the therapist to avoid awareness of important transference/countertransference material. Racker did not strongly advocate disclosure of countertransference, but rather saw it primarily as a tool for gathering information about the patient's unconscious and internally managing one's own reactions in order to be maximally responsive to the patient's needs.

Wilfred Bion explicitly made a link between the mechanism of projective identification as it worked in the dynamics of inner objects in fantasy and the use of projective identification in the therapeutic relationship (and often ubiquitously in other relationships) actually to induce feelings, behaviors, and experiences in the other person.[54] This "induced countertransference," as Bion called it, might be felt by the therapist as manipulation or, at other times, simply as thoughts, fantasies, and emotional reactions to the patient that feel alien to the therapist's usual responses. Bion considered the therapist's role in such primitive psychic interactions to be that of a "container" for the split-off parts of the patient, which the therapist could hold, analyze, and then return to the patient in the form of interpretations. Bion even went so far as to assert that, especially with psychotic or severely character disordered patients, "for a considerable proportion of the analytic time the only evidence on which an interpretation can be based is that which is afforded by the countertransference."[55] Bion also developed this theory extensively in relation to unconscious group dynamics.[56]

American Developments

Countertransference was a subject of interest in the United States in the 1950s, largely through the influence of Harry Stack Sullivan and his "interpersonal theory of psychiatry."[57] Sullivan and others who worked with him, including Frieda Fromm-Reichmann[58] and her husband, Erich Fromm,[59] shifted from an exclusive focus on patients' intrapsychic material to an interest in the actual interpersonal dynamics between patients and others in their lives. Sullivan and Fromm founded the William Alanson White Institute, where the therapist's own contribution to the analytic relationship—and fallibility as a real object—were highlighted in training from as early as the late 1930s.[60] Sullivan attempted to depathologize the attitudes of psychiatrists toward patients, preferring the term *difficulties with living* over *mental illness*. In his influential teaching over many years, he conveyed that "we are all more human than otherwise."

Sullivan, Fromm, and Fromm-Reichmann all focused a great deal on the problem of anxiety in both helper and helpee, reflecting a growing cultural preoccupation in American psychology with anxiety around the time of the Second World War, both as an existential philosophical category and as a growing psychosocial problem. Fromm-Reichman in particular considered that the result of self-neglect in the helper would be insecurity, leading to acute anxiety in the helping relationship. She considered working through fear and anxiety in reaction to the helpee to be a central task of the helper. Resistances on the part of helpees were empathically reframed by Fromm-Reichmann as "security operations" born of anxiety.[61]

Sullivan did not actually use the terms *transference* and *countertransference*, but rather referred to "parataxic interpersonal experiences," understood as distortions created by carryovers from either the patient's or the therapist's childhood. Both he and Fromm-Reichmann remained closer than the British school to the classical view of countertransference as a hindrance, but the acknowledgment of the therapist's contribution to the therapeutic dynamic was a significant advance.

Sullivan would have had ample opportunity at Harvard to engage in dialogue with colleagues from other scientific disciplines. Heisenberg's uncertainty principle and Einstein's theory of relativity generated a new interest in indeterminacy and a rejection of the idea of a purely objective scientific observer. No doubt influenced by these philosophical controversies in other sciences, Sullivan introduced the notion of the therapist as a "participant-observer," one who is influenced and also influences what is observed. For Sullivan and his followers in the "interpersonal school," therefore, careful listening to both self and other was at the heart of all effective helping.

The 1960s and 1970s: A New Focus on Empathy

In the 1957 movie *Funny Face*, an earnest Audrey Hepburn tells Fred Astaire that he could use some lessons from a famous "empathicalist."[62] The 1960s have been considered by some to be another hiatus in the study of countertransference.[63] But there was at least one very significant development that continued to advance the understanding of transference and countertransference toward a greater appreciation of intersubjectivity. This was a surge of interest in the concept of empathy. The screenwriter of *Funny Face* had accurately caught the psychological tenor of the times!

A number of writers from varying perspectives were taking up the question of empathy.[64] Terms such as *capacity for empathy* had already begun to appear in classical literature.[65] The concept of empathy was elevated to an unprecedented level of interest and controversy, however, with the publication of Heinz Kohut's "Introspection, Empathy and Psychoanalysis," first presented in 1957 to the Chicago Institute for Psychoanalysis.[66] In this paper, Kohut differentiated himself sharply from the classical ego psychology that prevailed in American psychoanalysis, and embarked on the project that would eventually be known as "self psychology." Kohut called for a revision of traditional notions of the therapist as a blank screen or neutral observer, in favor of an empathic stance that attempted to enter into the patient's own inner experience. Empathy, from Kohut's point of view, is not sympathy or warmth (as it is often misinterpreted), but rather the most effective source of information about the patient, a form of data gathering through vicarious introspection.[67]

Kohut believed this adoption of an empathic stance was necessitated at least in part by a changing patient population. At least initially, he believed that a classical analysis was still appropriate for the treatment of classical oedipal neuroses.[68] However, Kohut found that these methods did not work and at times hindered the treatment of patients with very early narcissistic wounding, resulting in enduring self-defeating personality structures.[69] He understood the origins of such pathology not in classical Freudian terms of internal *conflict* between unconscious wishes and conscious prohibitions, but rather in terms of *deficit*. He ascribed narcissistic characterological problems to insufficient emotional provisions by primary caretakers during the earliest years of life.

Kohut identified two serious lacks in the early upbringing of patients for whom classical analysis was not working: "mirroring" and "idealization." In Kohut's usage, mirroring is not simply good feedback, as the term is sometimes used. Rather, it involves positive, warm expressions of pride and admiration for the infant or toddler during the period in which the child needs to be able to strut and glow and be recognized as special and wonderful just for being him- or herself. Mirroring is the gleam in the mother's eye, the father's "Wow, you did that!" and must begin essentially from the child's birth.

Second, parents must allow for "idealization," at first by reliably and consistently providing physical and emotional nurture. Later, idealization involves parents' modeling wholesome values and behaviors and, importantly, tolerating and not deflecting the young child's idealizations of them.

In this way, parents become effective "selfobjects" for the child—that is, fulfilling the role of nurturing others (objects) who can gradually be internalized in the child's developing sense of self as a secure feeling of identity, solidity, and self-cohesion. The absence of such provisions on either the mirroring or the idealizing "pole" of self-structure would result in the opposite: a sense of inner fragmentation or lack of cohesion, narcissistic vulnerability, and depressive emptiness. It was such individuals that Kohut saw in his practice, and classical analysis seemed not to address the particular nature of their difficulty with living and internal suffering.

In his first book, *The Analysis of the Self*,[70] Kohut described the therapist's role as a "selfobject" for the patient—that is, an object used for the maintenance of a fragile sense of cohesion and equilibrium of the most central, irreducible core of the personality, or "self." Empathy was central to this process of understanding and interpreting what was lacking in the patient's childhood experience and resulting self-structure. In this process, the therapist must be able to tolerate being viewed and utilized narcissistically by the patient as an archaic object.

Kohut also made a unique contribution in his understanding of the role of the patient's experience of empathic failure by the therapist. No matter how empathically attuned the therapist is, such ruptures are inevitable. By tolerating the affective experiences engendered and interpreting the underlying infantile need, the therapist can help the patient eventually begin to build internal structure that was lacking on the mirroring and/or idealizing poles of the personality. The empathic exploration and interpretation of disruptions and failures in both their contemporary and genetic settings are precisely what effect cure, a process Kohut named "transmuting internalization."[71]

Kohut's ideas had many parallels with earlier British Kleinian and object-relational thought and practice. But Kohut's proposals were better known in America, where they were first introduced. They were simultaneously met by much greater controversy and had far greater influence—far beyond psychoanalysis proper into arenas of counseling and also pastoral care.

The 1980s to the Present: Consolidation and Divergence

By the end of the 1970s, a consensus began to emerge in the psychoanalytic literature about the nature of countertransference and its uses as well as its perils.[72] Elements of this consensus may be summarized as follows:

- The therapist's identifications with aspects of the helpee's experience have increasingly been recognized as a useful aspect of countertransference.
- Countertransference has come to be understood as not *necessarily* pathological per se.
- Countertransference responses may be divided into pathological and non-pathological aspects, with an important task remaining to sort out which is which.

- Intense emotional reactions are not necessarily a sign of pathological transference or countertransference. In other words, the therapist is no longer expected to be neutral and unresponsive emotionally.

- The totalist view of countertransference as encompassing all the therapist's responses to the patient has become increasingly accepted in the mainstream of psychoanalytic theory and practice.

At the same time, the long hegemony of psychoanalysis was over, and its power to define terms and concepts, or even to determine what concepts were central to the helping enterprise, were seriously diminished by a number of factors. Psychodynamic theory and practice continued, and with it, interest in the phenomena of transference, countertransference, and empathy, but psychoanalysis no longer could speak from the privileged position of a monopoly. Alternative therapeutic paradigms, including humanistic, behavioral, and family systems approaches, were becoming increasingly accepted. In part, this was due to public disillusionment with the length and cost of psychoanalysis, as well as to wider cultural movements toward democratization of institutions and the penetration of eastern and humanist-existentialist philosophies into the world of psychotherapy. The concept of countertransference itself began to be largely ignored in nonpsychodynamic treatment paradigms.[73]

Psychoanalysis as a movement also began to splinter into numerous competing schools of thought, and there was a sharp increase in new journals and alternative institutes and organizations. The proliferation of training institutes, journals, and mental health disciplines created an atmosphere in the helping professions of widely divergent beliefs and practices concerning the nature of the helping relationship itself. Since the 1980s, at least four significant influences affected psychoanalysis from within, and two broad influences of political and philosophical movements had an impact from without. Influences from within included the following:

1. Self psychology by the early 1980s had begun to be institutionalized as a cohesive movement under the mentorship of Kohut before his death in 1981.

2. British object relations theory was enthusiastically appropriated in America in tandem with vigorous growth of neo-Kleinian and "middle school" thought in Britain.

3. New research appeared in the field of infant observation, primarily through the work of Daniel Stern.[74]

4. There was a growing interest in French psychoanalytic thought, particularly appropriations of the work of Jacques Lacan[75] by feminist and other French and American theorists.[76]

Two further influences came from without:

1. A variety of strands of feminist thought and political action
2. The rise of postmodernist philosophy and social constructivism

(Sadly, the civil rights and antiracism movements have even to this day had very little impact, and nearly all psychotherapeutic disciplines deplorably remain the province of relatively privileged white professionals. All the helping professions, including pastoral counseling and psychotherapy, need to address this reality seriously.)

Of all these factors, the rise of social constructivism has perhaps had the most influence on the evolution of the concept of countertransference. This postmodern trend will be described in detail in chapter 3. A new "relational school" of psychoanalysis has begun to conceptualize countertransference as embedded in a "two-person" paradigm,[77] in which both individuals involved are understood as reciprocal subjects. This is held up in contrast to all earlier therapeutic paradigms, conceptualized more in terms of subject–object interactions. In this model, transference and countertransference are no longer distinct entities, but rather two ends of a spectrum of mutual interaction, including both conscious and unconscious dimensions. Meaning is no longer viewed as the interpretive work of one observing subject closely paying attention to an "other" or object, but rather something that is coconstructed uniquely in that particular twosome. Meaning arises not in either subject or object, but in the shared wisdom, conscious and unconscious, that arises in the "between," somewhere along the spectrum of transference and countertransference, of "I" and "Thou." This understanding both parallels and intersects with many advances from feminist theory. We will turn to this relational paradigm in chapter 3. But first, it is important to review how this history of the development of countertransference came to be appropriated in the pastoral care and counseling tradition, as this lays the foundation for how most pastors and pastoral counselors understand countertransference to this day. The next chapter presents a review of this history.

CHAPTER TWO

The History of Countertransference in Pastoral Care and Counseling

COUNTERTRANSFERENCE had its origins as a concept in Sigmund Freud's own writings, as described at length in the previous chapter, and is therefore an intrinsically psychoanalytic concept. Most of the significant contributions to the development of the concept have been in the psychoanalytic literature, and differences in conceptualization have arisen largely in debates among various psychoanalytic schools.

As a discipline, pastoral care and counseling has for the most part been little concerned with generating constructive proposals for conceptualizing countertransference or refining the use of the term. Both areas of the pastoral field—pastoral care and pastoral counseling—have, however, appropriated the concept from psychoanalysis and utilized it in training and practice in various ways. Most pastors, especially those who graduated from seminary in the last two to three decades, have come to experience and examine firsthand in Clinical Pastoral Education (CPE)[1] their own countertransference, that is, the personal blind spots and emotional baggage originating in childhood experiences in their families of origin. Virtually all certified pastoral counselors are further trained in the concepts of tranference and countertransference as classically defined. Before proceeding to the most recent constructivist developments (discussed in chapter 3), it therefore may be helpful to examine how the concept of countertransference has traditionally been incorporated into the pastoral theological disciplines. This history encompasses virtually all of the previous century.

Early Influences

Countertransference was imported directly from Freud into the pastoral literature around the turn of the twentieth century. Freud's ideas were first disseminated in America in about 1908 by A. A. Brill and others in New York and Boston who were interested in the psychoanalytic movement.[2] The Clark University lectures of Freud and C. G. Jung further stimulated this interest. It was in this context in 1909 that the rector of Emmanuel Episcopal Church in Boston publicly took a pro-Freudian stance.[3] The "Emmanuel movement" had begun five years earlier, promoted by the associate rector of Emmanuel, Elwood Worcester. Worcester was a cosmopolitan cleric interested in new ideas. He had received his B.Th. at General Seminary in New York and also received a PhD from the University of Leipzig. He was the first to advocate blending psychotherapy with religious instruction, as part of a larger philosophical agenda of reconciling religion and medical science in general.[4]

Scientific studies of the mind were increasingly of interest in religious circles at this time. At this time, "psychology" was regarded as a somewhat suspect offshoot of the neurological sciences. However, in religious circles, it was recognized as relevant to the investigation of spiritual experience. William James gave his lectures on "natural religion" in Edinburgh in 1901–1902, and these were published as the widely read *Varieties of Religious Experience.*[5] James's work spanned the areas of neurology, anthropology, and philosophy with his exploration of "man's religious constitution" and the "indispensable beliefs that arise from its functioning." There were further efforts to bring science and religion together, as in Mary Baker Eddy's "Christian Science" movement, and the "New Thought." All these trends created a more hospitable environment for psychoanalytic thought. For many decades, transference and countertransference continued to be mentioned in the pastoral literature in the sense in which Freud introduced them. Then, in the 1930s, the focus of pastoral care and counseling began to shift from concerns with "adjustment" and "insight" to "freedom." E. Brooks Holifield, in his comprehensive history of pastoral care,[6] attributes this in part to the influence of World War I chaplains returning from war with a more success-oriented, pragmatic approach to pastoral care and counseling. This was the era of the founding of the American Foundation of Religion and Psychiatry (AFRP) in 1937.[7] AFRP grew out of the first clinic specifically created to integrate psychiatry and religious concerns, the Religious-Psychiatric Clinic. This clinic, known today as the Blanton-Peale Institute, was established at Marble Collegiate Church in New York City by the parish's very popular preacher, the Rev. Dr. Norman Vincent Peale, together with a psychoanalytically trained psychiatrist, Dr. Smiley Blanton.

This was also a time of strong existential influence in theological circles. Anton Boisen, in his widely read *Exploration of the Inner World,*[8] believed in the existential value of psychoanalytic self-exploration, now valuing introspection for its own sake and no longer only for the cure of symptoms. Boisen's personal experience as an inpatient in a psychiatric ward strongly shaped his convictions about avoiding the dehumanization of psychiatric patients and about taking their spiritual concerns seriously. Boisen advocated "the study of living human documents rather than books."[9]

The 1950s: Responses to Secular Psychology

The 1950s saw the rise of popular psychology. Two major figures in the field of pastoral care and counseling at this time were Wayne Oates[10] and Seward Hiltner.[11] Both men critiqued the infiltration of a "cult of reassurance" (Oates's expression) and manipulative techniques that did not foster real growth (Hiltner). They reasserted the distinctiveness of the pastoral perspective in offering a more meaningful form of counseling based on traditional biblical and theological principles that would address people's deeper moral and spiritual needs.

Partly in response to the counseling trend at large, and partly to differentiate the clergyperson's role from popular models, there was in this era a flurry of activity in training clergy as counselors. The 1950s also saw the rise of the Clinical Pastoral Education movement, which adopted a confrontational encounter-group method to root out unconscious personal barriers to more effective pastoral care. In general, many authors with a clerical/pastoral identity began to feel the need to fight harder to retain a distinctive theological identity amid pressures to secularize and psychologize pastoral care in the church.

Thus, in the 1950s, two divergent trends marked the pastoral field—secularization via the incorporation of popular psychology versus a trend toward reasserting more classical theological paradigms. Countertransference was virtually never addressed explicitly in the pastoral literature of this era. The pastor's own role and experience were sometimes addressed, mostly concerning the propriety of personal moral conduct and also with a view toward avoiding contaminating the parishioner's or counselee's own movement toward growth with the pastor's own biases and needs.[12]

The 1960s and the Human Potential Movement

In the 1960s, most pastoral counseling authors turned to Carl Rogers[13] and the human potential movement for their inspiration. In this period, although there were some very significant contributions to the pastoral literature,[14] there were virtually no references to transference and countertransference at all. There was a growing trend toward distinguishing between the domains of pastoral care (the parish) and pastoral counseling (a separate professional setting, or in the parish but conducted by a specially trained religious counselor) and knowing when to refer to a professional therapist.[15] The American Association of Pastoral Counselors (AAPC) was born in 1963 amid the ferment of debate about the proper context of pastoral counseling (parish or separate professional office) and fears about the secularization of the pastoral role.[16]

Howard Clinebell's *Basic Types of Pastoral Care and Counseling*,[17] first published in 1966, was the reigning textbook for generations of seminarians. In this influential training text, Clinebell promoted a strongly Rogerian client-centered framework.[18] Clinebell outlined four pastoral functions (adopting these from a similarly Rogerian work by authors William Clebsch and Charles Jaekle):[19] healing, sustaining, guiding, and reconciling. Clinebell's premise was that the proper domain of pastoral care and counseling was a "relational, supportive, ego-adaptive, reality-oriented approach," which he included under the umbrella term *relationship-centered counseling*. Clinebell advocated maximizing positive resources and present-day coping mechanisms, not delving into childhood roots of present difficulties. Countertransference, in keeping with this emphasis on conscious problem solving, was not a focus.[20] The method, following Rogers, was "reflective listening," with the goal of helping each person achieve his or her fullest potential. Clinebell advocated both individual and group modalities for promoting growth in the pastoral context.

Countertransference in the 1960s: The Influence of Karl Menninger

A few pastoral authors did address transference and countertransference directly in the 1960s. Nearly all cite the work of Karl Menninger, whose book *Theory of Psychoanalytic Technique*,[21] first published in 1958, was widely read in pastoral counseling circles. A number of early leaders in the pastoral theology movement trained at the Menninger Clinic. Menninger himself was an active Presbyterian elder. He welcomed religious thinking at the clinic, including the creation of a chaplaincy position, first held by Thomas Klink, and later encouraged Klink to create a division of religion and psychiatry at the Menninger Clinic.[22] Menninger's own writings, including *Whatever Became of Sin?*,[23] *Man against Himself*,[24] and *Love against Hate*,[25] also took up existential and theological issues. He even collaborated with Seward Hiltner on a book entitled *Constructive Aspects of Anxiety*.[26] Menninger's formative influence on the pastoral psychology and theology movement in the 1950s and 1960s is therefore significant. His willingness to entertain religious themes and his basic respect for spiritual and religious issues in his work opened the door for more dialogue between pastoral and psychoanalytic paradigms. Menninger also conveyed a combination of personal warmth and clinical pragmatism that was attractive to pastoral counselors. Therefore, Menninger's view of countertransference strongly influenced the training of a generation of pastoral psychologists and theologians.

Menninger's explication of transference and countertransference relied primarily on the point of view of ego psychology. His definition of countertransference was decidedly classical. He regarded it as a hindrance to objectivity, based on unresolved personal neurosis of the therapist.[27] Menninger outlined twenty-two specific ways in which countertransference "makes its appearance—i.e., becomes an interference."[28] Following Menninger, pastoral writers in the 1960s who referred to transference or countertransference at all continued to use the classical definition of countertransference as a sign of the pastor's own unresolved neurotic conflicts, and therefore a hindrance, integrated to varying degrees with a more interpersonal approach to the helping relationship.[29] A number of authors pointed to the need for pastors to attend to their own feelings and health, without naming countertransference per se.[30]

The earliest article to appear in the pastoral literature specifically on countertransference was published in 1965 by E. Mansell Pattison.[31] Pattison's contribution was to define transference and countertransference and then to offer examples of practical application to pastoral care and counseling. Pattison took an interpersonal view of countertransference as "parataxic distortion,"[32] inherent in all relationships but especially risky in pastoral relationships due to the intensity of emotions relating to religious beliefs and commitments. He warned clergy against solving their own problems or finding vicarious enjoyment in the lives of parishioners. He took the entire list of possible countertransference manifestations from Menninger's *Theory of Psychoanalytic Technique*[33] and translated these into pastoral situations. He advocated for increased observation of transference-countertransference distortions, in the service of remaining more alert and reality-focused, while leaving the act of interpretation to professional (that is, psychoanalytically trained) therapists. A 1973 article by Maurice Wagner[34] was similarly educative in tone.

Two other pastoral writers in the 1960s briefly offered some new and original thinking about transference and countertransference. Paul E. Johnson[35] reframed Freud's recommendations about transference, stating that Freud showed the value of the transference—that by reliving the past intensely in the present, the person could become free of the past and live more fully in the present. He suggested an urgent need for "another transference" not taken up by any other writers: a transference of present learning into future behavior. He also advocated for the transfer of the pastor's own authority to the growing person. Charles Curran, a Jesuit priest, further suggested that transference, in the classical sense of distortion, might affect one's relationship with God the Father much as toward one's own individual father[36]—predating Ana-Maria Rizzuto's[37] psychoanalytic study of the childhood origins of God imagoes by a decade.

The 1970s: Increasing Definition of Clergy Role

In the 1970s, the pastoral counseling literature continued to focus on an effort to differentiate the role of clergy from other secular counselors. It also included a gradual and at times tentative reintroduction of the context of the whole faith community into the therapeutic enterprise.[38] A central area of exploration continued to be the pastoral person and the minister's role and moral authority.[39] Don Browning, in *The Moral Context of Pastoral Care,*[40] stated that pastoral authority is defined squarely in the context of the church: "It is my thesis that there is a moral context to all acts of care." For Browning, the word *secular* did not mean neutral. Therapy is always a human act. Browning's work called for a return to the nineteenth-century notion of preaching as stimulus to moral inquiry, and he integrated the importance of moral inquiry into the practice of pastoral care at all levels. Like others of this era, Browning did not refer to the dynamics of transference and countertransference in this work—although the minister's capacity for self-awareness as moral agent was implicit throughout.

The 1970s also were a time of continued expansion and integration of existential philosophy within both systematic and pastoral theology. In particular, the theology of Paul Tillich[41] had widespread influence throughout theological training across many disciplines. The writings of Rollo May[42] had already been influential in theological circles. Pastoral theologians began asking what Charles Gerkin identified as "the root question facing the pastoral care and counseling movement"[43] about the conjunction between theology and psychology. Influenced by their readings of David Tracy's "revised critical correlational" method,[44] Gerkin and Hiltner[45] both turned to the field of hermeneutics, which had venerable theological origins in medieval scripture studies, to propose new, dialogical methods of pastoral care and counseling focused on questions of existence and meaning. While this trend represented a move in pastoral counseling toward a more relational, two-person therapeutic stance, it was a further move away from psychoanalytic conceptualizations of the therapeutic relationship and from focus on countertransference phenomena.

Recent Decades: Critical Challenges

Carroll Wise, in *Pastoral Psychotherapy,* a book that represents the summation of a life's work, devoted six pages to the topic of countertransference.[46] While this amount seems small, it may represent a return of attention to the subject in pastoral care and counseling in the early 1980s after a period of relative disregard. Wise defined countertransference primarily in classical terms, as a "displacement of unconscious attitudes in the pastor to the person, attitudes which are inappropriate in the pastor or therapy relation."[47] He did incorporate the notion that countertransference can be evoked by the other person, particularly if this is a pattern in the person's relationships.

Wise's book represented a compilation of previous decades' thinking about countertransference. Much of the pastoral counseling literature from the 1980s forward, in contrast, has begun to focus in new directions. The major creative contributions in the recent literature have increasingly reflected a growing awareness of the white, middle-class bias inherent in previous decades of writing. In particular, the authoritative role of the individual pastoral caregiver has been challenged. Pastors have been urged increasingly to be aware of larger contextual issues for care in community[48] and to view themselves, in the words of pastoral theologian Bonnie Miller-McLemore, as "facilitators of networks of care."[49] Community, global, and ecological influences and contexts have been incorporated into the self-understanding of pastoral care and counseling.[50]

Attention to ethnic, racial, and cultural concerns in pastoral care emerged in recent decades as an important contribution to the pastoral literature.[51] With a growing body of pastoral literature from North America, Latin America, Asia, and Africa, the investigation of pastoral care from other cultural and ethnic perspectives remains an important frontier for further constructive work in pastoral care and counseling to this day.[52] Explicitly feminist models of pastoral care and counseling began to appear in the 1990s,[53] together with examinations of more specialized subjects in the pastoral care and counseling of women, including sexual and domestic violence, poverty, the tensions between work and family, and the impact of God images on women's self-esteem.[54]

In this recent pastoral literature, there has been very little mention of countertransference, as the focus has been on other issues. Greater attention to self-care, alternatives to models emphasizing sacrifice, and at times vehement discussions of boundaries in relation to professional ethics and sexual abuse[55] do, however, represent a bridge toward further integration of feminist insights with specific attention to countertransference as a topic.

Pastoral Research

Most journal articles on the subject of countertransference have applied a classic definition of countertransference to particular or problematic topics such as the dynamics of specific religious communities and congregations, cross-denominational counseling, countertransference and burnout, gender issues in pastoral counseling, countertransference with older clients, death and dying, and the practice of pastoral home visits by parish clergy.[56] Additionally, some articles have taken up the implications of religious affiliation and belief, in both therapist and patient, and the impact of religion on the dynamics of transference and countertransference.[57]

Of the empirical clinical research in the field of pastoral counseling, there is still little exploring the concept of countertransference per se.[58] In an early example of countertransference research, Howard Friend in 1977 applied the classical understanding of countertransference to the training of pastors and promotion of increased awareness of transferential dynamics in parish settings.[59] In the 1980s and early 1990s, most researchers continued to use an implicitly classical definition of countertransference (by virtue of viewing it as something to be "managed") in relation to the special topics of divorce and religiosity.[60]

At the New Millennium: New Interest and Emerging Definitions

A new appreciation for the importance of countertransference, including a broader definition of the concept itself, did, however, begin to appear in the 1980s. William Collins[61] was perhaps the first to refer explicitly, based on Otto Kernberg's much earlier psychoanalytic review article,[62] to the existence of two different general definitions of countertransference, "classical" and "totalistic," citing the most important exponents of each view historically. After a brief review of these definitions, he aligned himself with Joseph Sandler's important psychoanalytic contributions on countertransference and "role-responsiveness,"[63] stating that the specific emotional responses aroused in the therapist by specific qualities in the patient may lead to insight about the processes occurring in the patient. After offering three case vignettes, Collins advocated greater attention in pastoral psychotherapy to countertransference as a therapeutic strategy, and the use of supervision to enhance this work of self-examination. Five years after the publication of Collins's article, Gary Ahlskog[64] and Chris Schlauch[65] brought self psychological perspectives to bear on the practice of pastoral psychotherapy, suggesting that the transference was an appropriate focus for treatment and calling for more attention to self psychology in the pastoral counseling community.

Psychiatrist Richard Schwartz, in a 1989 review article in the *Journal of Pastoral Care,* took a middle position on these trends in the psychoanalytic literature. Schwartz wrote that the classical definition was too narrow but that an understanding of countertransference as all the therapist's emotional responses to the patient was too broad.[66] He proposed some specific transferences in pastoral relationships, based on the clergy caregiver's religious authority, the desire for forgiveness, and a view of the pastor as "more than human." These, according to Schwartz, come "preformed," not gradually developing as in secular psychotherapy, but existing from the first encounter based on the pastoral therapist's role as clergy. He questioned the resolution of the transference as an appropriate goal for pastoral psychotherapy[67] and concluded his article by drawing the connection between countertransference and the dangers of therapist–patient sexual contact, prescribing three approaches to minimize this danger: education, self-knowledge, and peer review or supervision.

In 1990, perhaps the first thorough and up-to-date discussion of countertransference appeared in the *Dictionary of Pastoral Care and Counseling.*[68] The author, Richard Bruehl, explained the evolution of both classical and more contemporary views of countertransference and their application to pastoral care and counseling, particularly with religious counselees.[69]

In the 1990s, pastoral research also began to reflect the more intersubjective totalist definition of countertransference. Hans-Friedrich Stängle[70] applied this definition to students learning hospital visitation skills in Clinical Pastoral Education. Stängle's aim again was awareness: to demonstrate the existence of countertransference in general pastoral ministry settings, to show that neglect of countertransference impairs ministry while attentiveness to it improves pastoral effectiveness, and to provide a research tool for training and evaluation.[71]

Two additional pertinent articles on countertransference in ministry and pastoral psychotherapy appeared more recently in an anthology entitled *Exploring Sacred Landscapes: Religious and Spiritual Experiences in Psychotherapy.*[72] This anthology represents some of the most psychoanalytically immersed writers in the fields of pastoral theology and psychology of religion. They include Ana-Maria Rizzuto, whose research book about children's projections of parental imagoes onto their concepts of God, *The Birth of the Living God,*[73] made a strong impression on students of ministry and pastoral counseling in the 1980s, and John McDargh,[74] whose work has brought object relations theory to bear on the phenomenological study of religion.[75]

Summary

In pastoral theology, the time seems ripe for a renewed attention to the understanding of transference and countertransference. As the first chapter has shown, however, the study of countertransference has changed even as the concept itself has changed toward a more mutual, intersubjective approach. The relational paradigm in contemporary psychoanalysis offers a rich mine of new understandings of self and other, toward a more complex understanding of the use of the self in pastoral care and counseling. The next chapter will explore this relational paradigm, grounded in postmodern, postpositivist, and constructivist challenges to Enlightenment notions of truth, subjectivity, and objectivity.

CHAPTER THREE
The Relational Paradigm
Postmodern Concepts of Countertransference and Intersubjectivity

Inscrutably involved, we live in currents of universal reciprocity.
—Martin Buber, *I and Thou*

HOW DO WE EVER really know another person? Or can we? For us as care-givers, this question takes on a particular poignancy. When, as pastors, we dare to take off our shoes and stand reverently on the holy ground before the burn-ing bush of another's experience, are we truly able to enter into that experience? And if we do, even fleetingly, apprehend something from the depths of those flames, how do we know that what we have perceived is a "true" representation of the other's experience, as opposed to something we have imagined or projected from our own experience? Then, as if these questions were not enough, how do we know that what we have come to know will help us to be helpful to the other person? Even if we trust that out of this reverent encounter we have come to know something "true" or "real" about the other, how will that help us decide what to do or to say in the next moment?

It may seem obvious, perhaps, from the way these questions have been framed, or from the changes over the last fifty years in our culture's general understand-ing of how human beings come to know anything, that our own subjectivity as helpers is central to our efforts to know and relate with other people. Yet the idea that the helper's subjectivity counts at all in the helping equation, as any-thing other than a possible hindrance, is still considered quite new and treated with a good deal of suspicion in most of the helping professions. The prevail-ing model of professional care, which has valued objectivity, neutrality, and a level of scientific detachment, is only a few hundred years old. But it is the model in which most European and American adults have been schooled, whether as practitioners or as patients or recipients of care.

Nearly everyone reading this book has probably been brought up to regard doctors, nurses, lawyers, bankers, government officials, police, and other helping professionals, even clergy, as holders of power, knowledge, authority, and expertise, toward which one as a patient, client, citizen, or parishioner is expected to defer. Different cultural communities will regard each of these "authorities" in very different ways, based on their experience of how power has been used—as benign and trustworthy or as discriminatory, threatening, or abusive. Some of us have been socialized to expect to be mainly on the receiving end of professional "help," while others of us have been socialized to aspire to join the guilds of those holding professional degrees, credentials, and an authorized body of knowledge. But whether we expect to be helpers or mostly to seek help, and whether we tend to construe professional helpers as genuinely helpful or abusive, there is a large social divide between those upon whom society has conferred the credentials of professional helper or caregiver and those who come to such professionals for care.

I do not agree with the most radical critics of this social situation that, therefore, all systems of professional training and expertise are de facto abusive, built on power over others and at others' expense.[1] (This book itself, in its very existence, participates in the notion that education and training of professional helpers has positive value for the genuine care of others.) I do believe, however, that the paradigm of the professional as supposedly *neutral and objective* has unnecessarily widened the gulf between helper and helpee, and even exacerbated abuses of power. It is this paradigm of supposed objectivity, also called *positivism*, which is critiqued and replaced by the intersubjective[2] or "relational"[3] paradigm[4] described later in this chapter.

How Do We Know? Postmodern Challenges

"Only connect."[5] E. M. Forster's prescription for the "salvation that was latent" in every soul has become a catchphrase in contemporary American culture.[6] Yet, consider how seldom, in spite of our generally extroverted and talkative culture, we truly feel a sense of intimate connection with another, even someone we see and work with daily, even someone with whom we share our bed or breakfast table. We cannot separate our subjectivity from any aspect of our knowing, and we "know" that "I" enters every equation, no matter how hard we strive to achieve a neutral, observing stance. Yet this awareness of the centrality of our own subjectivity is, in itself, evidence that there has been a paradigm shift away from the so-called Modernist, or Enlightenment, standard of objective knowledge.

Modernism[7] is seen by many as beginning with René Descartes' famous dictum in the seventeenth century, "*Cogito, ergo sum* [I think, therefore I am]."

This statement privileged the rational, as many postmodern critics of the Enlightenment have pointed out. It privileged reason over emotion, and mind over body, in ways that have infiltrated Western thought for three centuries, but also hearkened back to much earlier Platonic privileging of idea over embodiment, or ideal (or archetype) over representation in the world. However, Descartes' *cogito* not only privileged the rational. It also privileged the (supposedly) objective. It presupposed a separation between observer and observed, knower and known.

At the heart of the *cogito* was what has come to be called the "Cartesian anxiety."[8] Descartes was so shaken by his fear of being deceived into making an error that he pursued an absolute ideal of objectivity, which could establish an "unshakable foundation" of truth. A dread of ambiguity arose from the notion that either one knew something to an utter certainty, or everything would collapse into a wild relativism, with no solid ground on which to stand. Descartes's original conviction was that one could be certain only of the existence of one's own reasoning mind ("I think, therefore I am") and therefore of the existence of God as prime cause.

This narrow construal of knowledge was eventually expanded, however, even in Descartes's own work, to encompass many areas of rational, scientific inquiry. This, in turn, led to a conviction, around the time when Isaac Newton began his own scientific inquiries, that finally anything in the physical world could be known, given the right tools and formulas. The idea of knowledge, then, was guided by a dread of believing something that might not be "true," building one's theories on a false foundation, and a concomitant passion for trying to know what is really real. Further, if something was tested to be true in one situation, it was presumed to be true universally. Over the centuries, the belief in the superiority of mind over both body and emotion grew into an overconfidence in scientific rationalism, culminating in the nineteenth-century ideals of universal truth and progress.

Postmodernism has become the very large umbrella term for multiple critiques, beginning in the mid-twentieth century, of this confidence in objective knowledge and universal truth. The relational model from contemporary psychoanalysis is strongly informed by postmodernist attacks on the Enlightenment ideals of objectivity, ontological certainty, and universal claims to truth.

The scientific stance of the Enlightenment is called *positivism*. The tenets of positivism include the following statements: Truth is real, discoverable, knowable, universal, and eternal. Reality exists "out there," somewhere where we can look at it or examine it. One can positively know what is real through sensory perception, and if there are difficulties in discovering certain facts, the problem will be in the inadequacy of one's tools of measurement. Given sophisticated-enough tools and adequate experimental controls to isolate the phenomena being studied, any phenomenon in the universe can be studied, quantified, and understood. Phenomena also will operate according to discoverable natural laws that do not change over time. Patterns of cause and effect can be determined and will always apply the same way to the same phenomena in the same circumstances. Metaphors used to describe the universe in this model of thought tend to be mechanistic—that is, describing the universe in terms of known machines (for example, a finely tuned clock). Knowledge in this system is built accumulatively and slowly, by accretion, and much of the work of science is to improve and refine the tools and strategies of measurement to uncover more and more details of what is already there in nature to be discovered.

This rational approach to truth was seen as a great improvement over medieval thought, which was increasingly already regarded by scholastic philosophers of the twelfth and thirteenth centuries as governed by superstition and lacking in adequate, consistent methods for testing elements of the universe and reality. Human beings and, in particular, human reason were confidently elevated to the center of the universe as its masters. Progress was the assumed end result of positivist scientific discovery. This Modernist worldview has functioned for centuries, not perceived as a "worldview" at all, but simply as the unquestionable, unconsciously accepted "way things are." It is already a postmodern idea to relativize this view, dethroning it from the status of reality itself to the status of merely one possible worldview or paradigm, however dominant.

Postmodernism represents a many-sided assault on Modernist confidence. Many critiques arose roughly around the same time in the decades after World War II and together constitute the multiple factors leading to a revolutionary questioning of Enlightenment principles. True to its inherent rejection of universals, the movement of "postmodernism" actually represents a widely diverse set of political, cultural, literary, and scientific revolutions, termed by John Caputo a "post-paradigmatic diaspora."[9] However, it is precisely the cumulative effect of critiques from many disciplines that made the assault more devastating.

Multiple causes arose in the wake of World War II for disenchantment with Enlightenment thinking and the hegemony of scientific rationalism. Among these were the disillusionment with world powers' capacity to make life better for poor and oppressed people, disillusionment with "rational" and "scientific" thought in the wake of the atom bomb, and the undeniable evil of the Holocaust,[10] with its instruments of torture and death, invented by the most supposedly rational, scientific, and technologically advanced nations of the world. Postmodern political scientist Zygmunt Bauman wrote:

The unspoken terror permeating our collective memory of the Holocaust . . . is the gnawing suspicion that the Holocaust could be more than an aberration, more than a deviation from an otherwise straight path of progress, more than a cancerous growth on the otherwise healthy body of the civilized society; that, in short, the Holocaust was not an antithesis of modern civilization and everything (or so we like to think) it stands for. We suspect (even if we refuse to admit it) that the Holocaust could merely have uncovered another face of the same modern society whose other, so familiar face we so admire. And that the two faces are perfectly comfortably attached to the same body.[11]

A slow, sickening realization dawned that higher rationality did not equate with higher morality. In fact, as Bauman pointed out, the ultrarationality and efficiency of the modern age was not in opposition to the barbarism of the Holocaust but, in fact, fostered it.[12]

Beginning in the nineteenth century, Marxists and other political analysts, and more recently the civil rights movement and the women's movement, have further questioned the Enlightenment confidence in progress by asking, "Progress for *whom*?" At the same time these social and political questions were being raised, the advent of quantum physics and relativity theory in the realm of science threw Newtonian paradigms up in the air and reopened the questions, What is reliably known about the way the universe operates? How do we account for the many inconsistencies—for example, that quanta (discrete bundles of energy at the subatomic level) seem to operate as both particles and waves, things scientists thought were mutually exclusive?

Many key figures have been recognized as contributing significant elements in the postmodern revolution.[13] A few examples will suffice in this chapter to give a flavor for the sweeping changes in philosophy, science, and many other arenas. One important figure was the political philosopher Michel Foucault.[14] Foucault was a keen observer of social systems, in particular, institutions endowed with power in society. Foucault, following the seventeenth-century scientific philosopher Francis Bacon, believed that knowledge is power. But Foucault further saw the potential for violence in this power. In his studies of prisons and mental hospitals, he identified that professions develop vocabularies that confer membership in an elite. Professional language thus functions as an exclusionary jargon. Power is operationalized through institutionalization, and through what Foucault called "discourses of power," with the *dominant* discourse given a tacit label of truth. In this view, reason is actually conformity in the guise of common sense and natural law. Thus, in the words of one observer of postmodernism, "[Reason] produces an administered society, not a rational society."[15]

The dominant discourse includes not only terms for defining people and phenomena, but also rules, norms, and contexts. The "other" is defined by what "reason" must exclude to legitimize itself—madness and deviance from what is labeled as normal.[16] Any discourse that defines people and phenomena differently becomes a "dissident discourse." There is an expertocracy, in which experts trained in the dominant discourses define "human nature" and derive laws from what they have previously defined. This whole process is further obfuscated by calling each of these definitions and laws a "discovery."

Each institution has its own version of this process. In the institution of the church, for example, church hierarchies write dogma and doctrine in which those who are in power in the church define and legislate proper Christian conduct. This power is then obscured and denied by being called God's law. Within a given ecclesiastical system, there may be people who disagree with the hierarchy on a range of subjects, from rules governing personal sexual morality to stances on public issues such as poverty or war. Dissenters, however, are not given equal access to decision making and often are even pathologized or demonized. The effect of this is that "dissident discourses," to use Foucault's term, are effectively marginalized and have no authority except perhaps within the limited circle of a dissident subculture.

Complementary to Foucault's critique is the work of the literary philosopher Jacques Derrida.[17] Derrida's method, called *deconstruction*, revolves around the scrutiny of texts to reveal hidden meanings and biases and to observe gaps and inconsistencies. Feminist and other contemporary biblical scholars have used a similar "hermeneutics of suspicion" to uncover previously unquestioned biases and gaps in biblical texts that have reinforced the marginalization of women and other oppressed groups.[18] Further, what might be considered a "text" has been broadened by postmodern analysts of culture to include not only written documents, but also film, visual art, advertising, architecture, and even human bodies and behaviors.[19]

Derrida is particularly suspicious of universals. Total-*ity* is aligned with totalitarian-*ism*. Derrida has asserted that "every totality can be totally shaken," shown to be founded on what it *excludes* and what it *privileges*. Derrida plays with nineteenth-century philosopher Martin Heidegger's notion of *différence* or, to be specific, the difference between being (small *b*), a particular state of being, and Being (capital *B*), a more transcendent category denoting all being or the essence of being. Derrida says that in totalist discourse, particular differences are obscured or suppressed, so the dominant mode of being, which is actually only one particular state of being, comes to represent all Being and takes on the authority of transcendence. This has the effect of elevating particular truths to the stature of universal, essential Truth and subjugating alternative truths or visions as untruth. Derrida asserts that therefore no text has just one meaning, and it is the job of the exegete to uncover alternative meanings, especially those that may have been obscured, omitted, or excluded.

Derrida explicitly draws this analysis in relation to issues of race and Western culture. In his essay "White Mythology," he writes:

> Metaphysics—the white mythology which reassembles and reflects the culture of the west: the white man takes his own mythology, Indo-European mythology, his own *logos,* that is, the *mythos* of his idiom, for the universal form of that he must still wish to call Reason. Which does not go uncontested. Aristos *(Ariste),* the defender of metaphysics . . . finishes by *leaving,* determined to break off dialogue with a cheater: "I leave unconvinced. If only you had reasoned by the rules, I could have rebutted your arguments quite easily." White mythology-metaphysics has erased within itself the fabulous scene that has produced it, the scene that nevertheless remains active and stirring, inscribed in white ink, an invisible design covered over in the palimpsest.[20]

Woman has similarly been recognized as the "Other" in feminist postmodern writings. French feminism in particular has made significant contributions to postmodernist thought, beginning with Simone de Beauvoir, who wrote as early as 1953, "Representation of the world, like the world itself, is the work of men; they describe it from their own point of view, which they confuse with truth."[21]

Two of the most important contemporary French feminist writers are Julia Kristeva[22] and Luce Irigaray.[23] Both women are psychoanalysts, trained and strongly influenced by the influential French psychoanalytic theorist Jacques Lacan.[24] Lacanian theory has emphasized linguistics, semiotics, and the acquisition of language as the central influences on the formation of the self. In Lacanian terms, it is language that initiates each individual into culture, which he called the "law of the father." For the French feminists, following Lacan, there is no escape from the "law of the father," because we are all initiated into it before we are verbal and before we have the capacity for rational symbolic thought, through our very acquisition of the symbol system of language itself.

As we absorb the symbol system of our language, we absorb along with it a particular approach to truth that suppresses otherness and difference. These feminist theorists critique Western philosophy's obsession with "oneness" in favor of a revaluing of "otherness." They reframe the Enlightenment ideal of unity as "the logic of the same," in which otherness is tacitly equated with women, with persons of color, and, in Kristeva's theological writings, also with God—providing a theoretical opening for solidarity between God and the oppressed. The "Other" is the "blind spot" in Western discourse. Irigaray's approach to this problem is to subvert language by using it in ways that turn normal linguistic rules upside down and, like Derrida, to challenge unitary readings of text.

In addition to philosophy, political science, and literary theory, the field of science, particularly the field of quantum physics, introduced yet another assault on the notion of a measurable, unitary, stationary idea of truth. Early in the twentieth century, nuclear physicist Werner Heisenberg introduced what he called the "uncertainty principle," which grew out of the study of atoms, in particular, attempts to study and measure subatomic particles. Heisenberg's uncertainty principle resulted from the observation that if one sets out to measure one property of a subatomic particle absolutely accurately—for example, its position—one cannot avoid disturbing it, so other properties—for example, momentum—immediately become uncertain. In other words, *as soon as I study anything, I disturb it.*

This principle is radical precisely because it undoes even the possibility of the positivist notion of a "neutral observer," who could stand back and study a phenomenon without having any impact upon it. There is no "Archimedean point," the point at which Archimedes postulated that, given a long enough lever and a place in space to position oneself, it would be possible to move the earth.[25] The social sciences have seized upon this realization, because if neutral observation is impossible in the study of subatomic particles, how much more impossible such neutrality and detachment must be in the study of human phenomena. In the social sciences, including anthropology, sociology, and psychology, there has been a parallel recognition that it is often more honest for researchers to understand ourselves as "participant observers," who have effects, both intended and unintended, on our "research subjects." We cannot observe something without interacting with it. We cannot study another person without having a mutual effect on each other's lives, if only for a moment.

This realization that mutual influence is inherent in every encounter, however fleeting, is at the heart of relational psychoanalytic theory. Human relatedness and the relatedness of particles in nature even appear to participate in similar patterns of interconnectedness. In Carl Sagan's famous words, "We are made of star stuff."[26] The mutual influence of all human relatedness profoundly appears to parallel the discoveries of quantum physics at the most minute level (at least to date) of what is observable by human beings. As Cambridge physicist and Anglican priest John Polkinghorne has written about the level of subatomic particles,

> Once two electrons . . . have interacted with each other, they [forever] possess a power to influence each other, however widely they subsequently separate.

If one electron stays around the laboratory and the other goes "beyond the Moon" (as we say), then anything I do to the electron here will have an immediate effect on its distant brother...There's an intrinsic togetherness [in the subatomic world] that cannot be broken.[27]

If we translate this into our own human situation, we realize that we are all interconnected, even physically, at the level of the molecules, atoms, and particles that make up our seemingly solid bodies. Both our seeming physical separateness and our subjective sense of individualism are illusions—illusions created by rationality itself. This illusion of human life as discrete and separate is taken for granted as reality (and reinforced in some cultures, such as Western European culture, even more than in others). Finally, however, contemporary science tells us that this reality does not exist at a subatomic level far beneath our surface sensory perceptions.

The question of reality leads, finally, back to the questions of how we know what we know, and how we come to know one another. From a postmodern view, gathering all the strands of critique just enumerated, knowledge and reality itself are radically reenvisioned. In the relational paradigm, there is no singular, solid, unchangeable reality. Reality itself is a *construction* of human rationality, human sociality,[28] human knowing.

The Social Construction of Reality

Named for this idea of reality as pure mental construction, *contructivism* represents the most radical of several alternatives to the positivist paradigm.[29] Constructivism finds its philosophical roots in the work of Immanuel Kant.[30] Moving beyond Locke, Mills, and the British empiricists who believed in the power of reason to discover truth through experience, and provoked by Hume's skepticism, Kant (treading a classical philosophical path that might be traced back to Plato) posited an absolute distance between *noumena* (reality as it is in itself) and *phenomena* (perceptions of that reality as it appears to the observer). For Kant, the noumenal realm of things-in-themselves was outside all human knowing, and phenomenal reality was what could be lived by human beings (still assuming one common, universal human experience). This increasing attention in philosophy to experience meant that increasingly "reality" was in the eye of the beholder.

Friedrich Nietzsche in the nineteenth century carried this into an assault on positivist science: "Against all positivism which halts at phenomena: 'There are only facts,' I would say, 'No.' Facts are precisely what there are not—only interpretations."[31] Nietzsche understood reality to be created, not discovered, and brought this to its most radical expression in relation to subjectivity and the sense of one's own self: "The fundamental false observation is that *I* believe it is *I* who do something, suffer something, have something."[32]

Constructivism rejects the notion that any reality exists outside the framework of some mental construct or theory. Objectivity is impossible, because reality is shaped by the interaction between observer and observed. Reality, finally, for constructivists, does not exist in any a priori sense but is literally created by interaction. Relativism replaces realism in this paradigm, as there is no fixed point of observation. Knowledge is approximated through hermeneutical and dialectical methods of inquiry, but there is no final truth, only consensus views, which emerge from local, particular, experience-near constructions, and these are therefore always open to transformation.

There is a more middle view between positivism and constructivism, called *postpositivism*. Postpositivism (also referred to as "critical realism" and "nonfoundationalism" in literary theory)[33] retains the Enlightenment belief in a reality "out there" that obeys natural laws, but it rejects positivism's confidence that it is possible to know that reality in an objective, distanced way. Postpositivist epistemologies emphasize the impact of the observer on the observed, and the impossibility of ridding oneself of bias or embeddedness in context. There are no a priori foundations or standards existing apart from nature by which knowledge or truth can be authoritatively asserted.

A related movement named *critical theory*[34] shares these assumptions of postpositivism but further emphasizes the importance of social and political context and, drawing from Karl Marx, Max Weber, and Émile Durkheim, the impossibility of value-free knowledge. Critical theory attempts to uncover hidden values and biases in stated truth claims, particularly those that contribute to social, political, and economic oppression. The Frankfurt school of philosophy, French structuralism, literary poststructuralism, sociology of knowledge, cultural Marxism, and feminist theory all utilize this epistemology. Social constructionism, from the field known as sociology of knowledge, asserts that reality is socially constructed.[35] Moreover, certain groups have the power to name and define reality (and, hence, nonreality) for other groups. These definitions of reality become the dominant paradigm, or "discourse" (borrowing Foucault's terminology), effectively marginalizing oppressed groups and dismissing alternative views of reality.

Table 1 summarizes the three main positions with regard to reality, "truth," and how we come to know what and whom we know: positivism (or Modernism), postpositivism as a middle position, and constructivism as the most radical departure from Enlightenment positivism.[36]

Table 1. Three Positions toward Reality

	Positivism	*Postpositivism*	*Constructivism*
Nature of reality	Reality exists "out there," and one can know reality as it is positively perceived through the senses.	Reality exists "out there," but one cannot know reality positively through the senses because these are subject to distortion, bias, and contextual influence.	There is no reality "out there"; what we perceive as reality is continually constructed within mental frameworks or theories of meaning, and these are further coconstructed in relational interactions.
Scientific worldview	Newtonian physics— The world operates according to regular mechanical laws of cause and effect (like a clock).[37]	Drawn from both Newtonian physics and chaos theory—How the world operates depends on the level or nature of what is observed (clocks or clouds; inanimate, animate, or human phenomena).	Chaos theory (from quantum physics)—The world operates according to multiple mutual influences among particles and forces (like clouds).
Method of knowing	"Scientific method"— objective, empirical observation, also called experimental design; laboratory settings preferred as most "neutral." Quantitative (i.e., statistical) research only. Questions are generated deductively, from theory through hypothesis testing to confirmation of theory.	"Quasi-experimental" designs in which observation of natural occurrences replaces strict manipulation of controls and conditions on data; "naturalistic" rather than laboratory settings preferred for observation; combination of quantitative and qualitative methods of research. Questions move both deductively and inductively.	Dialogical, hermeneutical, or narrative explorations of meaning through shared interaction between observer and observed; participant-observer designs in which observer is immersed in setting; qualitative research only. Questions are generated inductively, from observations to proposals of theory.
Theory of truth	"Correspondence theory"—What is proposed as true must correspond with empirically observed reality.	← both/and → Perception of truth is always context dependent.	"Truths" are multiple, fluid, local, particular, changing, and cocreated.
	"I see, I know, it is real." Seeing face-to-face is possible in the here and now. Confidence is placed in the revelations of received scientific and rational tradition.	"I see ('in a mirror dimly'). It is real, but 'my' perceptions are distorted by inner biases and external influences."	"I/we/you see/feel/experience. I know ('in part'). We change each other as we interact."

We might think of these three views of reality in relation to Paul's words to the church at Corinth in 1 Corinthians 13:12. The postpositivist position puts the emphasis on seeing "in a mirror dimly" *(en ainigmati)*—literally, as an obscure or indistinct image, or even (as in classical Greek) a riddle.[38] There is an external reality that may be dimly perceived, but for the postpositivist, awareness of one's own subjectivity means that one's vision is always clouded by one's own biases, projections, needs, and desires or, from a religious framework, one's own sin. There is a humility and circumspection in this position that therefore refrains from asserting that what one perceives is "the" truth. There is ample room left for mystery (the *enigmatic*), and a deep respect for the unknown.

Similarly, and to an even more rigorous degree, the constructivist position can be characterized by the statement, "Now I know only in part" *(ek merous)*—literally, a part in contrast to the whole, or even one's allotted portion, lot, or destiny.[39] The very most one can claim from a constructivist perspective is that one has a partial view of reality, and even this partial view is fleeting and highly suspect. One's view is always circumscribed by one's own local, particular situation—one's social location, one's context and culture, one's own awarenesses and blind spots. One's view is always subjective and contingent, so it is (or should be) open to revision through mutual influence and genuine engagement with the other.

Both of these positions acknowledge the limitedness and contingent nature of the human condtion in lived time. Philosophical, psychoanalytic, and scientific paradigms do not address the eschatological realm—Paul's "then," when we shall see "face-to-face." Christians may and do posit an eschatological fulfillment of all time in which there is full knowledge, recognition funded in the divine wisdom. We may glimpse this in the fleeting but genuine "I-Thou" encounter of which Martin Buber wrote,[40] when we sense in a momentary true meeting with another the inbreaking of the eternal Realm of God into the fleeting present moment—*kairos* (time-in-eternity) breaking into the *chronos* (ordinary measurable clock time) of our daily lives. But in the lived day-to-day of *chronos* time, we are unable to sustain such kairotic meeting.

The fallacy of the positivist view is to confuse the dim and partial view of one's own *chronos*-bound perceptions with the eternal, universal wisdom of the divine. This is as good a definition of sin as any—that by nature we humans must inevitably collapse back into our own limited perception and then mistake it for the eternal. The positivist view insists that we see "face-to-face," we "know fully" *now,* not in some deferred eschatological moment. The Modernist view believes in progress, learning built cumulatively upon prior learning in an ever-upward advance of knowledge. The truth about reality is conquerable, given the right tools and powerful enough instruments. The only limitation of which a strict positivist view will admit is the limitation of its tools and instruments, so much scientific exploration is then devoted to the invention of better instruments and more sophisticated technology for the testing of hypotheses generated within the operant paradigm.[41]

What is missed in this view is that solutions to problems are always bounded by the paradigm that generated them in the first place. That is, positivist research, because it is deductive, ignores the assumptive nature of the theories that generate the questions of research. It thereby confuses particular answers to these theoretically bounded questions with universal answers to supposedly universal questions. The fallacy of the positivistic view, then, is finally narcissistic, because it confuses the eternality of the eschatological "then" with the partiality and dimness of one's own human view.

The Relational Paradigm and the Nature of Subjectivity

Finally, to return to the relational paradigm, writers in the relational school of psychoanalytic theory appear to fall to varying degrees between the postpositivist and constructivist ends of the spectrum of viewpoints challenging positivism. Explicitly feminist work by Jessica Benjamin[42] and others incorporates elements of critical theory and social constructionism. Most relational analysts tend to agree, based on their clinical practice, that there is some basis of reality in terms of actual, external events in the lives of helpees. They agree further that not every statement is reducible to a purely subjective construction of reality, but that the meaning of such events is multiple, fluid, and continually under revision. Much therapeutic work is therefore understood as dialectical and hermeneutical (as in narrative therapy models).[43] Meaning, and therefore reality itself in the form of one's worldview, is continually being coconstructed in relationships (including all helping relationships). Subjectivity is also no longer understood solely as the product of individual consciousness, but rather as a shared experience of reality in any given moment. Individual subjectivity is relativized in importance, in favor of a view toward *intersubjectivity*[44] as a central (if not the central) area of knowing and experiencing of reality.

The relational model reconceptualizes the very nature of subjectivity itself[45] and begins to conceive the natures of both consciousness and unconsciousness in new, more fluid and dynamic ways. Most previous psychoanalytically based theories constructed consciousness in terms of "depth," originating in Freud's topographical model of consciousness-preconsciousness and the unconscious. Although Sigmund Freud's *Interpretation of Dreams*, written in 1900, is popularly known for his detailed illumination of the symbolic meaning of dreams, this work actually represents one of Freud's most significant achievements as his first explication of his "discovery" of the unconscious, particularly the concepts of repression and unconscious conflict. Over the next decade and a half, Freud worked out the details of what has come to be known as his "topographical" model of the mind. According to this model, conscious-preconscious and unconscious are conceptualized as separate spatial areas of mind, divided by the repression barrier, but each having its own strong influence on behavior, cognition, affect, and sensation—and potential pathogenesis. It was this model that was first transmitted to pastoral caregivers in America. Freud's later contributions—the stages of infantile psychosexual development, the oedipal situation, and the structural model with its tripartite institutions of the mind (ego, id, and superego)—further strengthened the notion of repression as the central mechanism by which certain contents of mind, conceived of as unacceptable or even intolerable, could be swept from consciousness into the "infernal regions" by the "higher powers" of a well-civilized, well-socialized ego. This model of conscious-preconscious and unconscious divided by a repression barrier had a powerful and formative influence on pastoral psychology and pastoral theology from its earliest days.

Over the decades, various schools of thought increasingly came to differ as to the precise contents of the unconscious domain and the mechanisms by which feelings, thoughts, sensations, and fantasies came to be in the unconscious (in particular, whether by repression, following Freud, or some other form of splitting, as in Kleinian and object relations theories). Even so, the unconscious was consistently viewed as something deeper, to be plumbed for insights that would cure psychic pain.

In the relational model, in contrast, the process of dissociation has come into greater focus, alongside earlier models of repression and splitting. In part, this has been due to the experience of a number of relational theorists in treating survivors of childhood sexual abuse, and their familiarity with traumatic dissociation.[46] But relational therapists in general have come to view dissociation as a nonpathological phenomenon, placing it alongside or even replacing repression altogether as the primary model of mental geography.

Jody Messler Davies has summarized this aspect of relational theory "that has begun to conceive of self, indeed of mind itself, as a multiply organized, associationally linked network of parallel, coexistent, at times conflictual, systems of meaning attribution and understanding."[47] Concerning multiplicity of consciousness, she also wrote:

> Not one unconscious, not the unconscious, but multiple levels of consciousness and unconsciousness, in an ongoing state of interactive articulation as past experience infuses the present and present experience evokes state-dependent

memories of formative interactive representations. Not an onion, which must be carefully peeled, or an archeological site to be meticulously unearthed and reconstructed in its original form, but a child's kaleidoscope in which each glance through the pinhole of a moment in time provides a unique view; a complex organization in which a fixed set of colored, shaped, and textured components rearrange themselves in unique crystalline structures determined by way of infinite pathways of interconnectedness.[48]

In this view, dissociation is not necessarily regarded as pathological per se, although it may become problematic, as in severe post-traumatic states in which continual experiences of fragmentation interrupt the normal sense of a seamless continuity of consciousness. However, dissociation, or multiplicity, is increasingly being recognized as inherent in mental functioning, and not only a consequence of trauma. The idea that the mind begins as a unitary phenomenon and is gradually fragmented by traumatic experience is itself increasingly being challenged. Philip Bromberg, a relational psychoanalyst who has written considerably about dissociation, the unconscious, and clinical process, has observed:

> The process of dissociation is basic to human mental functioning and is central to the stability and growth of personality. It is intrinsically an adaptational talent that represents the very nature of what we call "consciousness." Dissociation is not fragmentation. In fact, it may be reasonably seen as a defense against fragmentation, and in this regard, Ferenczi's struggle with whether fragmentation is merely a mechanical consequence of trauma or may actually be a form of adaptation to it was brilliantly ahead of its time. The answer to his question, however, took 60 years to appear. There is now abundant evidence that the psyche does not start as an integrated whole, but is nonunitary in origin—a mental structure that begins and continues as a multiplicity of self-states that maturationally attain a feeling of coherence which overrides the awareness of discontinuity. This leads to the experience of a cohesive sense of personal identity and the necessary illusion of being "one self."[49]

Bromberg and others point to a body of psychoanalytically informed research based on infant observation. Researchers such as Robert Emde,[50] Daniel Stern,[51] and Beatrice Beebe and Frank Lachmann[52] have observed that the earliest experiences of the self appear to be organized around a variety of shifting self-states that encompass cognitive, affective, and physiological dimensions and appear to include internalized representations of relational or interactive experiences.[53] A central aspect of the developmental process, then, consists of being able increasingly to move smoothly and seamlessly from one self-state to another with an increasing sense of self-continuity and an increasing capacity for self-regulation. This process is facilitated (or not facilitated) by primary caretakers' responsiveness (or lack thereof). The quality of the boundaries between self and other also gradually comes to be established, through mutual recognition and regulation or, in less desirable scenarios, impaired by parental nonrecognition and/or intrusion.

This view in relational theory has also been highly influenced by clinical work with trauma survivors, particularly survivors of sexual abuse. In fact, one of the central recent sources of disruption of Freud's topographical and structural models has been the reemergence of serious attention to the sequelae of severe trauma in mental life. Relational authors are to some extent reclaiming models of dissociation advanced by Freud's predecessors Jean-Martin Charcot[54] and Pierre Janet,[55] whose studies of hysteria took seriously the link between trauma and dissociation, as well as the writings of Sandor Ferenczi,[56] whose continuing emphasis on the actual impact of environmental trauma contributed to his ejection from Freud's inner circle.

Subjectivity and Memory

Knowledge of self and other is deeply intertwined with past as well as current events. How the past is remembered—embodied, internalized, symbolized, and codified—will affect and shape each individual's present subjective reality. The mutability or robustness of memory, particularly traumatic memory, is an arena in which questions of consciousness and unconsciousness have been hotly debated in recent years. Both "repression" and "dissociation" as terms have been appropriated—sometimes incorrectly—by combatants in recent wars about the reliability of memories of adult survivors of childhood sexual abuse. The politicization of issues surrounding trauma, sexual abuse, and so-called recovered memory therapy has unfortunately obscured or skewed a growing body of serious research on both traumatic and nontraumatic memory. We have already seen that "forgetting" is not conceived of within psychoanalytic models as a single process. Rather, it may involve repression (in Freud's original sense of banishing once-known but intolerable thoughts, particularly wishes), disavowal (in which something fully known but dystonic with one's sense of oneself is split off from everyday awareness), and dissociation (in which multiple arenas of cognition, affect, and sensation may be split off from consciousness for varying lengths of times and with boundaries of varying permeability). Exegeting beyond political rhetoric for valid evidence about the nature of memory, a somewhat less politically clouded but no less complex consensus may now be beginning to emerge. Some basic principles include the following:

- Memory is not a single phenomenon or process. Neuropsychological studies have determined that memory is "state dependent," that is, determined by whether the external circumstance is relatively calm or threatening.[57] Trauma specialists working in the medical and neurobiological fields are now validating the importance of dissociative processes on a spectrum from normal and universally experienced shifts in states of affect and cognition to highly fragmented states of consciousness resulting from efforts to adapt to extreme trauma.[58] Psychobiologists have also begun to offer evidence for the impact of a normative, nontraumatic early social environment on the brain, pinpointing neurochemical changes resulting from affect-regulating functions of the primary caretaker. They suggest a model of mind with greater developmental plasticity throughout the life span, and in some ways more in keeping with lateral moves among multiple mental states than a vertical model of repression as the sole mechanism of removing mental contents from awareness.[59]

- Not all memory is cognitively processed into a narrative, or even a symbolic, framework. Different types of memory are stored differently in the brain. Ordinary narrative or "declarative" memory is generally associated in neurobiology with the frontal lobe and the hippocampus, while nondeclarative memory (including emotional responses, reflexive actions, classically conditioned responses, and memories of skills and habits) appears to be associated with the central nervous system.[60] There is growing evidence that certain experiences, including severe trauma, may be encoded only in portions of the brain that do not primarily affect cognition, so they are accessible to consciousness only through visual fragments, intense waves of affect, or olfactory, auditory, or bodily sensations.[61] Hormonal hyperarousal resulting in chronic anxiety states, and dissociative responses, may themselves be memory traces.[62]

- The brain may encode an event, including affect, sensation, and cognition, in several separate domains at once, but subsequent cognitive processing may never connect the domains to make what we would ordinarily understand as a full narrative memory of an event by subsequent cognitive processing.[63] The capacity to process an experience is strongly influenced by the safety of the environment at the time of the event and immediately thereafter, as well as by whether the environment is hospitable or inhospitable to the act of processing into memory. Distortion may be introduced during the time period immediately surrounding the trauma. For example, in a situation of familial incest, the abuser may frame a painful sexual violation as something good and wanted, and other family members may treat the situation as unreal and unseen.

- Some memories may be fabricated or, more likely, elaborated from a kernel of actual experience. However, the heavily touted evidence that false memories

can be implanted by another person has frequently been overstated for political purposes.[64] In most cases, a core of memory persists, although it may not
have narrative form. At any given time, details of what is remembered may be
shaped in consciousness by the relational surround, including both personal
and wider societal canons affecting what is believable.[65]

• Perhaps most important in terms of its implications for clinical and pastoral
  work, memory cannot be divorced from *meaning*. Details of a remembered
  event may in fact shift and change, particularly in what is background versus
  foreground, depending on the meaning or multiple meanings assigned to the
  experience. This process of meaning-making is not a solitary one but is coconstructed (for good or for ill) in both therapeutic and nontherapeutic relationships. A constructivist framework for therapeutic and pastoral work does
  not imply that original events are being "made up" by helper and helpee.[66]
  *What is coconstructed is not the core of experience, but what the experience comes to
  mean.* The process of meaning-making is not and should not be viewed as
  moving toward some single, incontrovertible truth or concrete certainty. The
  "truth" of an experience, when given an open, nonleading, and nonintrusive
  exploration in a context of mutual, empathic curiosity, will usually become increasingly rich, complex, and multiple over time.[67]

Increasing recognition of the complexity of memory, traumatic and otherwise, leads to more complex understandings of consciousness itself as influenced by the vicissitudes of loss, grief, and desire and by the coconstruction of
reality in the context of relationships.

A Postmodern Subjectivity/Intersubjectivity

This view coincides with investigations on the nature of subjectivity(ies) currently being advanced on the philosophical front by postmodernism. Postmodernist thinkers have, from a slightly different vantage point than the discipline
of psychology, also called into question the whole notion of a unitary self. Some
have drawn analogies between the mind and cyberspace, which Graham Ward
has described as "an undefined spatiality, like the contours of a perfume."[68] A
somewhat parallel paradigm shift in cognitive science is a movement variously
called "connectionism" or "parallel distributed processing," which draws analogies between "human information processing" and digital computers.[69] Such
constructs are problematic, however, if taken to extremes. The metaphor of
cyberspace and computers is mechanistic and may tend back toward a more abstract Cartesian conception of mind, in which time and the body again are
disregarded.

Drawing both from the feminist writers Luce Irigaray and Hélène Cixous and from contemporary psychoanalysis, Jane Flax presents a critique of Modernist conceptions of a unitary self as potentially repressive of subjugated inner voices:

> I believe a unitary self is unnecessary, impossible, and a dangerous illusion. Only multiple subjects can invent ways to struggle against domination that will not merely recreate it. In the process of therapy, in relations with others, and in political life we encounter many difficulties when subjectivity becomes subject to one normative standard, solidifies into rigid structures, or lacks the capacity to flow readily between different aspects of itself... No singular form can be sufficient as a regulative ideal or as a prescription for human maturity or the essential human capacity... [I]t is possible to imagine subjectivities whose desires for multiplicity can impel them toward emancipatory action. These subjectivities would be fluid rather than solid, contextual rather than universal, and process oriented rather than topographical. Emancipatory theories and practices require mechanics of fluids [a phrase from Luce Irigaray] in which subjectivity is conceived as processes rather than as a fixed atemporal entity locatable in a homogeneous, abstract time and space [Flax's reading of the Cartesian idea of the self]. In discourses about subjectivity the term "the self" will be superseded by discussions of "subjects." The term "subject(s)" more adequately expresses the simultaneously determined, multiple, and agentic qualities of subjectivity.[70]

As a psychoanalyst, Flax includes in her work a deep respect for mental contents that exist both in and out of awareness. Her conception of a multiple, fluid, contextual conception of self and subjectivity opens the possibility for greater passage between conscious and unconscious, along with a sense of mental contents shifting in and out of awareness as contexts and subjective states shift and change. Freud's "return of the repressed" gives way to a more variable process in which we move in and out of multiple areas of our own knowing and unknowing. "Knowing" itself may be understood as more than cognitive appreciation alone, or even cognitive and affective experience together, which usually can be verbalized. It also may encompass nonverbal mental contents that are only symbolic, or even presymbolic, the knowledge of the body and physical sensation—in Christopher Bollas's words, "the unthought known."[71]

Admittedly, we may feel unsettled by a more multiple, fluid, and spatially conceived model of mind. But advances in psychoanalytic clinical theory, grounded in listening to patients' inner experiences, and in neurobiology, especially research into the aftereffects of traumatic experience, suggest that the postmodern view may be a more generous and apt description of the true complexity and multiplicity of mental life. In fact, given the complex, pluralistic nature of our postmodern world and society, mental health may depend as much on the capacity for "identity complexity"[72] and the ability to entertain multiple meanings as it does on unity, integration, and a capacity to synthesize. Postmodernist writers also highlight the emancipatory implications of such theories of mind, especially as they influence the social construction of self and others, and the resulting social construction of categories such as gender, race, and class and the distribution of power.[73]

Countertransference: The Helper's Subjectivity and the Use of the Self

At its heart, then, the so-called countertransference is the helper's subjectivity. Even in the classical model, it was understood as such. However, in the classical model, subjectivity was not viewed in a positive light. In the scientific belief system in which Freud and most subsequent theorists throughout most of the twentieth century were embedded, the helper was automatically conceived as the subject who observed and knew, and the helpee was always the object to be observed and known. Objectivity was what the helping professional strived to achieve in his (or, less often, her) observations of the other. Subjectivity was devalued as containing contaminating elements of emotionality, irrationality, and unconsciously motivated acting out. Thus, in the classical model of countertransference as described in chapter 2, countertransference was understood as a hindrance to the helping process, something to be analyzed so that it could be done away with, or at least set aside while engaged in the work of helping.

Figure 1 shows a diagram of the positivist view of the helping relationship as lines between helper and helpee. The lines represent the contacts between self and other that constitute the potential for relationship. However, in the positivist paradigm, these lines are clearly polarized, with "I" always depicted on one end, and an "It" on the opposite end. In Buber's terminology, this is not an "I-Thou" relationship, but one in which the other is objectified, as "I-It."[74]

In this conception, the subjectivity of the knower is to be denied. The professional does so by attempting to purge his or her own view of anything irrational or even creative, in favor of appeals to tradition and a body of empirically tested knowledge agreed upon by scientific consensus. Thus, the "subject" in the positivist paradigm is supposed to be "objective" (that is, rational), while it was left to the "object" of knowledge to behave in "subjective" (that is, irrational) ways.

In the relational paradigm, by contrast, subjectivity is revalued as representing the whole spectrum of ways in which both one's own and the other's realities can be understood. Subjectivity does not exclude the rational sense[75] but also incorporates affect and bodily sense as ways in which both self and other

Figure 1. Positivist View of the Helping Relationship

can be known. The relational paradigm also replaces the positivist paradigm's depiction of the relationship between helper and helpee as a one-sided relationship with something vastly more reciprocal. Both helper and helpee in this new model are subjects. They both observe and are observed, know and are known. Moreover, what becomes knowable exists not only in each individual but is made most fully accessible in the potential space that grows up between the two. Knowledge, not only rational but also emotional and embodied, becomes a shared and coconstructed pool in which the two are equally deeply immersed, at both conscious and unconscious levels, in the "between" of their shared interaction.

In the relational sense, then, countertransference is no longer something that belongs exclusively to the helper at all, but rather is the helper's own subjective *experience* of a coconstructed body of knowledge about both self and other, and about the shared relationship in which they mutually participate. If "self" and "other" exist in some sense as equal subjectivities on opposite ends of a spectrum of relatedness that extends from one subjectivity across the gap of knowability to the other, then countertransference is simply a term to describe the subjective experience of the one designated as the helper from his or her end of the spectrum. Transference, similarly, is the subjective experience of the helpee from his or her end. From the perspective of either end of the spectrum, then, there is an "I," perceiving a "Thou," on the other or opposite end. There also is a "We" that spans the entire spectrum and bridges the gap between them.

In the relational paradigm shown in Figure 2, both helper and helpee are simultaneously both "I" and "Thou." Subjectivity and objectivity, rationality and irrationality are shared as both are conceived as being able to feel, experience, and examine what is being shared in their interaction. Instead of one expert and one client, both subjectivities are honored, and both contribute to and, in fact, construct the knowledge shared between them. From a theological perspective, such shared knowledge participates in the "infinite conversation"[76] of which Buber wrote: "Extended, the lines of relationships intersect the eternal Thou."[77]

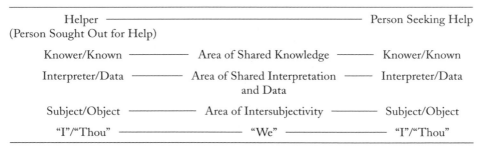

| Helper ——————————————————————————— Person Seeking Help |
| (Person Sought Out for Help) |

| Knower/Known ————— Area of Shared Knowledge ————— Knower/Known |
| Interpreter/Data ————— Area of Shared Interpretation ————— Interpreter/Data |
| and Data |
| Subject/Object ————— Area of Intersubjectivity ————— Subject/Object |
| "I"/"Thou" ————— "We" ————— "I"/"Thou" |

Figure 2. A Relational View of the Helping Relationship

In this model, in fact, as much or more is going on in the *middle* of the spectrum as at either end. In the positivist model, the locus of activity in the relationship is conceived as primarily cognitive, and the activity occurs in the transmission of what is known by the helper to what is eventually received or stimulated as "insight" (a word that itself tends to privilege the visual as a metaphor for the rational) in the helpee. In the relational model, in contrast, insight (or, perhaps in its literal sense, *re-cognition*—thought that goes out and returns influenced, to be rethought again) flows back and forth between the participants. And because knowledge is not construed as only rational, glimmers of comprehension and creative construction of meaning may spark at any point along the spectrum at any time. Recognition also may bubble up in one or both participants in the form of rational thought, affective feeling, and/or bodily sensation or behavior. Sometimes a recognition or realization will occur very focally in just one of these aspects of subjectivity—cognition, affect, sensation, or behavior.[78] At other times, it may occur in multiple areas of awareness or even as a holistic sense of flooding of all one's faculties of perception. Such realizations may occur similarly or differently for each participant at any given moment. Thus, the helper *uses his or her own self*, not only as a channel of information about his or her own inner knowledge and experience, but equally as an empathic receiver of the other's affective state and the shared meaning that is emerging between them.

The Valuing of the Nonverbal and Enactments

Because in the relational model knowledge is not understood only as rational, but also involves affect, sensation, and behavior, this newer model has also given much greater attention to the nonverbal as well as verbal aspects of what occurs from moment to moment in the helping relationship. Most forms of pastoral care, and especially counseling, following influences from the positivist therapeutic model, have generally privileged words over behavior. Exceptions in the realm of pastoral care have often been in the form of anointing or laying on of hands for healing. In general, however, especially in pastoral psychotherapy, thoughts, fantasies, the flow of associations, and the telling of life stories and the narration of dreams have constituted the main arena of healing and change. This served an important purpose, especially in long-term therapeutic relationships in which unconscious material was intentionally elicited and attended to. It allowed for the irrational, the preposterous, and even the dangerous—all the most threatening contents of the unconscious—to be safely admitted into investigation without the threat of enactments that could exploit and harm the helpee.

Relational theorists now argue, however, that this privileging of the verbal in psychotherapy has led to an unintended ignoring of nonverbal communication.[79] In a relational model, attention returns to the concept of *enactment*. In the relational sense, *enactment* is used as a technical term referring to the important but often overlooked nonverbal cues and communications that occur in a helping interaction. The relational school of psychoanalysis gives greater emphasis to the mutuality of therapeutic interactions, recognizing that words and actions are not as distinct as previously conceptualized. These theorists find support for this understanding especially in the work of Ferenczi and his interest in the role of activity in the therapeutic relationship, as well as of the philosopher Ludwig Wittgenstein,[80] who argued that language itself is an action using words as tools.[81] Enactments, following Theodore Jacobs,[82] are not equivalent to the more pejorative term *acting out*. "Acting out" is traditionally considered to represent a failure of the process of reflection and verbalization. But many actions are subtler than the types of behavior labeled as acting out. They may be as nuanced as a glance, a tone of voice, or the momentary slight tremor of a foot. They are generally not conscious. Nor are they the exclusive domain of the patient, as in a more classical paradigm, where only the patient is regarded as saying or doing anything of diagnostic interest.

Enactments are inevitable, continual, and part of an ongoing dance of mutual influence—an "intersubjective" relationship both conscious and unconscious—between helper and helpee. When regarded in this light, virtually every action may have meaning, and often some of the most powerful work of the therapy may be carried on at the nonverbal level.

This new appreciation for the power of enactment is not an open invitation to helping professionals to become more "active," or more personally involved on a social level with individuals who come to them for help. On the contrary, a new appreciation for the potentially multiple meanings that any action can represent at multiple levels of consciousness and unconsciousness, as well as for the fluidity and revisability of meaning over time, constitutes a good argument for continuing to be as conservative as possible about one's level of activity. Only the reason for refraining from overactivity or overinvolvement has shifted. It is no longer adherence to a classical standard of neutrality and objectivity but, rather, an appreciation of the inherent complexity of all interactions and the need within the helping relationship to focus as much as possible on the immediate presenting needs of the helpee. Enactments are inevitable in any case, and there is always more than enough occurring at multiple levels of consciousness and unconsciousness for the helping partnership to "handle" in a way that ultimately will benefit the helpee. Helping professionals do not need to muddy the waters by introducing or allowing themselves to be pulled into a greater level of activity than already exists. This raises the question of how to understand and reenvision ethics in the relational paradigm.

Professional Ethics in the Relational Paradigm

Because of the fluidity of subjectivities in the helping relationship as understood in the relational paradigm, it might be construed that traditional norms concerning boundaries and ethical behavior by helping professionals should be revised. Some writers have, in fact, challenged traditional standards relating to boundaries and professional ethics as perpetuating a harmful power-over dynamic,[83] even rejecting the concept of pastoral care as a profession on the same grounds.[84]

Relational theorists, however, virtually unanimously stress that rigorous attention to ethics is not diminished by the new paradigm. If anything, the new appreciation of intersubjectivity requires an even greater attention to ethical integrity on the part of the helper.[85] One of the most rigorously constructivist relational theorists, Irwin Hoffman, has written, "The kind of authenticity that I have been talking about should not be confused with . . . damaging actions. On the contrary, that authenticity actually incorporates the special kind of discipline that the [professional helping] situation requires."[86]

In the positivist paradigm, there were qualitative differences between helper and helpee, as illustrated above in Figure 1. The helper was the knower and interpreter of the data, which was provided by the helpee. The helper was the knowing subject, the helpee the known object. All this is revised in the relational paradigm, in which helper and helpee coconstruct meaning through the mutual exploration of their shared subjectivity. The hierarchy of knower and known is vastly diminished, and the primary remaining difference between them is not in the validity or quality of the subjectivity or even the objectivity of each, but in their different roles and responsibilities.

Professional training and experience are not erased in this equation, but the use to which professional training is put differs from the positivist model. In the positivist model, training and education are used to maintain the helper's status as expert and objective knower of the other. In the relational model, in contrast, training and education (at least in the ideal) shape that subjectivity in ways that will enhance the helper's capacity to share ideas, observations, and possibilities that can stimulate a mutual curiosity about what is happening in the subjectivity of the helpee and what it might mean to him or her. There is still a difference between the helper and the helpee, and it is primarily an ethical one: the helper has been entrusted with the responsibility to care for the other. Because of this, the professional helping relationship, unlike other, more reciprocal peer relationships and friendships, is focused as a matter of contractual trust to benefit the one seeking help. Both may in fact derive benefit, but the stated purpose of the relationship, and the reason it exists, is to help the helpee.

The totalist understanding of countertransference does not undo the classical understanding of countertransference but incorporates it into a wider subjective experience of both self and other. The helping professional, because of his or her own childhood experiences, will have a unique "role responsiveness" to the helpee's own projections and expectations, conscious and unconscious.[87] As the helpee's projections meet up with the pastor's unconscious role responsiveness, a subtle dance is engaged in which both partners in the therapeutic process begin to recapitulate dynamics from both the helpee's and the helper's past. The pastor or pastoral counselor *is* a professional helper in this dance, not just another dance partner, because of his or her training and experience in recognizing that a dance is happening and in bringing the steps of the dance into conscious awareness in order to make decisions about how to respond so as to be as truly pastoral (focused on the growth and healing of the helpee) as possible.

Relational theorists have begun to reframe this difference in roles from one of hierarchy to one of *asymmetry*.[88] While the participants share a mutuality of subjective experience, there is nevertheless an asymmetry in their respective roles and responsibilities. It would be naive and potentially even dangerous to try to pretend that no power differential exists in this asymmetry. However, the authority conferred on the helper exists not because of any intrinsic superiority, but because of a disproportionate fiduciary (that is, entrusted) responsibility for the welfare of the other. In this sense, there is power in the helping role, but when it is exercised faithfully, it is exercised in the sense of power-for rather than power-over.[89] Abuses are most likely to occur, paradoxically, not when the helper acknowledges this power calmly and openly but, on the contrary, when this power is ignored, denied, or exploited for the gratification of the helper.

Thus, the ethical requirement *primum non nocere* (first to do no harm), with its origins in antiquity in the Hippocratic oath, is no less compelling than it ever was. What has shifted in the new paradigm is not the need for professional ethics and boundaries, but a new understanding of why such ethics and boundaries matter and how to think about them. Many of the values informing professional ethics have been inherited from the positivist framework, including confidentiality (as understood in the sense of who "possesses" information) and a preoccupation with "correct" technique and "accurate" interpretation. This preoccupation with technique presupposes the ability of the helper to "control for" all his or her own internal factors and create a neutral field in which only the helpee is to be changed by the well-intended manipulations of the professional. In the relational paradigm, responsibility shifts from issues of ownership, control, and technique to something that is perhaps even more ethically demanding: a commitment to authenticity, integrity, faithfulness to focusing on the growth and well-being of the one seeking help, and a new form of self-discipline that is framed less around perfecting one's technique than a scrupulous commitment to self-examination—especially because one's own subjectivities have come to be understood in the relational model as simply one point of observation of the entire intersubjective field that lies, continually in flux, between both participants in the dance.

Even classical views of confidentiality are reframed from contractual notions of ownership of information to a concern for "protecting the integrity, the mutual sense of privacy, and the intimacy of one's engagement"[90] with the helpee. Because, finally, in the relational paradigm, much more is going on at any given moment than what appears at the level of conscious interaction, and the meaning of any action is likely to be more multiple, spatial, and revisable than even a classical model of consciousness and unconsciousness.

CHAPTER FOUR

The Relational Paradigm in Pastoral Assessment and Theological Reflection

WHAT ARE THE implications of this new relational, intersubjective paradigm for pastoral practice? This chapter proposes a method of pastoral assessment and theological reflection that focuses on the pastoral caregiver's subjective experience as a way of understanding the experience and needs of the other. This case vignette, and those in the two chapters that follow, are continuations of the case vignettes introduced in the Introduction.

Linda

Linda went home the night of the council meeting uncomfortably aware that she had missed most of the discussion of the agenda. Both Yvonne's face and her grandmother Eleanor's floated in her mind, each one as if superimposed on the other. Linda greeted her husband, Ben, and teenage son, Alex, in the living room but quickly made excuses to be by herself and went up to the small third bedroom that had become her study during seminary. Looking at the shelves of textbooks, she tried to find wisdom or, failing that, comfort from the familiar titles, but nothing could calm her distress. She picked up a framed photograph of her grandmother and herself, taken years before at her wedding. Her grandmother was smiling, sitting bolt upright in a chair set in a place of honor at the reception. She was the picture of a strong elder of the family, a mother of her church, and an influential leader in the local African American community.

Linda began to think of one of Grandma's favorite hymns, "I Want Jesus to Walk with Me,"[1] and tears stung her eyes. All through seminary she had been so busy and so distracted by multiple tasks and responsibilities! The guilt she had felt during Grandma's last two weeks in the hospital and in the months following her death washed back over her as if no time had passed. All the what-ifs flooded back: What if I had just set my studies aside more and been more available to Grandma and the family? What if I had told Professor Shackley that

I just needed to take that fifth course another year, or at least allowed myself to get a C in it? What if I had let myself drop everything and sit at Grandma's bedside like my sister Janet? What if I had used my connections with the hospital chaplain to see if there wasn't one more treatment option they didn't even try because Grandma was considered too old . . . or "too black"? What if . . . ?

Linda went off to bed, where Ben was already fast asleep. She tossed and turned, her stomach churning. She felt frustrated, helpless, and alone.

The next morning Linda awoke early from dreams in which she had been fighting with a hospital administrator over getting new, experimental treatments for Yvonne. Feeling a surge of energy and determination from the power she had felt in the dream, she drove past the church office and on to Yvonne's home. Looking tired but pleased to see her, Yvonne invited her in and offered her a cup of coffee. But Yvonne's pleasure at Linda's pastoral visit soon cooled, as Linda's opening prayer veered quickly into her own agenda for alternative treatments for Yvonne and Linda then began to pepper Yvonne with medical questions and suggestions.

Suddenly, Yvonne realized what was likely going on in the mind and heart of her earnest pastor. Yvonne, too, had grieved when Eleanor had died. Eleanor had been a close friend since childhood, and as others had come and gone in the neighborhood, Eleanor had always been there. They had fought together against crime in the neighborhood and against redlining.[2] They got neighbors involved in community policing to keep their streets safe, and got banks and stores to reinvest in the community. They had also worked to keep the church alive when it seemed that many persons in the neighborhood had either died or moved away. She missed Eleanor terribly, and imagined that Linda must be thinking of her, too. Yvonne felt a wave of fatigue wash over her, but summoning the energy to sit up straighter, she looked Linda kindly in the eyes: "Pastor," she said slowly, "I'm not Eleanor."

Linda sat back, momentarily feeling caught off guard and defensive. "Of course you're not, Yvonne. I just want you to get the best treatment!"

Yvonne closed her eyes and decided to give it one more try. "*Linda*," she said, "don't try to save me. My doctors are doing that already, and believe it or not, I think I can trust them."

Linda felt her anger rising. Interrupting Yvonne's last statement, she burst out, "*Trust* them!? Yvonne, you mentioned Eleanor yourself. Do you really think she got the best treatment? I wish I had fought harder for my grandma, and now I only want what's best for you!"

Yvonne averted her eyes and fussed for a moment with her housecoat, still unused to this much bluntness from the younger generation. Linda had spoken out of a place of truth and righteous anger. There *was* plenty of reason not to trust. No one knew better than Yvonne herself how an older African American woman could be dismissed by the medical system.[3] But Yvonne also knew how to ask the right questions. She believed she had advocated well for herself in this situation, and that her doctors were fine. In spite of Linda's sincerity and her desire to care, Yvonne felt wary. She wondered if Linda was trying to do what she felt she couldn't do for Eleanor by pushing her way into Yvonne's business now. She saw herself at a crossroads, deciding what to say next—as an elder in the church giving Linda a little guidance but also as a parishioner in need of a pastor, especially now that the cancer was back. But could Linda be that pastor, or was her mind still too much on what she had or hadn't done for Eleanor? Yvonne felt herself bristle and draw her mantle of privacy around herself a bit more closely. "Pastor," she said, "everyone appreciates what you tried to do for Eleanor, and I appreciate what you're trying to do for me. But I'm very tired now, and I think we had better just talk another time. I'll certainly let you know if I need anything."

Linda felt the sting of Yvonne's polite dismissal and stood up. "Well," she said, floundering for words. "I only wanted to help."

"I know," said Yvonne, now looking at her pile of newspapers and mail. "It's very kind of you to come. Charlie, my nephew—you know him—he'll be bringing me to church the next couple of Sundays until I start the radiation treatments. I'll see you there."

Linda fumed as she walked down Yvonne's front steps, feeling worse than she had the night before. What had gone wrong? She had gone to visit spontaneously, just as one of her professors had described doing once, full of love and hope and good ideas. But somehow things had gone wrong, and now she was out on the street with no idea of how to reach out to Yvonne a second time. "OK, Linda," she thought as she threw herself into her car and started to drive away, "try to think through the meeting the way you learned in CPE. Try to pinpoint when things started to go downhill . . . Hmm, wasn't it after the first mention of Grandma's name?" As she drove, she continued to ponder this. Had Yvonne taken offense, somehow thinking she was comparing Yvonne's experience with her own grandmother's? Linda's speculations took flight as she tried to rationalize what had gone wrong: Had she stepped on some competitive feeling between Yvonne and Eleanor after all these years? Why had her help been so summarily rejected?

∽ ∽ ∽ ∽

As we enter this first case study, bear in mind that all the cases in this book are fictional composites, designed to illuminate certain common transference-countertransference dynamics that arise in ministry. As examples, they are intended to provoke thoughts and questions about past, present, and future situations they resemble or differ from. Of course, every real-life situation is unique, not only for the internal and interpersonal dynamics at work in the relationships involved, but also for the myriad contexts and social locations in which every relationship is embedded.

Traditional one-on-one models of pastoral care, based on the medical model, have tended to operate in the arena of the individual psyche and perhaps—as influenced by family systems theory—that of the family. But this approach ignores larger dimensions of human experience, including the social, political, economic, racial, ethnic, and cultural surround in which any individual's life is embedded, and which brings additional pressures, stresses, and traumas, both acute and ongoing, to bear on an individual's growth and life. As the increasing awareness of these contextual realities has led pastoral theology into an aware-ness of the connection between pastoral care and the work for justice, there has been a shift, in the words of Larry Kent Graham, beyond "relational human-ness," which emphasizes the individual, to "relational justice."[4] As shown in Figure 3, family theorists Betty Carter and Monica McGoldrick[5] graphically illustrate how such external stressors originate both vertically (as enduring pressures) and horizontally (from challenging or traumatic events occurring chronologically across the life span).

Social, economic, racial, gender, age, and other factors have *extrinsic* influ-ence on the dynamics of the relationship in any given situation—for example, in the type and quality of education, available work, access to power and deci-sion making, and the high or low expectations and demands from others in the individual's social and political milieu. These factors also have *intrinsic* influ-ence, operating at the level of each individual's internalized object relations, sense of self, and socially constructed aspects of self-worth and ability. Racism, sexism, and other forms of oppression also operate most insidiously at the level of the unconscious. For example, many readers may have simply assumed that the subject of the first case, Linda, was white, until her grandmother was iden-tified as African American in the second portion of the narrative.[6] The absence of racial-ethnic labels in speech and writing signals that the subjects are white in a culture where white is assumed as the norm.[7] This is only one example of the unconscious shaping of subjectivity to absorb thought structures of racism and other forms of oppression by presenting the dominant culture as norma-tive, rather than as simply one culture among many.

For Linda, then, being African American will influence her experience of grief and loss in ways that are unique both to herself as an individual and to the responses, reactions, and support she can expect to receive from other family members, from the church, and from the wider community. At the same time, Linda's gender will also affect her grieving process and her experiences in all

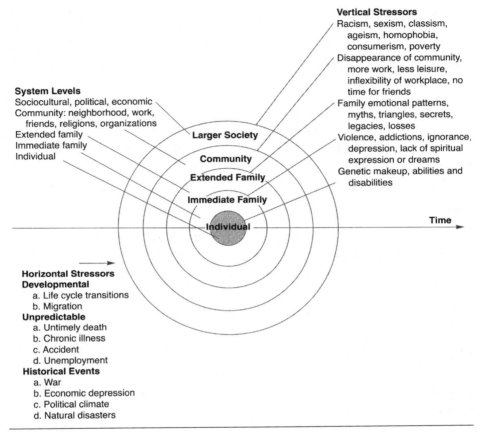

Figure 3. Flow of Stress through the Family

From: Betty Carter and Monica McGoldrick, *The Expanded Family Life Cycle,* 3d ed. (Needham Heights, Mass: Allyn & Bacon, 1999), 6.

these concentric circles of relationships. Age, education level, the urban setting (which also may not have been in the reader's mind at first), and a myriad of other social factors will similarly have their impact. All these, in turn, will affect the particular dynamics of loss of her elder, female, African American grandparent and the anticipated loss of an elder, female, African American parishioner.

The reader is therefore invited beyond the immediate case reflections offered in this book to "play with difference"[8] and ask, "How might this case play itself out differently if each individual in the narrative were [this race], [this gender], [this sexual orientation], [this age], [this socioeconomic class], [this sociogeographical setting], etc.?" Without resorting to stereotypes, how could context and social location influence how the power dynamics might shift internally and externally? How would the clergyperson feel about his or her own ministerial identity and authority? How might the clergyperson feel, experience, or react differently? How might others in the environment respond differently?

Although Linda's case will speak to each reader's own situation differently, it may nevertheless offer some instructive examples of how the intersubjective dynamics of the transference-countertransference relationship can work in a given pastoral situation. Even across great cultural differences and social locations, each individual's situation will be like all others, like some others, and like none others.[9] What might be learned from Linda's painful experience?

Classical Countertransference and Pastoral Assessment

For each case, it may be helpful to examine first the countertransference that is operative in the classical sense—that is, what unresolved issues, particularly at the unconscious level, may be impacting Linda's capacity to enter fully into Yvonne's experience? What "unfinished business" may be interfering with Linda's ability to read Yvonne's current feelings accurately and respond empathically? These questions already constitute an important aspect of reflection that Linda, in spite of adequate, classical pastoral training, failed to take the time to do when her own emotions about her grandmother's death became overwhelming. But let us return to the point at which Linda arrives home from the church council meeting and enter into a process of reflection that might have helped Linda determine how best to deal with the mass of feelings she was experiencing and how best to respond to Yvonne.

The first step, as in any classical pastoral training, would be to separate Linda's "own stuff" from Yvonne's situation—or would it?

Self-Care Comes First

I propose that the first place things went awry in the pastoral relationship between Linda and Yvonne was in Linda's quick bypassing of her family members and her rush to sit in her study alone, churning with feelings but unable to do anything productive about them. What if, instead, Linda had come into the house and sat down in the living room with Ben and Alex? Again, recognizing how particular each case story is but assuming a good-enough family relationship in which Linda can count on some warmth and support, what if Ben had said, "You look beat. Tough meeting?" and Linda had been able to let go and cry a little (or a lot) as she told them about Yvonne's news (assuming Yvonne had not sworn the members of the council to secrecy)? What if the family had hugged and cried together and talked a little about their sadness for Yvonne?

Linda already had a preconscious awareness that her grief for her grandmother was mingling with her processing of Yvonne's news. But this awareness was not yet fully conscious, so that she could articulate it to herself or to others. Possibly, in the warmth and security of her family, as Linda allowed her tears to flow, these feelings might have surfaced more fully. Then she might have been able to recognize how much her own unresolved feelings of grief, guilt, and anger were affecting her ability to respond helpfully to Yvonne—as well as to others on the church council, who also might have needed her pastoral support upon hearing Yvonne's disclosure.

This first step, then, is the step of self-care. If Linda lived alone or did not have a supportive home situation, she might accomplish this step differently, but it would be no less important. She might have called a close friend with whom she knows it is possible to have late-evening conversations. Without disclosing inappropriate confidences, she might have been able to process her feelings from the meeting with this trusted confidante. Failing that, she might have made a note in her appointment book to call one of the members of her clergy peer support group the next day, or a veteran pastor in the community who has served as a mentor to her in the past. In one way or another, because of the strong feelings evoked in the church council meeting—evidenced by her distraction, lack of focus, tearfulness, and the churned-up feelings in her stomach—Linda must claim some time and space, seeking the safe support she needs to process her initial reactions and responses. And this must happen *before* she engages in pastoral care with Yvonne.

Fast-forward to the next day. Linda is in her study, a cup of hot tea on her desk, and the Bible open to the psalm appointed for the day in a book of devotions she uses for her morning prayers. Linda is feeling somewhat refreshed by a good night's sleep, prayer, and the love and care from her family. Still, she remains very sad about Yvonne's news and aware of some still-raw emotions surrounding the loss of her grandmother. At this point, Linda is ready to ponder what in her own life situation may be getting in the way of her seeing Yvonne's situation as clearly as she can.

Using Classical Countertransference

Linda is now fully aware that during the time of her grandmother's death, she sometimes chose her studies and other priorities over caring for Eleanor. There are many things she now wishes she could have done differently. But in pondering deeper, she also sees that at the time of Grandma's illness, she had internalized Janet's not-so-subtle criticisms. Janet, the younger sister, had, in turn, internalized their mother's expectations about a "proper woman's role in the family" and had always competed with her. Janet had resented Linda's professional interests and achievements, and expected Linda to do more family caretaking, although Janet garnered much of the family's approval for being the "good girl" who stayed closer to home and looked after everyone. Linda, everyone said, took more after her dad, a high school principal, and she had thrived on his admiration and encouragement. With the help of the pastoral counselor she saw during seminary, on recommendation of her denominational ordination committee, Linda had come to recognize the good-girl/bad-girl underachiever/overachiever splitting in this situation. She knew it had served neither herself nor Janet well and that both would lead more whole lives if they could come to appreciate and even integrate some of the other's gifts into themselves.

By recalling this good work in therapy, Linda is now further able to recognize how falling back into the split of overwork and guilt toward the end of seminary got in the way of her fully grieving Eleanor's death. In a sense, she had used the perfectionistic drive of her work habits to "sweep the grief under the rug." Her grieving process had gone underground, in a sense, allowing the unconscious guilt feelings to fester. "OK, then," she is able to think now, "it's like it's always been. I'm probably not as bad and self-centered as Janet (and Mom) have sometimes portrayed me, but the regrets I do have are real, and I need to ask God's forgiveness and learn to forgive myself for those. In the meantime, I also have to remember that Grandma was proud of what I was doing, like Dad is, and she would have been proud of my work at the church now. There's that, too."

As she comforts herself with this realistic insight, she may even be able to catch a glimpse of how she was projecting some of this split onto Yvonne in her fruitless "analysis" on Yvonne's doorstep the day before. This is the point at which a pastoral assessment of Yvonne's needs becomes more useful. This is congruent with a classically conceived pastoral care approach. The old, unresolved personal baggage needs to be cleared out before any relatively objective assessment (recognizing the impossibility of absolute objectivity) can even be attempted.

After Linda has recognized how much her grief for Eleanor is still affecting her, she may be able to take a step back and reevaluate her preliminary observations and interpretations of Yvonne from the day before. Who was being competitive, really? Yvonne and Eleanor? Had she ever really seen much sign of that? Well, maybe just a little—just enough hook to hang the projection on (as her counselor used to say). Yvonne was always a "prideful woman," Eleanor used to say. But Eleanor had said it mostly in admiration, not envy or resentment. No, there was little evidence for this interpretation of competition. "That's really my own issue, with Janet," she concedes to herself. Why, then, had Yvonne sent her away, at least until another day? "I got pushy," she can now acknowledge. "I went in there with a big agenda, and all it did was wear Yvonne out. I hope I can go back and do a better job of just listening next time, really be there for her and not play out all my old stuff instead."[10]

Preliminary Pastoral Assessment

What *does* Yvonne need now? Linda must acknowledge that she actually knows little up to this point about what Yvonne needs from her or the congregation. She actually hasn't taken time yet to ask or to listen. What she knows of Yvonne gives some helpful background, to prepare her to be a better listener. As she would do in her pastoral care classes and CPE, Linda can now consider a *preliminary* pastoral assessment of Yvonne's needs:[11]

Yvonne, an eighty-one-year-old African American woman, a widow for the last ten years, raised five children and has twelve grandchildren. She has lived for forty-eight years in the same well-maintained small house in a mostly African American urban neighborhood near the church. Yvonne was baptized as a teen in her parents' Baptist church, and she has been an active church member all her life, active in neighborhood political work, and regarded by the community as a spiritual, moral, and political leader. Her personal faith is strongly rooted in her parents' Baptist tradition, Bible-centered, personally convicted, and evangelical. But in her older years, she has increasingly come to appreciate some of the Afrocentric, ecumenical, and Muslim traditions of others in her community and doesn't like the "hard-line TV evangelists." She believes in a "tough love" approach to raising children, and raising the neighborhood.

If Yvonne has any vulnerability that Linda can see, it is in her dogged determination to be self-sufficient. Linda knows this was born both from decades of political struggle with economic, racial, and gender violence and from the internal values of a strict, tough parental environment that expected much of her. In this, Linda suddenly may also recognize a further kinship with Yvonne: her own father's pride in her accomplishments is not so different from Yvonne's parents' expectations of Yvonne when she was growing up. Knowing what this feels like from the inside, Linda is now ready to spend time with Yvonne in a different, more receptive way. She is ready to listen for Yvonne's possible struggle with pride and need as she faces the recurrence of her cancer. But most of all, knowing how important self-determination is to Yvonne, she is all the more ready to listen and be guided by Yvonne's own expression of what she wants and needs now.

These paragraphs constitute a useful pastoral assessment from a classical standpoint, adequate to reenter the relationship from a more circumspect and potentially helpful point of view. However, Linda's pastoral assessment need not stop here. This is where a more contemporary constructivist approach to pastoral care can be enlisted, additionally, to consider what Linda might have learned from her countertransference reactions about what Yvonne herself was possibly feeling, at a deeper level, and what Yvonne further needed from her as her pastor.

Totalist Countertransference and Further Pastoral Assessment

Linda's pastoral assessment at this point will likely become more complex, more mutually determined, and more open-ended. Any assessment at this point must, of course, be understood as contingent upon what happens when Linda actually engages with Yvonne and can mutually process Yvonne's own experiences and responses, both verbal and nonverbal. But this can begin with a playful, imaginative, free-roaming exercise of holding the individual for whom one is caring in mind, simply noting what feelings, physical sensations, thoughts, fantasies, and images come floating into awareness. This is allowed to unfold completely freely, without imposing any second-order interpretation, analysis, or judgment. Patrick Casement uses the analogy of a pianist who practices scales before playing full pieces of music.[12]

In considering one's interpretations of both one's own countertransference and what is observed in the other person, it is often helpful to allow the imagination to roam freely, as in the analytic process of free association.[13] Often the images, thoughts, feelings, and fantasies that arise in such an exercise of playful introspection can illuminate the pastoral situation at hand. It is the sum of these thoughts, feelings, and images that constitutes the definition of the countertransference in a contemporary totalist sense. Reflections on whatever comes to mind (and heart and body) can bring to light certain elements in the situation, or in the transference-countertransference dynamic itself, that might be missed in a more classical, systematic analysis of the situation.

These reflections still focus on the contents of the caregiver's own subjectivity and cannot be assumed to be a perfect mirror of the subjectivity of the care recipient. On the other hand, if one accepts the most constructivist understandings of subjectivity as described in chapter 3, one cannot any longer regard "my own" thoughts, feelings, and so on to belong only to oneself. My subjectivity inevitably draws from, and is influenced by, the pool of thoughts, feelings, etc., conscious and unconscious, that has been created *intersubjectively*, between the other and me. This cocreated pool of thoughts and feelings now exists between us and within both of us, a pool from which both of us can continually draw inferences, and which influences us both at conscious and unconscious levels.

Table 2. Layers of Conscious and Unconscious Communication

Level of Consciousness	Form of Communication	How Communication Received
Conscious verbal level	Message sent in clear words	Heard at conscious, verbal level Easily processed cognitively Accompanying feelings felt and easily named
Preconscious level	Message both stated and implied (verbally and nonverbally)	Heard at conscious verbal level and "read between the lines" Takes some work to interpret or understand Feelings felt, not all named
Unconscious level	Message mainly enacted nonverbally, symbolically, and/or ritually May be congruent or dissonant with what (if anything) is verbalized	Message not registered at conscious, verbal level May be experienced as seemingly unrelated thoughts, fantasies, emotions, images, and/or bodily sensations May engender sense of cognitive confusion, if verbal and nonverbal signals do not match Meaning may need to move first through symbolic thoughts and images before being verbalized Accompanying feelings not easily named; anger, frustration, or anxiety possibly present as surface feelings, in reaction to the state of confusion engendered

How might this play out in Linda and Yvonne's situation? Linda's strong feelings during the church council meeting are the first signal that important information may already be stirring in the pool of intersubjectivity between Linda and Yvonne (and, potentially, all the members of the council). Because Linda experiences these feelings mostly nonverbally and even finds them difficult at first to articulate and understand, we can further infer that this information is likely dwelling more at the level of unconscious than conscious communication. These layers of communication might be shown schematically, as in Table 2.

In fact, at the church council meeting, Yvonne sent a combination of conscious, preconscious, and unconscious messages. The conscious message is, simply stated, "My cancer is back. It has metastasized to the liver. I have been given six months to a year to live. I plan to resign from the council after this meeting, but I wanted to come and deliver this news in person." Yvonne's dignity, maturity, and integrity are apparent to everyone as she quietly shares the news and demonstrates her dedication and care for the group itself by doing this in person. She speaks of death matter-of-factly and calmly, grounded in her strong faith and her long experience with matters of life and death over the course of a richly lived life. She does not dwell, however, on issues of pain and weakness or the details of her medical care.

At the preconscious level, Yvonne is aware but not articulating to herself and especially to others her level of fatigue and physical decline. Yvonne is also aware of, but not focused on and certainly not sharing out loud, her dread of nausea from the treatments ahead. She knows she will soon have some difficult treatment decisions to make. Her dignified bearing precludes members of the group from asking detailed questions out of respect for her privacy. She is not at all aware of fearing pain but knows from her previous treatments that the nausea is, for her, one of the hardest things to have to go through again. Many of these preconscious feelings, especially the fatigue and physical decline, are fairly evident to many in the room, as they observe her graying skin tone and loss of energy. Many are also likely to be feeling empathic waves of sadness, loss, even defeat, as they identify to varying degrees with this strong leader's new vulnerability. Her own sense of loss resonates at this level with their own sense of loss of her presence, as they anticipate her declining participation and eventual death.

Finally, we might speculate that at the unconscious level, Yvonne is subliminally communicating but not experiencing directly emotions she has not welcomed throughout her life: fear of loss, of giving up, of being a "victim," and of being a burden or dependent and at the mercy of others, and the experience of weakness itself. Pain is something she has likely walled off to a deep recess in the unconscious, where it is experienced at the conscious level as little as possible. And the sadness of grief is mostly denied, tucked into a far corner much of the time. None of this is being articulated in the moment, even in Yvonne's own self-perception. If asked directly if she were feeling some of these things, Yvonne might have been able to share them in the context of her depth of religious faith. In the moment, however, no one felt permission to ask her. Nevertheless, Linda, and some others in the council may be experiencing some of these emotions as unconscious communication.

As Linda reflects on her own reactions during the meeting, she may be able to identify some of these unconscious communications. Linda's tears were not only for her grandmother, and not only for other losses in her life (because every loss does, indeed, recall every other loss), nor were they only for herself, in anticipation of her own death someday (although this classical psychoanalytic understanding does account for some of every person's sadness at times of grieving). Linda's tears were also likely an expression of the tears of Yvonne's own unexpressed grief and sadness, welling out of the pool of shared but unconscious communication between the two women.

Linda also experienced an unusual amount of distraction and inability to focus, both during and after the meeting. Was this simply Linda's preoccupation with her own unfinished grief, which so flooded her cognitive capacities that she could not concentrate? Linda's distraction, in fact, may have had the character of some mild dissociation. One speculation might be that Yvonne has suffered through so many battles, so many traumas born of racism and other social and economic threats to her survival, that the recurrence of cancer is, for her, a restimulation of past traumas and threats. Yvonne has not only repressed but unconsciously split off her awareness of vulnerability, fear, and pain, in a process of traumatic dissociation. Her businesslike demeanor is not only a cover for "deeper" feelings but comes out of a different affect state, or part of herself, the one that operates successfully in the world most of the time. The only times Yvonne really dwells in the part of herself that holds her traumatic experience are the times when she feels helpless, frustrated, and out of control—as when she felt nauseated by chemotherapy. Even then, she finds it hard to ask for help, so she often feels isolated when she is hurting most.

When Linda went to bed the night after the meeting, she tossed and turned, her stomach churning, feeling frustrated, helpless, and alone. Linda's distracted state, her feelings of frustration, helplessness, and isolation, and perhaps most telling of all, her physical nausea, were resonating with a part of Yvonne that was rarely shown to the world but that held some of Yvonne's deepest soul need.

Reflecting on these reactions would not in and of itself reveal all the details of what Yvonne was going through. And because Linda's own unconscious is deeper and wider than just those elements she has already touched upon in therapy, it is important to remain circumspect about the origins of these feelings: Are they Linda's? Yvonne's? Or a combination of both? However, with a proper amount of caution and openness to further information, such feelings may provide clues to understanding that might then pave the way for a much more closely attuned listening and practice of the presence of ministry the next time Linda can spend some pastoral time with Yvonne.

This reflection has been even more helpful to Linda in preparing to visit with Yvonne. But there is still one more, very important step she needs to take before her pastoral reflection and assessment can be considered complete: theological reflection on both Yvonne's situation and Linda's own countertransference to it will likely bring some further insights to light. These insights may help to illuminate for Linda what her next steps might most fruitfully be.

Theological Reflection

There are many processes for theological reflection that pastors can profitably use to deepen their spiritual understanding of a pastoral situation.[14] Sometimes the process may be informal, simply prayer and meditation on a given individual or family, seeking God's guidance. But in situations that evoke strong feelings, it is often helpful to take the time to engage in a more formal or structured method of reflection. The method I am suggesting here continues the free-associative process just described with regard to the reflections on one's countertransference, as a way of further enlisting the unconscious as a partner in one's critical thinking about a case.

Note that the process of theological reflection recommended here is not undertaken until after a thorough reflection on the countertransference and the implications for a pastoral assessment. The reason for this goes back to the postpositivist/constructivist understanding, described in chapter 3, that "truth" is not abstract but is always located in the particular details and context of a real, lived life situation. *Pastoral theological reflection always begins with a human situation* (the "case" at hand), not an abstract idea, image, doctrinal proposition, or social or psychological theory to which cases are then made to fit, like a procrustean bed. Reflection begins with the richness of the real person—the "living human document."[15] It begins by searching in one's mind among the nuances, hidden details, "thick description"[16] of the case situation. (If one were doing a written theological reflection, every case study would similarly begin with a detailed description of the pastoral situation, initial intervention[s], reflection on one's own countertransference from both classical and totalist perspectives as previously described, a discussion of one's own social location, the authority it may confer, its commonly unquestioned norms and assumptions, and a pastoral assessment, including drawing from relevant social, psychological, and political/contextual information and resources.)

Once these reflections are in place, the actual process of theological reflection can begin. To break it down initially, this process involves three steps—although, over time, these "steps" tend to become more fluid and automatic, and less strictly sequential.

Step 1: Free Association

The first step in this process is to free-associate. At this point, we may simply allow the rich details of the case to roll around in our mind, while also holding in mind the open, general question "What theological, spiritual, religious themes pop into my mind as I simply sit with this case?" What comes to mind through this associative process might include the following:

- *A biblical story* that resonates with the story line of the case—For example, a person who feels he always relates to others at somewhat of a distance might remind you of Zaccheus in the tree. A woman who feels her talents have been overlooked or even that she has been criticized for her gifts might remind you of the woman with the alabaster jar.

- *A biblical image* that resonates with the case—For instance, a person seeking refreshment and renewal might remind you of biblical images of flowing streams, clear water, even baptismal waters.

- *An overarching biblical theme* that addresses the person's experiences and needs—Possible themes include bondage and liberation (as in the entire Exodus narrative), exile/alienation and return (the Babylonian exile or the Prodigal Son), hospitality to the stranger (numerous examples in Old and New Testament), justice (the prophets and the Gospels), lamentation (the book of Lamentations, many Psalms), wisdom and mystery (consider Job, Ecclesiastes, Ecclesiasticus, Proverbs), sickness/brokenness and healing/salvation (numerous examples in the healing narratives), God's inseparable love (expressed in the Song of Songs, Psalms, Gospels, Epistles), discipleship (many examples in the Epistles), and God's love, mercy, and divine providence (numerous examples).

- *A broad theological theme or emphasis* from one's own religious *tradition*—This might involve Martin Luther's understanding of grace and justification, Richard Hooker's understanding of participation in the Body of Christ, John Wesley's understanding of sanctification, evangelical and Pentecostal understandings of the workings of the Holy Spirit, or Ignatian/Catholic understandings of vocation and formation, among many possibilities.

- *A sacramental theme* or emphasis—Possibilities are baptismal waters of rebirth, cleansing, dying, and rising; Eucharistic fellowship, community, communion; the threefold pattern of breaking-blessing-giving and then sending; and "lesser" sacramental or sacrament-like (depending on one's tradition) aspects of reconciliation of a penitent, healing/unction, and so forth.

- *A theological image, metaphor, or story* from *contemporary literature*—There are many possibilities from novels, poetry, essays, and devotional readings.

- *A theological theme*—This may be drawn from one's readings in social analysis, literature, or political commentary.

- *A theologically rich visual image or music*—Different cultures offer a myriad of possibilities from the arts, including film and all types of music.

- *A theological metaphor or image* drawn from the *physical or biological sciences or science essays*—Essays such as Loren Eiseley's "star thrower," Barbara Kingsolver's "Creations Stories," or Stephen Hawking's reflections on "the mind of God" may resonate with the issues and images in a given pastoral situation.[17]

As with all forms of free association, this process, like the process of developing a guiding image or story for a sermon, assumes that the person doing the reflection is well versed in the Bible and the theological themes of one's own religious and spiritual tradition, and well read in rich, meaningful literature and the arts. Taking time to read widely is a significant element of self-care and a wellspring for greater theological depth and perceptiveness. Reading outside the theological literature is not simply an indulgence. The breadth of one's own life, experience, and education will more and more deeply fund resources from which it is possible to draw in any reflective process. This, in turn, enriches and deepens one's capacity for good ministry.

In this initial step, it also is important to try not to censor or rule out whatever comes to mind. Often, as with the "free-floating attention" one gives to the other in the course of pastoral listening, some of the insights that might be dismissed as extraneous actually hold important clues to the unconscious dynamics and important material in the case. Theological reflection is not done apart from one's countertransference; it is not an objective, purely rational process superimposed on the intersubjective dynamic of the pastoral relationship. On the contrary, theological reflection must proceed out of the same shared pool of conscious and unconscious knowledge as one's reflections on the countertransference and emerging pastoral assessment.

Step 2: Critical Thinking

The second step is to bring critical thinking to bear on the interrelationship between the theme, story, or image that came to mind through the process of free association and the specifics of the case itself. At this point, it is useful to highlight points of correspondence between the case and the story or theme. (Usually some bridge will present itself as the reason for the association in the first place.) It is also important, so the theme or image does not begin to take precedence over the case itself, to consider places, if any, where the story or image or theme might not completely fit. Moving back and forth between the case and the image, theme, or story may allow some new insights about the person and the pastoral relationship to emerge. It should then become possible to put into words how this theological theme helps illuminate the inner experience of the person being described or provides a window into greater understanding.

One caveat: it is important at this juncture not to "fall in love" with the theme or one's own creativity or cleverness! The theme will only be a fit to the extent that it suggests deeper and more empathic ways of engaging authentically with the person seeking care.

Step 3: Planning for Pastoral Care

With this caution in mind, the third and final step is to consider how the theological theme might inform how you would plan to respond to this person pastorally. (If you are using this process to reflect on a past case that is not ongoing, in this step it may also be helpful to consider what one might do differently, as a result of reflections on the case in retrospect.) Consider, for example, a situation that involves caring for a patient who has a terminal illness. If the predominant theological theme seemed to be illness and healing, one might think of a healing story in the Gospel in which the true healing is one of restoration to the community, not just physical "cure." But with another patient suffering a similar terminal illness, the predominant theme as presented by the patient might rather be one of "unfinished business" and alienation from certain family members. Then the theological theme that emerged from this process might be a very different one of exile and return, and the pastoral interventions would be more focused on helping the individual overcome internal and interpersonal barriers to healing broken relationships.

Revisiting the Process

A fourth step might be considered as well: to loop back around and reengage this process after every fresh encounter with the person seeking care. This can be a useful check against becoming too fixed within the metaphorical world of the initial theological reflection and can offer corrections or revisions to one's theological view of the case. Revisiting the process again and again infuses new transference/countertransference information, which may also surface new information or reflect important changes occurring in the person seeking care, in the caregiver, and/or in the living dynamic of the pastoral relationship itself.

Some Additional Guidelines for the Process

A few more general principles are also useful in engaging this process. First, the best theological reflection will be "experience near" to the other person's own spiritual and/or theological beliefs and language. If the other person has actually expressed a theme or image him- or herself, this will often provide the best starting point for further theological reflection on the case.

Also, it is important to be aware that one's own religious or spiritual tradition may differ from that of the person receiving care. Do not impose biblical or theological images or doctrines from your tradition on the other person.

This reflection is mainly for your own benefit, to help you get closer to the spiritual depths of the case, but is not necessarily intended to be shared directly with the person. Nor is it necessary to try to squeeze the other person's different framework into one's own in order to judge it as "good" or "bad" theology. In pastoral practice, it is important to accept the spiritual framework of the other on his or her own terms. What *is* helpful to one's thinking is to allow images and ideas from your own tradition to flow freely, in order to inform one's understanding and interventions from a place of groundedness in your own particular faith. This approach honors and values the particularities of faith of both the pastor and the parishioner or other person.

In the second step, where critical thinking is brought to bear on the materials surfaced in one's free-associative process, it is necessary to differentiate among first-, second-, and third-order theological statements. Following Theodore Jennings's helpful distinctions,[18] in pastoral theological methodology, *first-order religious language* is the set of words and phrases that express one's basic sense of relationship to God: "Jesus loves me," "God is punishing me." These may recall and even quote favorite liturgies, hymns, or Bible stories, but the emphasis is personal faith. This is the level at which we quote bits of pastoral conversation, as well as our own guiding faith statements, but it is not yet the level of theological *reflection* (reflection, by definition, requires not just thinking, but thinking *about* thinking).

The second step of this process enlists *second-order theological thinking*, which is the work of doing theology per se—words *(logos) about* God *(theos)*. This is the propositional level within which many first-order statements are gathered, critically understood, and/or codified as a more universal truth claim—with which others may then vigorously agree or disagree. So, for example, the first-order statements in the previous paragraph might be codified in second-order propositional language: "God is a God of love," and, "God's judgment is expressed in the evils that humans experience in life." This is one level of theological reflection, in which the individual's experience is compared and contrasted with theological beliefs, propositions, and judgments from his or her own theological traditions. Taken together, the second-order theological statements that are subscribed to by a group who identify as belonging to a particular religious tradition become *doctrines*. A coherent set of these doctrines comprises a set of dogmatics, a belief system, and/or "the theology of" that particular religious tradition.

The third step of this process engages *third-order theological thinking*, which involves a comparison and critique of those various belief systems, propositions, judgments, doctrines, and theologies made under second-order thinking. (This order of thinking is also used extensively along with second-order thinking in the practice of systematic theology.) In *pastoral* theological reflection, third-order thinking would further determine whether "God is a God of love" or "God's judgment is expressed in the evils that humans experience" is a true, sufficient, and coherent faith statement in relation to *understanding the case at hand.* "Third-order thinking is also used in pastoral theology, specifically, to evaluate whether and what language and tools of the other person's tradition, my tradition, and/or other traditions that might be drawn upon are helpful in guiding praxis—that is, offering direction for *the most facilitative pastoral intervention* in this case. It is the level of critique of propositions, their sources and norms, and their coherence and relevance, not for the sake of critique, but for determining what set of theological propositions will best help to shape a genuinely facilitative pastoral response. This process, of course, at times may also call into question some of our own cherished beliefs and assumptions, and this becomes something we must take back to our own prayer and contemplate as part of our own ongoing spiritual and pastoral formation!

Linda Reflects

Linda begins her theological reflection by gazing out the window of her study at the tree growing up between her house and her next-door neighbor's. Accompanied by lively background noise of children boarding a school bus on the street below, she allows her mind to float freely around the question "What theological, spiritual, religious themes pop into my head as I sit here with Yvonne in mind?" Soon the same hymn comes into her awareness that she found herself thinking of the night before in her state of distress, her grandma's favorite: "I Want Jesus to Walk with Me." "What are all the words, and what do they have to do with Yvonne's need, now?" Linda wonders, and she begins to sing the familiar spiritual to herself:

> I want Jesus to walk with me;
> I want Jesus to walk with me;
> All along my pilgrim journey,
> Lord, I want Jesus to walk with me.
>
> In my trials, Lord, walk with me;
> In my trials, Lord, walk with me;
> When my heart is almost breaking,
> Lord, I want Jesus to walk with me.
>
> When I'm in trouble, Lord, walk with me;
> When I'm in trouble, Lord, walk with me;
> When my head is bowed in sorrow,
> Lord, I want Jesus to walk with me.

Linda's thinking flows easily from this first-order recollection of a familiar hymn to two related second-order thoughts: Yes, our faith tells us that we are not alone in our troubles, but that when we call on him, Jesus is near and does sustain us. And as Yvonne's pastor, it is my calling to walk with the people in our congregation, as a sign of Jesus' own nearness, and also help the whole community to walk with those who are hurting and living alone. Linda pauses to thank God for the richness of her African American tradition, in which hymns and spirituals have offered people such encouragement and hope—perhaps especially to women like herself, her grandma, and Yvonne in their times of need.[19] The hymn flows powerfully out of her tradition and Yvonne's, speaking to both their generations.

Linda's thinking again turns naturally toward third-order theological thinking: How might this hymn be speaking to Yvonne's particular situation and to the pastoral responses she might make? The hymn is the clue to Yvonne's deep, unspoken need: Yvonne needs someone—Yvonne needs Jesus—to walk with her. Linda realizes that the hymn is therefore also the clue to the most appropriate thing she could have done and still, by God's grace, may be allowed to do, if she approaches Yvonne again with due humility and respect. Linda needs to set her own agenda aside and simply be present to Yvonne.

Yvonne may find it hard at first to acknowledge any need, and even harder to say it out loud. But if Linda is quiet enough and open enough, perhaps just by being there, she can help Yvonne dare to give voice to the need she so often has kept walled off from awareness. Yvonne needs to know that, in spite of her self-sufficiency and dignity and her long history of "making a way out of no way,"[20] she does not need to make this last "pilgrim journey" alone.[21] She does not have to face this new trial, this sorrow, this trouble by herself. Even as her most secret heart seems almost to be breaking, from this loss and all the other losses and traumas and hardship of her life, she can be accompanied by her pastor, her extended family, and her community. They can rejoice as they remember the love of her family, the strength of her faith, and all her accomplishments and hard-won victories; grieve the work that is unfinished; and pray together for healing and peace.[22] Together, as "where two or three are gathered," Jesus will be in their midst, and Yvonne can experience the sustaining presence of her Lord.

Summary of This Pastoral Method

To summarize, the pastoral method proposed in this chapter consists of the following steps:

1. *Self-care,* including seeking out sources of relational support and consultation as needed, quiet time to reflect, and *centering prayer*

2. An examination of *countertransference in the classical sense,* as one's own "unfinished business" and tender spots in one's own personal history that might distort or impede an empathic understanding of the other's reality

3. A *preliminary pastoral assessment* focusing on the other's actual needs

4. A further examination of one's own *countertransference in the contemporary totalist sense,* recognizing that one's own subjective feelings and experiences of the other may be drawn from the shared reality and wisdom between them, both conscious and unconscious, and may contain insights that open one up more empathically to the reality of the other

5. *Theological reflection,* beginning with a free-associative process and moving toward a new openness to previously unconsidered dimensions of this unique pastoral relationship and expanded possibilities for *pastoral praxis*

Throughout this process, the uniqueness and particularity of this pastoral connection is honored, and care is understood as contingent on the contextual realities of both self and other. Therefore, there is no one solution, nor even a single understanding of a problem to be solved or ill to be "cured." The process of pastoral reflection itself is to be revisited, again and again, as feelings are stirred and new meanings mutually emerge in the pastoral relationship.

This process may seem very systematic and time-consuming at first. Over time, however, and with practice, the process becomes second nature and simply flows. The steps in the process will occur naturally and fluidly, at times overlapping or even shifting in sequence, as evoked by the details and dynamics of each particular pastoral situation. The key elements, however, will always pertain: attending to self-care and centering prayer, examining the significance of one's own subjectivity, one's countertransference in both classical and contemporary senses, and allowing one's own inner creativity to play theologically with multiple meanings and implications. Taken together, these elements can generate more openness to the shared wisdom that is generated at both conscious and unconscious levels in the intersubjective relationship, and ultimately open greater possibilities for empathic listening and liberatory pastoral praxis.

Replaying the Vignette

Roll back to the night of the church council meeting. How might things have gone differently if Linda had taken the time to reflect before going to visit Yvonne? In the following replay of the vignette, notice that Linda is not suddenly the perfect pastor, nor are her countertransference reactions suddenly gone. The vignette is intended to demonstrate, on the contrary, that the process of reflection does not in any way diminish the intensity of feelings in the intersubjectivity of the pastoral relationship. What it does is offer an additional element of circumspection that enables a pastor to *use* what she can learn from within her own subjectivity, her countertransference, toward the practice of a more genuine and unencumbered listening—to both one's own subjectivity and the expressions of the other.

Also note that as a result of greater reflection and self-care, Linda makes a more boundaried approach to Yvonne. Rather than rush to Yvonne's home unannounced, she calls first, allowing Yvonne to determine when and whether she would like Linda to come. This reduces the possibility of intruding upon Yvonne and gives Yvonne a more equal partnership in the pastoral relationship from the outset. Although it may seem like a small thing, it signals a level of respect and mutuality. This replaces a heroic but one-sided model of care represented by Linda rushing in unannounced and with her own agenda.

Linda also does not make the mistake of sharing all her reflections with Yvonne. This, in itself, would likely be experienced as intrusive and presumptuous. Linda remembers that her entire exercise of reflection is like playing scales before practicing a piece of music. All her thoughts, all her assessments, all her analysis are still entirely provisional, depending on what she hears and senses from Yvonne in the actual moment of meeting. To share her psychological or theological reflections out loud might very well have the effect of trying to impress Yvonne or convince herself of her own powers of discernment. Linda uses her reflections, rather, to guide her own subjectivity into a place of greater clarity and openness. In this way, rather than becoming the focus of her meeting with Yvonne, the process of reflection creates an imaginal openness to whatever may spring up in the intersubjective pool of experience that flows between them. It facilitates a ministry of presence.

Linda, Redux

Linda went home that night from the meeting uncomfortably aware that she had missed most of the discussion of the agenda. Both Yvonne's face and her grandmother Eleanor's floated in her mind, each one as if superimposed on the other. The guilt Linda had felt during her grandmother's last two weeks in the hospital and in the months following her death washed back over her as if no time had passed. All the what-ifs flooded back: What if I had just set my studies aside more and been more available to Grandma and the family? What if I had told Professor Shackley that I just needed to take that fifth course another year or at least allowed myself to get a C in it? What if I had let myself drop everything and sit at Grandma's bedside like my sister Janet? What if I had used my connections with the hospital chaplain to see if there wasn't one more treatment option that they didn't even try because Grandma was considered too old . . . or "too black"? What if . . .

Linda greeted her family when she arrived home. They saw on her face that something upsetting had happened at the meeting. As Linda recounted Yvonne's news, Ben and Alex stood up and hugged her, and they talked and wept together. After Alex had gone to bed, she found further comfort and insight talking things over quietly with Ben. She recognized the power of the feelings she had about Grandma and how a good deal of "unfinished business" she still felt about her grandmother's death was deeply affecting her reactions to Yvonne's news. She found herself thinking of Eleanor's favorite hymn, "I Want Jesus to Walk with Me," which began playing in her head as she got ready for bed. That night, she had a dream in which she and Alex and Ben and Janet and Yvonne were all sitting at Eleanor's bedside, holding hands, praying, and singing "I Want Jesus to Walk with Me."

The next morning Linda awoke feeling somewhat refreshed by a good night's sleep, prayer, and the love and care from her family, although she was still very sad about Yvonne's news and aware of some still-raw emotions surrounding the loss of her grandmother. After seeing Ben and Alex off to work and school, she went up to her study with a cup of hot tea. She opened the Bible to the psalm appointed for the day in a book of devotions she used for her morning prayers: "God is our refuge and strength, a very present help in trouble. Therefore we will not fear, though the earth should change, though the mountains shake in the heart of the sea; though its waters roar and foam, though the mountains tremble with its tumult" (Psalm 46:1-3). In prayer and meditation, she took some time to ponder what in her own life situation might be "getting in the way" of her seeing Yvonne's own situation as clearly as she could. She spent time in theological reflection, remembering again the hymn that came to her the night before, "I Want Jesus to Walk with Me," and the clues it held for how to approach Yvonne in the most open, helpful, respectful way possible.

Feeling clearer and more centered, she drove to her office at the church and dialed Yvonne's number. "Yvonne, hi, it's Linda. I was wondering if you would be feeling up to a pastoral visit sometime today." Yvonne felt tired but was pleased to have Linda come. Linda thanked her, saying, "I know you are feeling pretty tired, so I won't stay long."

Once she was seated in Yvonne's living room, Linda shared a quiet prayer recalling the words of the psalm and praising God for always being their refuge and strength. Linda then gently asked Yvonne how she was feeling. As Yvonne shared more of the details of her diagnosis, Linda started to experience some of the same feelings of outrage and sadness she had felt at the council meeting the night before. Although she knew from her morning meditations that she was likely to be reacting out of some of her feelings about her grandmother, Linda heard herself begin to move the conversation more and more toward medical interventions and encouraging Yvonne to "try everything possible to fight this!" Trying to catch herself from blending these two strong grandmother figures together in her mind, she added, "I wish I had said more of that to my grandmother—you know?"

Yvonne understood what was likely going on in the mind and heart of her earnest young pastor. Yvonne, too, had grieved when Eleanor had died. Eleanor had been a close friend since childhood, and as others had come and gone in the neighborhood, Eleanor had been there as an ally in all the neighborhood's struggles. She missed Eleanor terribly and knew that Linda did, too. Yvonne felt a wave of shared compassion wash over her. She looked kindly into Linda's eyes: "Pastor," she said slowly, "I understand how you might wish you could have done more for your own grandmother, but I'm not Eleanor."

Linda sat back, aware of her habitual tendency to react out of her old feelings. Slightly embarrassed at this, she said, still feeling some tension, "Of course you're not, Yvonne. I just want you to get the best treatment!"

Yvonne smiled, recognizing Linda's care and also sensing her wrestling with old guilt feelings. She also knew that Linda had spoken out of a place of truth and righteous anger. There was plenty of reason not to trust the medical system. No one knew better than Yvonne herself how an older African American woman could be dismissed by the system. But Yvonne also knew how to ask the right questions. She believed she had advocated well for herself in this situation and that her doctors were fine. "Pastor," she said again, "don't try to save me. My doctors are doing that already, and believe it or not, I think I can trust them." Yvonne paused, then trusting Linda's sincerity, added, "And as you well know, I also trust in the Lord to guide me through this."

Linda looked abashed, and tears of concern filled her eyes. "I don't know what to say, Yvonne. I guess I've been coming off as pushing you. I didn't mean to. I want to be helpful, but now I'm not sure how I can be."

Yvonne averted her eyes and fussed for a moment with her housecoat, moved by Linda's emotional vulnerability. Touched by Linda's nondefensive response, Yvonne was able to see past Linda's relative youth and inexperience to her sincerity and desire to care. She also recognized a bit of her own pride and how it sometimes got in the way of getting to know other people better, or even giving them a chance. She saw herself at a crossroads, deciding what to say next—as an elder in the church giving Linda a little guidance, but also as a parishioner in need of a pastor, especially now that the cancer was back. Finally, sensing

Linda's openness, she decided to trust the decent, caring woman sitting in front of her and said, "I do need you, Linda. I need you to be my pastor." Linda's eyes again filled with tears of appreciation, empathy, and care. She said, "Maybe we could start by your just telling me more about all that's happening." Yvonne nodded. "All right—and then, would you pray for me?"

CHAPTER FIVE

The Relational Paradigm in Pastoral Care

THIS AND THE NEXT chapter will illustrate the use of the method of reflection given in chapter 4 for both pastoral care and pastoral counseling/psychotherapy, respectively. As in the preceding chapter, these chapters will expand on case vignettes together with analysis of each case using the relational method described in chapter 4, and conclude with recommendations for the use of the self, in pastoral care, and in pastoral counseling, respectively.

Gary

At the end of the day, Gary[1] squeezed his six-foot frame into his one-year-old metallic-blue coupe and opened the sunroof. Still feeling churned up about Daniel and the social worker's request, he gunned the engine and zoomed home, ignoring the speed limit and enjoying the feel of the wind in his hair. He let himself into his townhouse and greeted the cats, Luther and Calvin, who wreathed their bodies around his legs. "OK, guys," he said and filled their bowls, careful not to spill oil from the cat food cans on his new hardwood kitchen floor. He poured himself a large glass of white wine and tossed a frozen quiche into the microwave.

As Gary felt the usual warm, relaxing effect of the wine, Daniel's face floated back into his mind for what seemed like the fiftieth time that day. As the cats noisily slurped at their tuna, Gary sighed and allowed himself to think about his wish to take care of Daniel. He knew, on the one hand, that hospital policy and all his prior training completely forbade his offering to take Daniel into his own home. "But," he thought, "the social worker did ask for my help[2] and wanted a church person at that. It would be a lot easier for me just to take him myself than to call around to a bunch of parishes and possibly get nowhere or have to wait days for an answer." He pulled his dinner out of the microwave and cursed as the steam hit his hand. Tossing the quiche on the kitchen counter, he felt his irritation rise. "Some rules are meant to be broken, anyway!" he fumed. "It's unfair that this poor kid, who's been through so much already, should be basically stranded by the system just because his mother is still in the hospital and can't take care of him. That jerk, Stan, should be strung up by his . . . toes!" He looked at Calvin, contentedly pawing the tuna oil off his whiskers. "Calvin," he said out loud, "some humans are just not very nice!" Sitting down to his dinner, Gary mused that if he were Daniel's father, none of this would have happened.

He finished the second glass of wine he always allotted himself—no more, no less—and stood up from the table with a sense of new resolve. He felt more energized than he had for some time working in this job. Preferring not to wait until morning, he dialed the social worker's number and left a message on her voice mail: "Cora, I've thought about your request. It will take too long to get hold of someone in one of the local parishes, but I would be happy to take Daniel. I have plenty of room here, and since I'm on the professional staff, I may even be able to help him begin his healing from the trauma of the accident. I'll go see the mother first thing tomorrow morning and get the paperwork started. OK, well, that's it. Thanks, Cora. Talk to you tomorrow."

Classical Countertransference

Following the process detailed in chapter 4, what classical countertransference issues seem to be operating in the classical sense in Gary's strong desire to care for Daniel? What "unfinished business" may be interfering with Gary's ability to assess Daniel's needs more objectively and respond with an appropriate plan to meet them?

Gary is seeing in Daniel many of the same struggles he had endured growing up as an only child in a blue-collar white family.[3] His parents had tried to have more children, but other pregnancies resulted in miscarriage and, more traumatically, a stillborn baby girl when Gary was five years old. These losses were not talked about in the family. Gary's father worked in the same Detroit auto factory for forty years until disability forced him to take an early retirement. His mother worked part-time as a grocery checker, trying to time her work hours to the children's hours in school. Gary did not realize until seminary, after taking Paul Fussell's "Living-Room"[4] test in a sociology of religion course, that his family was working-class. Even then, it took years for him to wrestle with what the label meant and how it did and didn't accurately describe his personal experience. His family would have described themselves, if asked, as middle-class, a *Leave It to Beaver* family, motivated by the American dream of translating hard work into moderate comfort, a home of their own, and high respectability.[5]

Gary's college and seminary education, made possible by a large scholarship and even larger loans, catapulted him into class confusion.[6] Upon graduation, he was initiated into the "professional class"[7] by education and training but was functionally quite poor by debt and low income. His parents had been proud of his college education, as Gary was the first in their family to attain this, but then found it increasingly difficult to talk with him and were perplexed by the changes in values and ideals that his education seemed to have wrought. They worried that his idealism, which at times sounded strident to them, and his attachment to ideas in general might "ruin him for living in the real world."[8] Gary eventually felt uncomfortable and somewhat alien in his parents' home and neighborhood but equally uncomfortable and alien among professional colleagues from upper-middle-class backgrounds—at least at first.[9] Over the seventeen years since earning his M.Div., and as his income and professional status have risen, his conscious identification with his new class status has grown. His anxiety about his class origins has receded into the background, a place he no longer likes to visit in his mind, barely conscious and mostly disavowed.

Daniel's family has struggled even more than Gary's. In the roughly four decades since Gary was born, the security and many of the comforts of working-class life have greatly diminished.[10] Daniel's mother has been working two jobs to make ends meet, and Daniel has often been left alone to tend his two younger siblings. Alternating with Daniel's anxiety about his mother's exhaustion and loneliness has been a greater dread of the new boyfriend, Stan, who seems surly and unpredictable. Stan has been taking Daniel's mother out drinking. Starved for adult companionship, she has gone along, although she has never been a heavy drinker and is allergic to the smoke in bars.

Gary also is having a strong gut reaction to the issue of Stan's drinking and driving. His father, Bill, was a heavy beer drinker—strictly weekends only, but consuming two or three cases from the time he got home from work on Friday night until he stumbled into bed on Sunday night (if he made it to the bed-room).[11] Bill used to lecture Gary about the evils of alcohol during the week and instructed Bill on the importance of never drinking on the job. For this reason, Gary's family always adhered to the belief that Bill was not an alcoholic, because he "controlled" his drinking and never touched "hard liquor." His mother, a strict teetotaler herself, professed scorn for a more affluent neighbor who was often seen drinking a martini in his yard on warm summer weeknights.

All Gary knew growing up was that his dad's drinking spoiled many week-ends. His father spent most of the weekend on the living-room sofa in his good weekend flannel shirt and carefully creased casual pants, gazing at sports programs on the TV. Family outings had been canceled and promises broken so many times that by junior high, Gary's mother had stopped trying to make plans. Bill was never overtly abusive, so Gary's mother considered herself rela-tively "lucky," especially in comparison with her sister Ruth, whose husband periodically punched and threatened her. Mom tiptoed around Dad on weekends, did the grocery shopping, brought home the twelve-packs, and stayed busy with household chores until Monday came and she could have the house—and the TV, her own addictive form of self-forgetting—to herself again.

Gary felt too embarrassed to invite friends to his house on weekends and always made excuses to meet them somewhere else. As soon as he had his driver's license, he used his newfound freedom to borrow the family's one car and literally steer friends away from his home, as well as to escape. Both he and his mother found church to be a welcome respite on Sunday mornings. In fact, the feeling of relief and of belonging that Gary came to associate with the church community, especially through his youth group, was a major subliminal motivation for seeking ordination.

Again, it was not until a seminary class on pastoral care and addictions that Gary came to the painful realization that his father was actually an alcoholic, classified as a binge-drinking type.[12] Conversations with the campus chaplain and his CPE supervisor helped him work through the initial grief and anger of this discovery. But it left Gary with a raw place in his heart concerning abuse of alcohol. This was especially easily triggered by situations involving parents who drank and neglected their children. He also had a particularly strong reaction toward beer drinking. Influenced by his upper-middle-class peers, he had come to associate beer with a class stereotype of the sloppy, loud, and demanding man with a "beer belly" protruding from a sleeveless undershirt, who spends the day in a recliner chair.[13] Objectively, he knew that people of all class backgrounds are equally affected by drinking and that alcoholism is not more prevalent among the working class—although it may be better disguised and treatment more privatized among wealthier families.[14] The stereotypical image, though not a fair replica of his own father, was just close enough to arouse feelings of shame, disgust, and anxiety, which in turn reinforced his preconscious tendency to disavow his family of origin.

Gary's own white-wine habit was not, in his own mind, inconsistent with these negative feelings toward "beer-drunk" fathers. His habitual imitation of classmates and professional colleagues over the years had planted the idea of wine as both harmless and sophisticated.[15] His carefully rationed two glasses in the evenings after work represented for him, at a mostly preconscious level, his desire to differentiate himself from his father both in terms of drinking habits and class identification. The same two glasses, however, also appear to be a symptom of an inherited tendency toward alcohol abuse, which at the present time remains buried in Gary's unconscious. Gary's ritualized, nightly use of alcohol to relax and his conscious efforts to control his drinking are both, in fact, symptoms of alcohol abuse and possible addiction.[16] The repetitive, rationed use, al-

though with a different choice of alcohol than his father's, reflects a similar effort
to deny any problem, and even to portray himself (mainly to himself) as prin-
cipled in his drinking habits. If this tendency were suggested to him directly, he
would have vigorously denied it, with some feelings of indignation: "I'm not
my father, and I'm well aware of my father's problems."

Let us return to the end of Gary's workday. What might Gary have done
differently, beginning with the way he might choose to deal with his own anxiety, and moving through a process of reflection toward a different outcome?

Again, the first step would not be for Gary to engage immediately in a process
of critical analysis of the situation. At this point, Gary is too stressed, both
emotionally and physiologically, to engage his intellect fruitfully beyond some
form of unconsciously self-satisfying rationalization. As is seen in the vignette,
before processing his reactions, Gary's intellectual abilities were recruited merely
in the service of a rationalization of what he was already feeling pulled to do.
Gary needs first to attend his own self-care and well-being.

What if, for example, instead of driving too fast as a form of release, Gary
had taken a few moments at the end of the day, in his office or perhaps in the
hospital chapel, and prayed or meditated on the day's events?[17] Perhaps before
heading home Gary also might have gone running, or swimming, or played
racquetball, in order to relieve some of his stress and to clear his mind for more
fruitful reflection on the day's events.

Allowing himself this time to de-stress, and to process the day, might have
helped Gary avoid putting himself and others at risk behind the wheel. Gary
might still use the drive home to help further relax and center himself, perhaps
by listening to a favorite news or sports program on the radio, music, or an audio-
tape of an engaging book, and, yes, enjoying the sunroof—within the speed limit!
Gary's cats also are a pleasant source of comfort and companionship. Gary
might have played with the cats and eaten his quiche, but without the two
glasses of wine, and then called a friend. (Note that unwinding in front of the
television, while not dangerous, would likely not be an optimal choice for Gary
at this point, given Gary's family's addictive use of television as a form of self-
soothing, escape, and avoidance of the stresses and conflicts beneath the surface of the family's relationships.)

At this point, with at least this modicum of appropriate self-care, Gary is
much more likely to recognize that he is having an unusually strong, emotional
response to Daniel. The feelings he has about this child are not simply objectively
aroused responses to a heart-wrenching situation, but also constitute unconscious "pulls." In the language of relational psychoanalysis, the term *pulls* refers
to powerful unconscious feelings that draw one toward another person in an
enactment that meets unconscious needs. Recognizing the presence of such

pulls is a necessary first step toward uncovering unconscious dynamics that otherwise, if left out of awareness, might result in inappropriate actions that could be countertherapeutic or even harmful to both parties. This is not to say that such pulls are in and of themselves pathological. Strong feelings of all sorts are common and, in fact, inevitable in caring relationships.[18] The potential problem is impulsively acting on such pulls, not the pulls themselves. The strength of such feelings, if one is in the habit of being attentive to one's own process as a source of information about the helpee, is precisely what can signal a time to step back, reflect, and, in many cases, to seek supervision or consultation.

Gary's first task, then, has been to center himself sufficiently to be able to recognize that his feelings about Daniel are unusually acute and seem to go beyond what he feels in other pastoral care situations. Once he is aware of that, even if he cannot yet name all of what is being stirred inside him, he is then in a position to be able to call a colleague with whom he is in a mutually supportive relationship of peer consultation or a senior professional consultant (perhaps a senior chaplain with many years' experience or a pastoral counselor or psychotherapist skilled in supervision) to set up a time for a paid consultation. This, of course, presupposes that Gary has either some individual colleagues or a peer group for ongoing mutual support and consultation and/or a formal relationship with a professional supervisor whom he can call when dealing with particularly difficult or stimulating cases. Some such mechanism for honest, supportive feedback and consultation should already be in place in every pastor's professional life.[19] Such supervision optimally would be provided from a depth-psychological perspective, so that the countertransferential considerations in any strongly felt case situation could be thoroughly, empathically explored. This type of supervisory process would offer the most benefit both to the pastor and to the individual or family receiving care. This, then, is the call that Gary should make, in lieu of impulsively dialing the social worker and beginning to enact a plan of unauthorized foster care.

Fast-forward to the next morning. Gary is sitting in one of the hospital's consulting rooms with Carol. Carol is an experienced pastoral psychotherapist in the community; Gary met her when she gave a workshop on grief counseling for the hospice staff of the hospital. She has provided Gary with professional consultation several times before. As Carol listens carefully, without judgment, Gary is able to describe his puzzlement over his strong feelings for Daniel. Over the course of this hour, Carol helps Gary make the connections between Daniel's situation and his own upbringing, especially his feelings about his father's drinking on weekends. Carol's empathic responses further help Gary to tap an even deeper wound that is stimulating his strongest countertransference feelings: Gary felt profoundly abandoned by his father. His father's hard work and physical exhaustion during the week, coupled with his drunken immobility on weekends, left Gary effectively without a father for most of his growing-up years. Through this part of their conversation, Gary is able to realize that there is, indeed, a large amount of unresolved baggage that has been influencing his impulse to bring Daniel into his own home. Gary is longing to rescue Daniel and care for him in a way he himself wished to be rescued and cared for as a child.

As Carol allows Gary's awareness and accompanying grief and anger to unfold, she herself becomes aware of how, in her own countertransference to this supervision, she is feeling a maternal pull of her own toward Gary. She recognizes this as a possible reenactment of the role of Gary's mother, the older woman who nurtured him, helped him find alternative sources of support (through the church), and attempted to be both father and mother to him as he grew. She also feels within herself a growing sentiment of judgment against Gary's father, in spite of her intellectual understanding of the many pressures and anxieties that motivated his drinking. She feels herself falling into a split, emotionally competing with his "bad father" and joining with or even outdoing his "good mother."

Carol sits with this for a while, and as the feeling grows stronger, finally voices it aloud to Gary. Gary feels the power of this intervention, naming the previously unconscious parent–child dynamic in the room at that very moment. This, in turn, allows Gary to realize what he has been trying unconsciously to accomplish with Daniel—he has been trying to be the better parent, the one who does not abandon him, the one who not only finds but provides the alternative source of support himself. And by so doing, he has actually been trying to re-parent himself.

At this point, as Gary has become open to this awareness, Carol may even be able to address the tone of judgment about drinking that has pervaded their conversation. Gary's resistance to awareness about the problematic aspects of his own drinking habits is likely to be very high at this time in his life, since he has not experienced many negative consequences for his drinking and regards himself as responsible. His control of his drinking also touches on larger issues of control and perfectionism, which have at times been problematic in his personal relationships but have served him well in terms of academic and clinical success. Carol therefore is probably not aware of Gary's specific drinking pattern. But she can begin to explore the issue of judgment.

"I've noticed," she ventures, "that we both seem to be experiencing a lot of judgmental feelings toward Dawn's boyfriend Stan, particularly around his drinking. Of course what he did was reprehensible, but I wonder if we're also tapping into something important that might be getting in the way of helping Dawn."

Together, Carol and Gary identify some of Gary's own charged issues around drinking, particularly in parental situations, and particularly beer.

"Have you ever done a genogram, Gary?" Carol asks.

Gary, somewhat surprised by the question, answers, "Yes, I did one in a seminary class once." Together they reconstruct Gary's genogram,[20] a family tree that shows intergenerational patterns of health, behavior, and relationship bonds (see Figure 4).

Carol notes that there seems to be a lot of alcohol abuse across the generations in Gary's family. Gary, in turn, is able to recognize that while his concerns about Stan's drinking and driving and Dawn's allowing her son and herself to be endangered are legitimate and must be addressed somehow by an appropriate professional, he has allowed his personal feelings to heighten his judgmentalism to a point that would be counterproductive in any work with Daniel.

At this point in the supervision, Carol has a decision to make as well. She has observed the intergenerational pattern of alcohol and other substance abuse in Gary's genogram. She wonders if Gary himself may have some issues with drinking but has no evidence of alcohol abuse on Gary's part. Her own countertransferential tendency toward "therapeutic ambition" (a wish to open up too much too quickly in the hope of curing her client), coupled with ethical concerns for Gary as a hospital professional, causes her to want to address it with him. Carol also notices Gary's mother's miscarriages and the stillbirth of Gary's only sibling, and she wonders how much these events in the life of the family may have affected Gary's feelings about children and his relationship with his own child-self.

Yet it is not the purview of supervision to do psychotherapy with Gary. Their focus has been on helping Gary gain insights in the service of his case. Carol decides to broach these issues, but very mildly, simply to open the door for Gary to think about these things further on his own. "We're almost out of time, Gary, but it looks like this issue of alcohol in your family is a pretty big one. And then," speaking sadly, "there are all these lost babies! Have you ever thought about doing some counseling around these issues?"[21]

Gary replies that he did some brief counseling during seminary, but "these issues never came up, really."

"Well, they might be worth pursuing at some point. Think about it."

Gary agrees, and the consultation concludes. Carol has only been able to plant a seed about how Gary's own drinking might be following an unhealthy family pattern and how the family's unprocessed grief about lost children may also have some bearing on this case. Still, she has helped Gary identify a number of personal issues that have been getting in the way of his ability to think clearly about his pastoral interventions with Daniel. Now that Gary is more

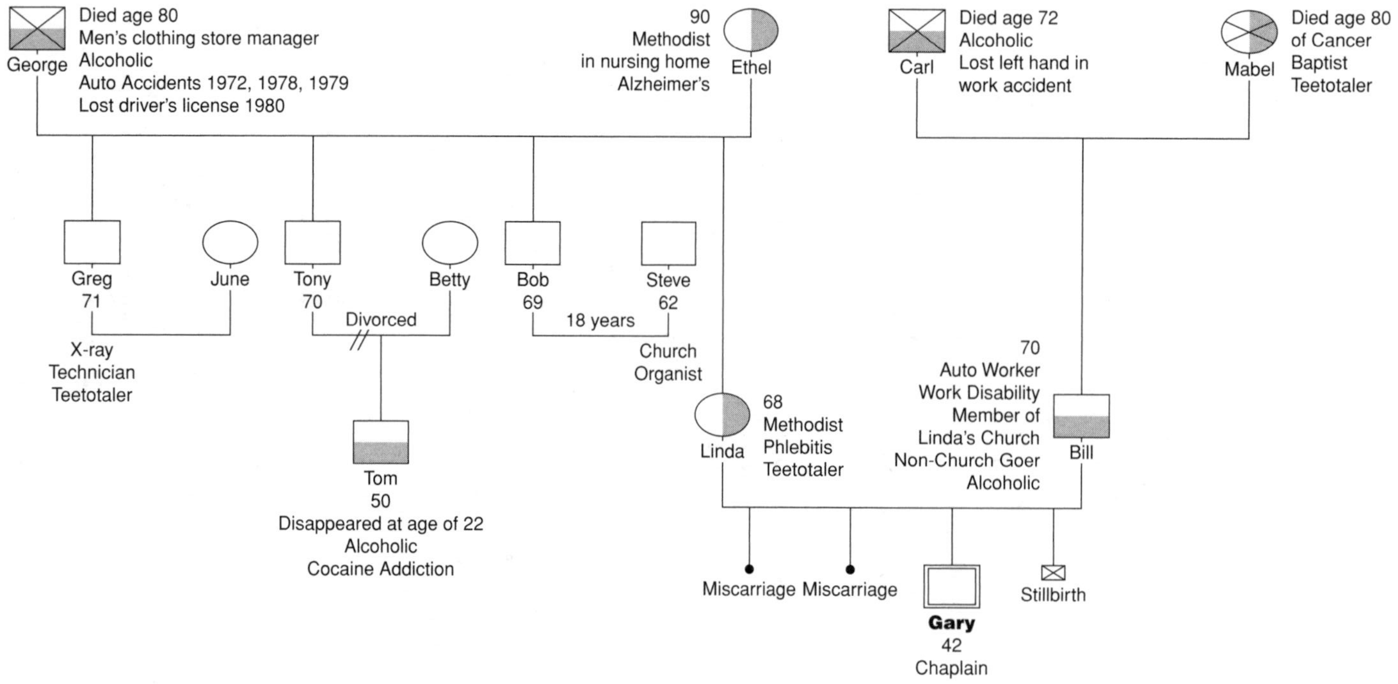

Figure 4. Gary's Genogram

conscious of these difficult aspects of his childhood, he may be more able to think deeply about their impact on his ministry and claim these painful memories as a foundation for greater empathy and sensitivity toward the child Daniel and toward Daniel's mother.

Pastoral Assessment

Gary is now at the point where doing a pastoral assessment becomes fruitful. He is now able to begin considering more objectively what Daniel's actual needs might be and, for the first time, as the hospital chaplain, also to consider the needs of Daniel's mother. He realizes that up to this point, because of his judgments about the accident, he has not even thought of her by her name, Dawn. He has been objectifying her as "the mother."

Daniel needs material assistance, temporary lodging with a responsible adult, and emotional support to help him to get through this period of Dawn's hospitalization and begin healing from the trauma of the accident. But none of these functions are properly within Gary's own domain as hospital chaplain. Gary can be of real help to both Daniel and Dawn, however, by responding to the social worker's actual request—and activating a network of possible community support for Daniel.

Daniel also needs to be helped to feel safe again in his relationship with his mother. By trying to play the part of the "better parent," Gary, on the contary, would have begun to set up a split between Daniel's family and the outside world, and a subtle wedge between Daniel and Dawn. For this not to happen, Gary needs to establish a supportive, rather than competitive, relationship with Dawn and to help Dawn herself obtain the material and emotional support she needs to provide an appropriate level of safety and care for her children. This needs to be done in a nonblaming way. To keep his feelings of judgmentalism from impairing his interactions with Dawn, Gary will need to work through his own feelings of judgment about men drinking beer, not directly with Dawn but in supervision, *outside* the pastoral relationship.

By so doing, Gary will become more available to listen to Dawn's feelings about what has happened, including her loneliness, her stress, and the real-life pressures that have caused her to be less available to her children than she knows she would like to be. Keeping his judgments out of the pastoral relationship may enable Gary to help Dawn reach a point where she can use Gary's pastoral presence to work through issues of forgiveness for herself and to initiate a process of reconciliation and healing of the relationship with her traumatized son. Depending on Dawn's own faith tradition, she may even be able to receive the sacramental rites of anointing for healing and of confession and reconciliation as part of this healing process. She can use what she has learned from the near-death experience of this accident to reevaluate her relationship with Stan and to resume her parenting role from a place of greater strength and renewed courage.

Without talking with Dawn, Gary does not yet have enough objective information to know whether Dawn's primary difficulties are, in the words of Carroll Watkins Ali, "truly, life,"[22] the sum of external economic, social, and gender stresses that press in on Dawn every day in an ongoing battle for survival, or whether they are also part of a more long-standing pattern of relational difficulties due to wounds experienced in Dawn's own childhood. Further pastoral conversation is needed to determine this aspect of pastoral assessment. A combination of external and internal factors is frequently at play, given the intergenerational nature and traumatic impact of such contextual stressors. It is again beyond Gary's purview to provide the ongoing pastoral support that would be indicated in Dawn's situation. But Gary can help Dawn find appropriate resources in the community both for economic and social advocacy and for emotional support through ongoing pastoral counseling or psychotherapy. Gary can also work together with the hospital social worker on finding resources to meet Dawn's needs, and to determine what social supports she already has utilized that might be reenlisted on her own and Daniel's behalf.

Totalist Countertransference and Pastoral Assessment

In this case study, Gary's consultant, Carol, has already used a contemporary, totalist approach to the countertransference in her supervision with Gary. By reaching into her experience during the consultation, Carol has become aware of deeper dynamics at work in Gary's responses to Daniel and has used these to help Gary achieve a more balanced approach. Gary himself can also go further in his understanding of both Daniel and Dawn by applying this method of examining his own countertransference.

In a second consultation with Carol or on his own, Gary is now in a position to consider what in his own responses might go beyond his own baggage to offer clues about what Daniel himself is experiencing. As with Linda and Yvonne, Gary's strong feelings are not only a signal that Gary's own internal issues have been stimulated. The strength of his reaction may also signal that important information may be stirring in the shared, unconscious relationship between Daniel and himself.

As Gary goes back over his pastoral care encounter with Daniel the day before, he may identify several responses in himself that could tell him more about Daniel. Gary normally feels awkward around children, yet somehow this did not happen with Daniel. Was this only because he identified with many aspects of Daniel's situation? Or was there something more going on in their interaction? Gary realizes that one reason he had little trouble communicating with Daniel was that Daniel did not seem entirely *like* a child. Daniel seemed to have wisdom beyond his years. He exhibited an unusually philosophical attitude that Gary could identify with as an only child who had often found his best friends in books. As Gary considers this further, however, he realizes that this is not only a gift in Daniel but a burden as well. Because of the many social and economic stresses on Daniel's mother and their household, Daniel has had to care for his siblings and also to care for his mother emotionally.

It might seem easy at this point for Gary to once again blame Dawn for Daniel's situation. But Daniel's mother is not "narcissistic" in her parenting;[23] she is overwhelmed by the external demands of keeping body and soul together for both herself and her children. She is doing the best she can. And Daniel, in turn, as a bright and sensitive child, is taking up some of the slack. It is nobody's "fault," but it does put Daniel in a less than healthy psychological position of being a "parentified adult,"[24] at times assuming the role of parenting partner and even emotional partner for his mother. Gary may both identify with this position himself and feel it empathically from within Daniel's own subjectivity as he relates to Gary in an adultlike manner in their pastoral relationship.

This insight is reinforced by Gary's further considering how he felt when he was about to leave work. "Yeee-hah!" was the feeling. Gary had been feeling more than a little burned out on his institutional responsibilities as a chaplain, especially his supervision of the CPE groups. Due to budget cutbacks two years ago, Gary was now the sole supervisor. He missed his cosupervisor, Donna, and the mutual consultation they shared in dealing with tough student situations. He also felt little support from the hospital administration to keep the CPE program alive. Although the seminary professors who referred students were available for occasional consultation, he felt very much alone, out on a limb and helpless in the face of institutional realities that often seemed to impede good care. He knew, intellectually, that these were classic burnout conditions,[25] but given the current economic climate, he did not envision any good job alternatives at present. And he still loved chaplaincy work in general—wanted more, in fact, of the visitation work, the actual hours spent directly with patients and their families, and the interdisciplinary collaboration with hospital staff in other fields.

Gary's "Yeee-hah!" was not only a reflection of his feeling of burnout. He had not even had any students that day. It was also an intersubjective reflection of Daniel's feelings. Daniel was actually experiencing his hospitalization as a moment of freedom from his heavy household responsibilities. Gary's speeding home with the sunroof open was an extension of this feeling, the desire for freedom and play. It was a desperate enough desire that it caught Gary up in a risk-taking mood, throwing caution literally to the winds. One of Daniel's deepest desires is to play, without having to remember all the duties he has been given in his life.

As Gary allows himself to go even deeper inside the feeling he got driving home, he contacts one additional, even more buried desire in his own life that also reflects Daniel's deepest need. Gary recognizes that part of his acting out by speeding in his bright blue sports coupe had to do with wanting to be noticed. He is lonely on the job—lonelier now since he is alone in his department—and lonely at home. Sometimes, he admits to himself, the company of cats just "doesn't cut it." His perfectionistic habits have spoiled two serious relationships, and his perfectionism has further inhibited him from forming close friendships or romantic ties, because no one is ever quite perfect enough to suit him. Gary's desire for attention on the road masks a deeper loneliness and desire to be loved and cared for, even as he longed for more attention and care as a boy.

This, in turn, empathically mirrors Daniel's deepest need. This is not only Gary's "stuff." It is Daniel's own subjective experience. Daniel is profoundly lonely. The hospital stay has been fun, not just because he was freed from responsibility. Daniel also received balloons and cards from classmates and teachers, and a couple of companions even visited—more personal attention than he had received the rest of the year.

The foregoing reflections can now lead Gary to another important insight in his pastoral assessment of Daniel: Daniel needs to be allowed simply to be a kid. Again, by working with his networks in the community, Gary may be able to find some appropriate structured youth activities and perhaps a big-brother or buddy program for Daniel, in which he can receive some surrogate fathering and also just have some fun. This, in turn, will necessitate helping Dawn to find appropriate child care for Daniel's younger siblings, so Daniel can be freed of this over-responsibility at least some of the time. Advocacy, including political activism, may become a part of the pastoral plan for Dawn, if child-care resources in the community are (as is often the case) either too expensive or simply inadequate.

Theological Reflection

Gary is almost ready to apply his pastoral assessment to an appropriate intervention with Dawn and Daniel. Theological reflection will further deepen his empathic openness to Daniel's and Dawn's spiritual needs and reinforce his pastoral understanding.

After his consultation with Carol, Gary sits for a while in the hospital chapel. This has always been one of his favorite places, together with the chapel at the local airport. He is always intrigued by the great variety of people who come in to use these chapels. These places are anonymous, private, wayside places. They seem to feel equally safe to the most disenfranchised and the devout. He finds the simplicity of the small room, designed for interfaith openness, peaceful and soothing. Gazing at candles placed in three niches at the front of the room, he allows his mind to wander, while lightly holding the question "What theological, spiritual, religious themes pop into my head as I sit here with Daniel and Dawn?" in mind. An old favorite film, *My Life as a Dog*,[26] comes to mind. He sets this aside twice, thinking it not suitably spiritual for his theological reflection. But it refuses to go away, and he finally accepts it as the theological image he has been given for this day.

In the film, a twelve-year-old boy, Ingemar, whose father abandoned him and his older brother, is set with the task of caring for his seriously ill mother. Although wishing to be careful and responsible, Ingemar continually finds himself in trouble and is finally sent away to a relative. There, in the company of eccentric villagers, he finds both an intimate friend his own age and the delights of simply being a child. Ingemar's reverie toward the beginning of the film offers the poignant title image, that of the dog Laika, who was sent into outer space to test the effects of space-orbit life. In his opening voice-over narration, Ingemar says:

> It's not so bad if you think about it. It could have been worse. Just think how that poor guy in Boston ended up . . . who got a new kidney. He got his name in the papers. But he died just the same. And what about Laika, the space dog? They put her in a Sputnik, and sent her into space. They attached wires to her heart and brain to see how she felt. I don't think she felt so good. She spun around there for five months until her doggy bag was empty. She starved to death. It's important to have things to compare with . . . It could have been worse. It's important to remember that. Just think about the train wreck I read about. A train ran into a rail bus at Glycksbo. Six people killed and fourteen injured. Just as a comparison. You have to watch those rail buses. It could have been me . . . It bothers me to think of that poor dog Laika. Terrible, sending a dog in a spaceship without enough food. She had to do it for human progress. She didn't ask to go.[27]

Reflecting on Ingemar's loneliness, parent loss, and overresponsibility, Gary again recognizes echoes of Daniel's life. But the image of Laika, with whom Ingemar resonates, also suggests another profoundly theological theme—that of connection and disconnection. Laika is in orbit, without food or comfort, sent into outer space to serve "human progress." She didn't ask to go. Daniel, like Ingemar, has been similarly thrust into a position of isolation and responsibility for the sake of others, but at the expense of his own nurture and development. He is disconnected.

Daniel needs to know both that he is not alone and that he is a valuable, lovable person in his own right: "Are not five sparrows sold for two pennies? Yet not one of them is forgotten in God's sight. But even the hairs of your head are all counted. Do not be afraid; you are of more value than many sparrows" (Luke 12:6-7; cf. Matthew 10:29-31).

Daniel needs both the connection of human community and the larger sense of connection with a loving God who sees and takes care of us. Gary's thinking moves from this "first-order reflection, that God takes care of us, to second-order reflection: in God, no one need feel "out in orbit." Process theologian Bernard Loomer wrote compellingly of the "size of God," large enough to contain all suffering.[28] Such a conception of God emphasizes that human beings are always, however isolated they may feel, held in the vastness of God's understanding and care:

> O Lord, our Sovereign,
> How majestic is your name in all the earth!...
> When I look at your heavens,
> The work of your fingers,
> The moon and the stars that you have established;
> What are human beings that you are mindful of them,
> Mortals that you care for them?
> Yet you have made them a little lower than God,
> And crowned them with glory and honor. (Psalm 8:1, 3-5)

Each person is profoundly known and loved by God from the very beginning:

> O Lord, you have searched me and known me,
> You know when I sit down and when I rise up;
> You discern my thoughts from far away.
> You search out my path and my lying down,
> And are acquainted with all my ways.
> Even before a word is on my tongue,
> O Lord, you know it completely.
> You hem me in, behind and before,
> And lay your hand upon me...
> For it was you who formed my inward parts;
> You knit me together in my mother's womb.
> I praise you, for I am fearfully and wonderfully made.

Wonderful are your works; that I know very well.
My frame was not hidden from you,
When I was being made in secret,
Intricately woven in the depths of the earth.
Your eyes beheld my unformed substance.
In your book were written all the days that were formed for me,
When none of them as yet existed.
How weighty to me are your thoughts, O God!
How vast is the sum of them!
I try to count them—they are more than the sand;
I come to the end—I am still with you. (Psalm 139:1-6, 13-18)

Gary now moves into third-order reflection by applying these reflections to Daniel's situation specifically. Due to circumstances beyond his and his mother's control, Daniel has been thrust into a situation with inadequate caretaking and too much reversal of the parenting roles. For Daniel, then, there is much value in an understanding that God never needs to be taken care of, but is always larger than any human dilemma and wide enough to inhabit every far-flung, lonely space in which a soul can exist. This understanding also applies to Dawn. God is big enough to absorb the hurts and mistakes of Dawn's life. Dawn can find compassion and comfort there.

In Gary's ministry of presence, it is not his job to provide the direct companionship Dawn and Daniel need over the long haul. But Gary can help both of them to give voice to their needs. His reflections have given him the sensitivity to be attuned to these needs and to hear them in the subtlest of communications. As chaplain, he can help them navigate the hospital system, which almost always seems impersonal, confusing, and intimidating to patients, especially those with little social status, economic security, or institutional power of their own. He can further connect them both with community resources, not only for the material needs they can address, but also for the sense of being reconnected with a wider circle of care and advocacy. The right temporary placement for Daniel can even help connect Daniel and his mother with a local church community, in which they may be able to establish a long-term, mutually contributive relationship.

Gary's theological reflection also gives him one more insight into his own countertransference and his own initial impulse to "adopt" Daniel. Gary, too, feels "in orbit" and wants to be reconnected to his own family, to others in the hospital system in which he works, and to others in the wider community. By fantasizing about taking in Daniel, Gary was unconsciously seeking to meet his own needs for human companionship and at the same time positioning himself to be admired by others in the community (and perhaps, ultimately, his own parents) as a hero who rescued the lost child.

Gary's new plan is appropriate: to listen openly and nonjudgmentally to both Daniel and Dawn, to determine their pastoral needs without imposing his own heroic projections, and to use his own responses to be more readily attuned to what they may be communicating at a deeper level. Then Gary is in a position to claim both the unique strengths and the limitations of his role as chaplain. He can offer sensitive pastoral support for their spiritual needs while addressing their material needs through advocacy and referral. Together with the hospital social worker and other individuals in his community network, he can help identify solid referrals and resources in the community to help both mother and son heal from their shared trauma. He can affirm the strengths present in their relationship. Finally, *conscienticized* by this personally challenging pastoral encounter, Gary may even find new energy to begin joining with others in the public arena who are organizing to change some of the external social and economic realities that have made Daniel's and Yvonne's lives so hard.

Terence

Terence ushered Elaine to a seat on the couch in his office and took her cane from her, propping it against his large desk. Drawing his rolling executive chair close to the couch, he sat opposite Elaine and offered her a box of tissues from the polished mahogany side table next to her left elbow. "How can I be of help, Elaine?" he asked in a gentle voice. Elaine began to speak and then bent over and broke into heavy sobs, her tears falling on her knees. "It's OK," Terence said, touching Elaine's shoulder lightly. "I'm here for you. Can you tell me what's happened?"

Elaine sat up and tried to compose herself. "After hearing your sermon Sunday, Terry, I knew I had to come talk with you. Jim still denies that he's having an affair, but there's just too much evidence. I . . . I find things. In his car, in the laundry. You know, all the usual stuff, lipstick stains, a receipt from the jewelry store for something I've certainly never received from him . . . And what's really killing me is that I think the kids are starting to suspect, too. In fact, knowing Emily and Peter, they probably knew before I did." She smiled ruefully. "It's all so trite I hate myself for even telling you any of this. It's like right out of a soap opera!"

"But it hurts, Elaine, doesn't it?" Terence murmured. She nodded, and new tears sprang to her eyes. Terence got up from his chair and paced the room once, then came back and sat next to Elaine on the couch. "The question is," he said, looking deeply into her eyes, "what do you want your life to be about? Is this the way you want to live? Is this the way *God* wants you to live?"

She shook her head. "I knew you would know what to say," she said, returning his gaze. "You always know what to say."

"God wants you to have the love you deserve," Terence said, more forcefully. He took a tissue and dabbed at Elaine's eyes. "Remember, Jesus said, 'I came that they might have *life* and have it abundantly'!"

"I wish I could really believe that, Terry. But you know, I don't think Jim has, you know, really *wanted* me for a long time, since my lupus got worse and I started to limp. I mean, who could blame him?" Elaine felt her face flush.

"You're a beautiful woman, Elaine. Don't you know that?" Elaine teared up again. Terence turned toward Elaine and leaned in a bit closer. "You can believe in Jesus' promise of the abundant life. You just have to claim the promise. So what are you going to do about this?" He looked again into her eyes and thought how soft they looked, not steely and sharp the way Jane's always seemed of late.

"Well," Elaine said slowly, "I keep telling myself I have to let Jim know that I'm not fooled anymore by his lies and his empty words about how he still loves me 'more than ever.' I need to stand up to him and tell him that either he stops this or I'm going to see a lawyer. I'm going to get a divorce, Terry. I know it will be hell on the kids and me, but it's the right thing to do."

"You have to trust that inner voice," Terence replied, and he drew Elaine into a sensuous, enveloping hug.

Elaine pulled back, suddenly startled by the feelings she was having toward Terence. "We shouldn't be doing this, Terence," she said in a shaky voice.

"Doing what, Elaine?" Terence pulled back slightly, looking hurt. "Can't a pastor give a parishioner a healthy hug?"

Elaine looked down at the shredded tissue in her hand. "Of course," she said. "How stupid of me. Now I'm embarrassed all over again. Maybe I'm imagining all kinds of things—with Jim, too. Maybe it's me who's really just not in love with Jim anymore."

"Don't be embarrassed," Terence said soothingly. "Your emotions are all churned up right now, that's all. I think it would be a good idea if we schedule a weekly appointment to do some counseling around this. My sense is that there are early-childhood issues at work in you. Doesn't it feel like some deep things are getting tapped in you?"

Elaine couldn't disagree with that. She nodded.

"Good! That's an important step. Now be a good girl and go home and think about what we've been talking about. You can set up a weekly time on my calendar with Betty on your way out. And while you're at it, why don't you ask Betty for a copy of that sermon? She always keeps a stack, since I get so many requests."

❧ ❧ ❧ ❧

I find my own self hard to grasp. I have become for myself a soil which is a cause of difficulty and much sweat.
—Augustine, *Confessions* 10.16.25[29]

It might be easy to dislike Terence based on this version of the case vignette. Terence has made an egregious mistake and is sliding fast down the "slippery slope"[30] of sexual boundary violation. While Terence himself considers that he has done nothing wrong,[31] he has already sexualized the pastoral relationship through inappropriate touch and physical closeness. Out of the confusion and pain Elaine is feeling about her marriage, she has idealized Terence and even perhaps signaled sexual attraction to him. In contrast to the emotional distance she feels from her husband, Terence's seemingly gentle attention feels like a balm to her wounds. This is not at all to say that Elaine is therefore to blame for the crossing of sexual boundaries between them. The all-too-common stereo-type of the divorced (or divorcing) female seductress and the myth of the pas-tor as "sitting duck" for women's sexual wiles[32] are forms of blaming the victim that ignore the professional ethics of care.[33] It is Terence's responsibility as the professional caregiver, not Elaine's, to monitor the boundary and to maintain a safe, facilitative environment for Elaine to explore her pastoral needs.[34]

Elaine's idealization, which is one normal transference reaction during a time of physical, sexual, and emotional duress, actually signals her need for healthy, safe pastoral support to help her gain a sense of direction and purpose in her marital relationship. It likely further signals her distress about her lupus diagnosis, her growing disability, and her fear of the future progression of the disease. Terence mistakes this transference communication for an invitation to enact a sexual encounter. He fails to attend to the deeper meaning suggested by her communications. He then takes advantage of the authority inherent in the clergy role and the power of her idealization to enact a sexual fantasy rather than explore the actual needs present. He rationalizes his behavior both to Elaine and to himself under the rubric of "giving a parishioner a healthy hug." This masking of the inappropriate enactment further confuses Elaine and increases Terence's power and control in the situation. But in this version of the vignette, Terence has been attempting to meet his own needs, not Elaine's. Terence has abused Elaine.

It is clear, perhaps, from the opening paragraphs of Terence's vignette in the Introduction that Terence is already at risk for some form of professional misconduct. Terence is himself experiencing stress and conflict in his marriage. He appears to be dealing with this by "stonewalling,"[35] literally shutting out the sound of his wife's voice, and externalizing the blame for their difficulties entirely onto her, rather than considering what his own shared responsibility might be. At the same time, he is indulging in fantasies about the parish treasurer, Susan. He disavows any direct wrongdoing with Susan, while secretly enjoying the feelings her pleasant manner arouses. Terence has unconsciously engaged in a form of splitting, in which his wife represents the bad woman in his life, Susan represents the good, and he experiences himself as an innocent victim of pressure, external demands, and conflict.

Terence's ambition also suggests a narcissistic vulnerability. Being on the short list for bishop is both stimulating and anxiety-provoking for Terence, because he not only feels it is a challenging and exciting call to ministry, but at a deeper level feels tantalized by the promise of affirmation and admiration he inwardly craves. He has already depended on external symbols of wealth and power, such as his luxury car, and has sought a "high-steeple" church position that would reinforce his self-image as powerful and successful. Terence's narcissistic vulnerability is a significant risk factor for boundary violations, following the profile of many clergy offenders.[36]

From the very outset of this case study, then, several significant risk factors are present. Risk factors, however, in and of themselves do not guarantee inappropriate behavior. The single most important predictor for any form of abuse is past behavior. Once a boundary has actually been crossed, rehabilitation is much more difficult, and prognosis is almost always poor.[37] Reinstatement in ministry or other helping professions at this point is a high-risk proposition. The fact of having crossed the line from fantasy into actual behavior demonstrates a level of impulsivity that signals a much deeper entrenchment of narcissistic character pathology.

Terence's behavior with Elaine in the vignette has crossed this line in a number of ways, some quite subtle. From the very first moment in which Terence takes Elaine's cane, Terence conveys paternalistic power over Elaine in the guise of kindness and pastoral concern. He does a number of things Elaine could be expected to do for herself, including positioning her cane, reaching for the tissue box even though it is closer to her, and telling her to ask for a copy of his sermon. His language, especially calling her a "good girl," is patronizing and disempowering.

These pseudo-solicitous acts of power are combined with an increasing physical proximity, beginning with rolling his chair close to the couch, presumably leaning across her to reach the tissues, then sitting next to her on the couch, and finally drawing her into an "enveloping hug." Only when Elaine pulls away does Terence quickly disavow his exploitative behaviors, reframing them as appropriate pastoral care and comfort.

Terence has behaved exploitatively toward Elaine, although his actions are ambiguous enough that Elaine would have difficulty proving misconduct if she ever attempted to bring ecclesiastical charges or legal action. Terence would deny any impropriety, likely claiming that Elaine had misconstrued his pastoral warmth as something more. His narcissistic vulnerability would cause him to believe his own protestations, needing as he does to be in the superior position, and would make him a believable witness in his own defense. Elaine would be blamed or even pathologized for bringing the complaint. Why is Terence so able to believe he is innocent or even, if threatened with the truth of his actions, believe he is victimized by Elaine?

Terence failed to engage in any sort of self-reflection during Elaine's office visit and gave in to his own powerful, only partially conscious needs and feelings. In the office with Elaine, Terence chose enactment over verbal understanding, because in some sense it was easier than facing his own painful inner reality. He used words skillfully, but his use of empathy was directed toward a careful step-by-step seduction of Elaine toward meeting his own sexual and emotional needs.[38] This was the way the ethical violation unfolded. But recognizing the ethical failure as such, and the exploitation of the power dynamics inherent in the helper–helpee relationship, does not explain *why* Terence failed, nor why, if confronted later, he would be vehement in defending himself with a clear conscience. To understand the why, it is necessary to understand Terence's underlying psychological makeup. The emotional exploitation of others described in the vignette is the hallmark of narcissistic pathology.

Narcissism is not simply, as it is understood in the popular sense, conceit or self-absorption. The symptomatic behaviors of narcissism do involve an inflated self-regard, ambition exceeding one's abilities (although many narcissistically wounded individuals are high achievers because of their inner drive for affirmation), and a strong sense of entitlement. The narcissistically wounded person believes at the preconscious level that worldly benefits should accrue, and rules should not apply, because he or she is special and deserving of special consideration and rewards. Conversations, agendas, plans, and behaviors generally revolve around getting other people to praise and affirm the narcissist. There is a heavy wall of denial and resistance to seeing beneath this preconscious self-regard, because the acknowledgment of narcissistic desires is almost always laden with deep shame.[39] However, carefully guarded beneath this preconscious self-absorption, there generally exists a deep void. In the right kind of empathic depth psychotherapy, narcissistically wounded individuals gradually peel off the mask of grandiosity and uncover deep depressive feelings of emptiness, worthlessness, and despair.

There are various psychological theories on the origins of such narcissistic wounding.[40] Simply put, most theories agree that the narcissistic individual did not receive the admiration and unconditional loving praise that was needed very early in life. Around the first birthday, a child begins to walk and talk and to enter into human community in new and powerful ways. When this is appropriately mirrored,[41] the child begins to build within himself or herself a well of self-confidence and a healthy pride in accomplishment. This begins even in infancy, with the infant's internalization of the ability to have impact on the big people in his or her environment. But when such basic needs are not met, sometimes even at a very subtle level, the well remains empty. This can happen in a number of ways. Most often, it occurs because primary caretakers are too preoccupied by their own stresses and external pressures to adequately affirm the child's developmental achievements. More pathologically, they may unconsciously appropriate the child's successes to prop up their own fragile ego needs, thus treating the child as a narcissistic extension of themselves.[42]

Eventually, the empty well of affirmation comes to be sealed over in the unconscious by a heavy veneer of performance-oriented behavior. But because the original parental situation did not fill up the child's internal place of self-confidence, the thirst for praise and attention begins to function something like an addiction. Applause and promotion become primary motivations for one's life choices and activities. Such children grow up learning how to read others acutely, in order to recruit praise and avoid criticism. Criticism is phobically dreaded, because it threatens to reveal the emptiness felt within, the unconscious but ever-present sense of oneself as an imposter, and is thus laden with the potential for arousing primitive feelings of shame. Empathy is thus skewed toward a form of self-preservation that uses others' feelings as a barometer for one's own self-advancement.

At the heart of the problem of narcissism, then, is not the lack of capacity for empathy per se, and many deeply pathological offenders manipulate others sexually, financially, or in other ways precisely *by* their finely tuned ability to read the needs and feelings of others. There is, however, in such entrenched cases of narcissism a serious lack of empathy for one's impact on others and an underlying arrest in moral development to the stage where "what's right is what I want."

Not all narcissistically wounded individuals behave that exploitatively. Some theorists now suggest that just as neurosis was considered universal in the earlier part of the twentieth century, narcissistic character pathology may be equally ubiquitous in late-twentieth- to early-twenty-first-century Western civilization.[43] Once an actual boundary violation has occurred, however, and especially in the case of repeated violations, the level of narcissistic pathology must be viewed as more deeply entrenched and problematic. As I have written elsewhere,[44] this degree of narcissism is on the extreme end of the spectrum toward sociopathy. Remorse is impossible, because one's own needs are so overwhelming that others' needs or the impact of one's own actions cannot even be seen, except in a view distorted by self-interest.

Terence, like Gary, has been seduced by the self-image of "special carer" and hero to his "flock." Terence's internal needs are quite different, however, and more active disavowal is at work. Terence can best be described in terms of what is known in self psychology as a "vertical split." The concept of the vertical split was first introduced into self psychology by Heinz Kohut in his paper "Two Analyses of Mr. Z."[45] It has lately been the subject of much discussion in self-psychology circles, and has been described in much greater clinical detail in recent writings by Arnold Goldberg[46] (a psychoanalyst currently in practice in Chicago, and one of Kohut's most important editors and early interpreters). The vertical split is conceived as a psychological mechanism of *disavowal*[47] (rather than *repression,* as in either Freud's topographical model or later structural model). Unlike the process of repression, in which mental contents are understood to be pushed downward out of consciousness into a deeper realm of the unconscious, where they are entirely inaccessible to consciousness (except by analysis), in the process of disavowal, certain aspects of oneself *are* accessible to consciousness but are so uncomfortable to one's own sense of self that they are normally kept out of awareness.

The difference between these two forms of splitting—repression and disavowal—is illustrated in Kohut's paper (see Figure 5).[48] The "vertical split" is so named because it divides consciousness into two areas, pictured on the same horizontal plane, which are not entirely inaccessible to each other. In contrast, in the horizontal layers of the topographical model, the deepest layer, the unconscious, is separated by a repression barrier that is normally impermeable.

The vertical split is usually identified with narcissistic pathology and is mainly manifested in behaviors, often compulsive acts that the person would ordinarily find completely alien. Thus, rather than splitting the personality into conscious and unconscious domains (as in classically defined neuroses), the vertical split is conceived to explain patterns of inconsistent behavior, in which different behavior patterns are governed by the two separate, different arenas of consciousness, and corresponding inhibition or disinhibition. Individuals whose subjective experience resonates closely with this concept of the vertical split often describe this much in the same terms as St. Paul's self-description in Romans 7: "I do

THE CASE OF MR. Z - HIS PSYCHOPATHOLOGY AND THE COURSE OF HIS ANALYSIS

As Seen in Classical Dynamic-Structural Terms in the First Analysis	*As Seen in Terms of the Psychology of the Self in the Narrow Sense in the Second Analysis*	

Overt grandiosity and arrogance due to imaginary oedipal victory.	Overt arrogance, "superior" isolation on the basis of persisting merger with the (nondefinsively) idealized mother. Mother confirms patient's superiority over father provided patient remains an appendage of her. ① ① ①	**V** **E** **R** **T** **I** **C** **A** **L**	Low self-esteem, depression, masochism, (defensive) idealization of mother.
① ① ①			② ② ②
REPRESSION BARRIER			REPRESSION BARRIER
Castration anxiety and depression due to actual oedipal defeat.		**S** **P** **L** **I** **T**	(Non defensive) idealization of his father; rage against the mother; self-assertive male sexuality and exhibitionism.

The analytic work done on the basis of the classical dynamic-structural concept takes place throughout the analysis at the line indicated by ① ① ① .

The analytic work done on the basis of the self-psychological concept is carried out in two stages. The first stage is done at the line indicated by ① ① ① ; Mr. Z confronts fears of losing the merger with the mother and thus losing his self as he knew it. The second stage is done at the line indicated by ② ② ② ; Mr. Z confronts traumatic overstimulation and disintegration fear as he becomes conscious of the rage, assertiveness, sexuality, and exhibitionism of his independent self.

Figure 5. The Vertical Split

From: "The Two Analyses of Mr. Z.," *International Journal of Psycho-analysis* 60 (1979): 11.

not understand my own actions . . . For I do not do the good I want, but the evil I do not want is what I do" (Romans 7:15, 19).

The vertical split has its origins, according to self-psychological theory, in the lack of parental provisions as "selfobjects," reliable (or unreliable) and internalizable figures upon whom the individual depended in childhood. Inadequate or inconsistent parenting over a period of crucial early years results in weak or lacking internal psychological structure, particularly on two poles:[49] On the "mirroring" pole, the child should receive recognition, warmth, unconditional affirmation, "the gleam in the parent's eye." On the "idealizing" pole, the child experiences the parental selfobjects as reliable, admirable, and idealizable—the core of values around which adult aspirations and ideals are formed. When all goes well, mirroring allows infantile grandiosity to be fed and gradually modified into a mature sense of affirmed identity, self-confidence, and appropriate pride in one's capacities and achievements. Likewise, idealizing allows infantile dependence to evolve into mature interdependence in relationships and pursuit of goals founded in a secure sense of ideals, values, and purpose. When all does not go well, however, the result is an inner experience of fragmentation, lack, and depressive emptiness, a sense that inside oneself "there is no there there." This deep insecurity is disguised by an external presentation of inflated self-importance, sensitivity to criticism, and narcissistic grandiosity and entitlement.[50]

With the vertical split phenomenon, the external presentation is the "me" the individual identifies with, often quite successful in some arenas, but also frequently unable to form genuine intimate bonds in relationships and baffled by the reluctance of others in one's world to recognize his or her superiority. On this side of the split, the individual finds himself or herself attempting to ward off depression and at times flying into inexplicable rages that are out of proportion to a perceived threat or criticism, but finally unable to soothe himself or restore a sense of proportion and harmony. The person becomes "a problem to himself."[51]

"I have become for myself a soil which is the cause of much difficulty and sweat" (*Confessions* 10.16.25):[52] When productive activity and the release of tension through rages fail to soothe, then the individual slips over onto the other side of the split and engages in compulsive behaviors in a frantic, joyless attempt at filling the inner sense of emptiness, or in its most sociopathic form, "the world owes me" (paralleling Winnicott's "antisocial tendency").[53] Sexual acting out, fetishes, alcohol and drug abuse, compulsive gambling, physical violence, and other behaviors destructive of self, others, or both can often be understood dynamically as behavioral evidence of this vertical split born of early narcissistic deficit or injury. The predominant affect associated with those moments in which the individual is aware of this "other side" of the vertical split is not guilt, as with neurotic behaviors, but profound shame: not "I *did* something bad," but "I *am* bad."

Classical Countertransference

How might an awareness of Terence's own countertransference feelings have prevented the unethical behavior described in the vignette and led to a more constructive pastoral encounter with Elaine? Let us rewind the scenario to the point where Terence is leaving the house for the day, and let us further assume that Terence has not yet actually violated any boundary.

It is important to note that the presence of sexual feelings does not automatically define a pastor as a sexual predator. A wide range of feelings is a normal part of working intensively with people around emotional and spiritual issues. However, acting on all feelings is not normal or appropriate. The capacity to become *aware* of one's own feelings and then to consider in a reflective vein what such feelings might be communicating—about both one's own needs for healing and the needs of the helpee—are the essential skills for maintaining ethical conduct for caring genuinely and empathically for another.

In Terence's case, before he would be in a position to safely help Elaine, a number of things would already need to be in place for him, including individual psychotherapy, spiritual direction, marriage counseling, and professional consultation. In the ideal, these would not be simultaneous, but sequential, and would have begun years before the present situation.

Of primary importance would be individual psychotherapy for Terence. The level of narcissistic wounding evident in the vignette would not be a recent development in Terence's life. Failures and losses in adult life, even severe blows to one's self-confidence, do not result in the type of disavowal and exploitative behaviors described in this story. Such a pattern of entitlement, unconscious need for acclaim, and exploitation of others must have originated in early childhood, as described in the previous section. For this reason, the pattern should have been evident, at least in some form, before Terence was ever ordained to the ministry. In the ideal, concerns about Terence's need to see himself as super-successful and possible clues to issues with entitlement or lack of appropriate boundaries should have become evident to someone who had authority in Terence's ordination process: a perceptive ordination committee, psychological evaluator, CPE or field education supervisor, or seminary faculty. It would be important for these concerns to be surfaced early, before Terence is ordained and while others still have a significant amount of authority to guide his learning and supervise his behavior.

Red flags that can help with recognizing and addressing narcissistic vulnerability can include an attraction by the candidate to assignments perceived as "glamorous, dramatic, or dangerous."[54] Such candidates do not like jobs they perceive as beneath their talents, preferring settings where they will be perceived as powerful and in the limelight. There is a strong tendency toward autonomous action and resistance to true accountability. When pushed by a church official or group carrying authority, the candidate will likely show resistance to self-examination and may have difficulty taking responsibility for past questionable behaviors without excuse or qualification.[55] There is frequently a tendency to frame wants as needs, to frame conflictual situations in terms of being victimized, and to deny having caused others any harm. Because manipulation and the projection of a star image are common in narcissistically wounded individuals, empathy and conscience are often convincingly feigned. But at the core of the person's self-experience, there is often overwhelming despair, emptiness, fear, and easily triggered rage. For this reason, there is often difficulty establishing appropriate intimate relationships and friendships with peers, leading to the "lone ranger" style of ministry. Other people are used compulsively and heed-lessly in a desperate attempt to keep the demons of worthlessness at bay.

If this vulnerability had been recognized early enough, Terence's ordination could have been postponed, and a course of depth psychotherapy recom-mended. Even long-term psychotherapy cannot guarantee that an individual with a severe level of narcissistic wounding will ever be a safe candidate for ministry. But in many cases, sufficiently deep and intensive therapy can uncover and begin to heal the pathology, with one of two results: The individual may be able to recognize his or her own vulnerabilities and choose a different profes-sion in which the person's needs can be met in a healthy way without putting others at risk for exploitation. Or the individual's grandiose needs can be modi-fied and met sufficiently that the person is no longer likely to seek inappropri-ate support and affirmation from those in his or her care.

Without such intervention, there is, sadly, little hope that an individual can break out of this entrenched pattern of need and use of others. The antisocial tendency will be toward more compulsive acts aimed at filling the internal void. This is futile, however. We cannot fill ourselves up. The most effective remedy is probably a process Kohut called "transmuting internalization,"[56] whereby rela-tionships with new selfobjects facilitate the process of structuralization. As the individual survives (usually over and over) the experience in this new relation-ship of empathic ruptures and being given an interpretation that allows "me" to see more clearly the nature and origins of the split self that caused the vulnera-bility to that empathic rupture, gradual growth or repair of the inner self-structure begins to occur. Through this process, given enough time, the vertical split with its accompanying unconscious habit of disavowal may gradually be recog-nized consciously and healed. In this way, one's behavior can gradually change from shame-laden, compulsive, hidden activity driven by a need for grandiose self-inflation and self-soothing, to behavior that is more integrated and gen-uinely relational.

The original damage is done. It cannot ever be undone, but transmuting internalization functions in a way like grace: it does not replace the original goodness that was intended and then lost in creation, but it does mediate a restoration of the capacity, however imperfect, to desire the good once again. While this process of transmuting internalization may not *necessarily* require the services of an analyst, the aim of any depth psychotherapy, as well as the potentially curative function of all loving relationships, is in the healing of the vertical split and the restoration of wholeness. This corresponds to the theo-logical notion of the healing power of grace.

To the extent that self psychologists increasingly view this conception of psychopathology, as narcissistic deficit, to be more or less true for everyone, this model even corresponds with the universality of the theological construct of original sin. No one gets out of childhood with a "perfect" self-structure, so no one can escape the propensity toward self-inflation and narcissistic vulnerability of one form or another, although this may be acted out to varying degrees and may not enter into overtly destructive behaviors. In the same way, in this theological view, no one can escape the consequences of the Fall, and although some individuals will behave worse than others, even the saints can no longer perfectly will the good without the mediating and redeeming power of God's grace.

Does this mean that every candidate for ministry should engage in some course of individual psychotherapy to address narcissistic vulnerability? It couldn't hurt! But certainly, this analysis weighs in toward the importance of careful psychological screening of candidates, erring on the side of urging all candidates to engage in a compassionately supervised process of guided introspection and self-care. As I have argued elsewhere, the profession of ministry inherently attracts individuals who likely hold a self-image as rescuer, protector, or caretaker. In the vignette of Terence, Elaine's vulnerability is a significant element in her attractiveness to Terence, not at all in spite of, but because of, her tears[57] and physical disability. Again, larger issues of social and political context are relevant in this dynamic. Female gender, race, physical ability, and other demographic characteristics that are vulnerable to oppression may constitute elements that stir the narcissistic wounded healer's compulsion to rescue—and simultaneously to exploit.

This is where committees screening candidates for ministry can be honestly confused by narcissistically wounded candidates for ministry. A candidate's tendency—or compulsion—to care for others may result in laudable altruistic activities, even an appearance of heroism and self-sacrifice, especially in men, or a high level of nurturing and compassion in women. But, as has been discussed at length in this chapter, the outward appearance of heroism, self-sacrifice, or compulsive caretaking is, in fact, a red flag for narcissistic vulnerability. While classical psychoanalysts might dismiss any notion of genuine heroism,[58] a Christian perspective acknowledges true heroes—saints. An important distinguishing mark of genuine saintliness, however, like true heroism, is not eagnerness but *reluctance*. A genuine vocation is often marked by authentic protest of one's incapacity, and genuine courage is marked by the presence, not absence, of fear. One does what one is called to do, in spite of feeling unworthy, inadequate, and afraid. This is the opposite of narcissistic striving, which is marked by bravado, a surface self-confidence, and sense of entitlement to an exalted status.

This leads to the second recommendation, that of spiritual direction. "Discernment of spirits" is necessary, both by candidacy committees and by the candidate himself or herself. Spiritual direction cannot fruitfully be engaged in before serious psychological wounding has been addressed and the individual is well on the path to recovery. However, at a certain point well along in the healing process, the issue of spiritual and vocational discernment should be incorporated into one's personal work, either through psychodynamic pastoral counseling in which the spiritual issues are integrated or through a separate course of spiritual direction with a psychodynamically sophisticated, well-trained, and supervised director.[59]

Spiritual direction can help address issues of vocational discernment and a "testing of spirits." A genuine calling may, in fact, include mixed motives, both worldly and "not of this world." By building a consistent discipline of listening prayer, one's sense of ministry should gradually become more genuinely Christ-centered, and less "me"-centered. Such a discipline of prayerful listening is not a form of "works righteousness," but rather a practice of gratitude for the grace that is already given, and allowing space for the Holy Spirit to enter into one's heart with healing and transforming power.

A regular practice of prayer also can have the effect of slowing one down and creating the introspection and calm necessary to interrupt compulsive behaviors and develop a greater capacity for self-observation without the kind of neurotic guilt or shame that drives self-knowledge back into the regions of the unconscious. A genuine building of relationship with God in prayer can begin to fill the depressive, shame-laden void of narcissism in a way that no other relationship can do, because true prayer does put one in contact with the compassionate love and acceptance of God. C. S. Lewis, in *The Problem of Pain*, named compulsive, addictive behaviors as human beings' misguided efforts to fill the "hole that only God can fill."[60]

Perhaps God's mercy and judgment are not opposites, as is commonly thought. Psychoanalyst and spiritual director Phillip Bennett has written:

Given the destructive nature of our self-judgment, what are we to make of all the images of God's judgment in our religious scriptures and traditions? How can we reconcile God's love with God's judgment? The most satisfying answer I have found is that God's judgment is God's love, in its penetrating, unremitting power. God's judgment is never divorced from God's love; it is not some angry part of God which is split off from God's mercy and gentleness. Instead, God's judgment is the way we experience pure and constant love which sees and knows us to our core. Being known so deeply is like [the] golf ball [remembered by a therapy client, with its miles of rubber band–like material and very small but dense core at the center]: our layers of self-deception and avoidance of intimacy must be unwound until love can touch us to our core.[61]

The third recommendation for Terence is marriage counseling. Assuming that Terence has done the work of psychotherapy and spiritual discernment during his ordination process and is no longer at risk for severe narcissistically exploitative behavior, conflict or stress in one's own marriage is still a risk factor for failing to provide appropriate pastoral care, especially to a parishioner experiencing marital difficulties. Terence's stonewalling is likely part of a larger pattern of difficulties in communication that have been building for some time. If, in spite of working through personal issues in his own therapy, Terence nevertheless finds himself indulging in fantasies about the parish treasurer, Susan, this is likely a sign that something is being unaddressed in his own marriage. Family therapists are in general agreement that having an affair, or fantasizing about having one, is not the cause of damage in a marriage, but rather a symptom.

The form of splitting in which Terence is unconsciously engaging, in which his wife is all bad and Susan is all good, suggests a dynamic in which Terence is actually waging some form of internal battle. Often, the most negative trait one identifies in one's partner is, in fact, the negative that one wishes to disavow in oneself. By externalizing certain negatives onto Jane, such as considering her to be controlling or demanding, Terence has managed to blame Jane rather than owning the controlling and demanding inner voices that plague him from within. Often, these inner voices are, again, voices from early childhood, internalized as a part of oneself but largely operating at the unconscious level. Couples' therapy, particularly with a psychodynamic focus,[62] should be able to help Terence and Jane not only to improve their communication style but also to withdraw the (likely mutual) projections that are impeding their capacity for a conscious, loving relationship. Terence can withdraw the projection of a critical, demanding controller from Jane and own it as part of himself. At the same time, he can withdraw the projection of the fantasied ideal woman from Susan, and recognize those positive aspects in Jane that caused him to love her in the first place. Especially if Jane can meet him halfway in this project, they can open their communication to share their vulnerabilities with each other. This, in turn, should help them to reconnect in a supportive way, with each partner more able to hold good and bad together in a more realistic perception of the other.

This, in turn, will greatly help Terence's capacity to listen helpfully to Elaine. Rather than jumping to take Elaine's side in a split against her husband, Terence may be able to offer a more thoughtful approach that respects both partners. Because he no longer needs to side with Elaine as a tactic to rescue or seduce her and is also no longer projecting his own marital splits into the marriage of Elaine and Jim, he can participate in an appropriate brief, cognitive-style care-and-counseling model that can help Elaine explore the possibility of seeking marital counseling herself.

Finally, as in the case of Gary, Terence would do well to seek professional consultation and/or peer supervision. Supervision can help Terence see dimensions of the transference-countertransference dynamic he is missing. Of course, supervision undertaken with a genuine desire for honest feedback is the first line of defense against unconscious impulses toward grandiose behavior, in the form either of heroism or of getting one's personal needs met through a parishioner. Supervision can catch tendencies to project an attitude of "I can do anything; rules don't apply." But supervision is not only for prevention of misconduct. Nor are sexual feelings in and of themselves signals of narcissistic pathology. Healthy pastors also on occasion experience sexual feelings toward parishioners.

In a healthy or "good-enough"[63] situation, these feelings can be acknowledged rather than disavowed and dealt with as useful information about the intensity of the pastoral relationship, rather than as an invitation to become sexually or romantically involved. Sexual feelings should automatically signal a need for consultation—not because they are bad and a sign of one's being a bad pastor. On the contrary, they signal a need for supervision because they herald significant developments in the unconscious relationship between the pastor and the parishioner that require a third professional perspective. This third perspective is not only for the purpose of avoiding "the slippery slope" of inappropriate enactments[64] but to help the pastor use these feelings to choose appropriate interventions, and imagine empathically what these feelings might mean about the legitimate needs and possible suffering of the parishioner.

Pastoral Assessment

Let us assume that Terence has utilized appropriate forms of counseling, spiritual care, and supervision as just recommended, both in the past and in the present. All this should help him recognize elements in Elaine's presentation that would enable him to make a caring, appropriate response. Having come through his own marital therapy to understand the power of mutual projection and splitting, Terence may consider that some of this same common process may be occurring with Elaine and Jim. He should notice Elaine's idealization of him as part of her transference to him as helper and, further, be alert to the likelihood that there may be splitting. In the absence of any evidence that Jim is abusive, in which case he would need to attend Elaine's safety and refer her confidentially to a battered women's organization for specialized support and advocacy,[65] Terence should be alert to the possibility that he is standing in for the "good husband" and Jim is being seen as all "bad." Jim is likely projecting some of his own internal issues onto Elaine as well, and perhaps as Elaine's illness has progressed, the tension caused by this has exacerbated longer-standing issues in their relationship. Jim has been unable to support Elaine fully, and for whatever reason, the couple has not been able to work through this with effective emotional communication.

Terence's goal in this situation, then, is not to try to "fix" Elaine's problem or even to alleviate her personal suffering directly. Rather, his goal is to listen to Elaine empathically, validate her feelings, help her identify what healthy changes might be possible, and refer her to the right kind of professional support to facilitate those changes. Such an approach also, by putting the power for decision making back in Elaine's own hands, empowers Elaine instead of patronizing or pathologizing her.

Totalist Countertransference and Pastoral Assessment

An examination of Terence's countertransference responses, as in the cases of Linda and Gary, can also do more than simply prevent inappropriate pastoral intrusions. If Terence can recognize his sexual feelings for Elaine consciously (so that they are not acted upon), but also without shame or self-indictment, he may be able to gain a deeper insight into Elaine's own suffering. Erotic elements in the transference-countertransference dynamic may signal more than sexual desire, frustration, or loneliness. Feminist theologians have convincingly noted and critiqued a pervasive denigration of sexuality and the body in classical theology, inherited from Greek mind-body dualism. *Eros* has been reclaimed in the affirmative sense as the life force, even the creative energy of God's own self.[66] The presence of *eros* in the intersubjective space between helper and helpee may signal not only sexual desire per se, but a deeper desire for life itself in all its possible excitement and fullness.

What might this mean specifically in Elaine's situation? Elaine is struggling not only with unhappiness in her marriage, but also with the reality of having lupus, a progressive disease. While there are many things Elaine can do to manage her illness and enjoy a good quality of life, she is no longer able to take her health for granted, as perhaps she once did before her diagnosis. Living with the reality of a progressive disability, Elaine must contend with her body, including issues of sexual desire and desirability, procreation, and mortality, in ways that many nondisabled individuals typically deny. She also may represent to other (temporarily) able-bodied persons the vulnerability of the body and the fragility of life.[67] For this reason, she may encounter unconscious hostility and projection of others' fears of illness and mortality onto her. This may, in fact, be a dynamic at work in the problems of her marriage.

Terence, as Elaine's pastor, may be able to play an important role in helping Elaine recognize and even celebrate the embodied life she is living, disability and all. By refusing either to deny, to sexualize, or to project his own fears onto Elaine's illness, Terence can stand ready to hear some of the underlying existential fears that Elaine is bringing into this pastoral relationship. By refusing to participate actively in a dynamic of splitting, at least to the extent that he can be aware of it, Terence can use his responses to hold up both positive and negative dimensions of Elaine's experience, of the marital dynamic, and of her struggles with her disability.

Theological Reflection

The biblical image of the "abundant life," which in the original vignette Terence used to join with one side of the Elaine–Jim split, exploit her sense of vulnerability with her disability, and seduce her, can now be understood as representing the true promise of God to all the parties in this story: Elaine, Jim, their children, and Terence and Jane themselves. The Gospel text from John 10:10, which surfaced in Terence's consciousness in connection with Elaine's suffering, applies to all of them equally: "I came that they might have life, and have it abundantly." God's promise of life, embodied, relational, and real, can prevent Terence both from splitting off his desires and from acting out compulsively to fill his own needs at the expense of his parishioners. This promise of God's grace, freely poured out for the sake of the whole world, can then be made available freely to Elaine, not as a tantalizing fantasy of escape, but as a true affirmation of her life as it is, both wonderful and terrible, with all its true potential for personal healing and for the healing of her marriage and family relationships.

What if all these insights had been available to Terence? In the following reworking of the vignette, notice, as with Linda, that Terence is not now the "perfect pastor." He experiences discomfort and temptation. The key differences have to do with Terence's being able to become aware of his feelings in the moment, to recognize them for what they are likely signaling him about Elaine's needs, rather than joining with Elaine's idealization of him and forgetting to address the wider needs of Elaine's whole family. He is also more able to be receptive to the possibility that Elaine's disability is at the heart of at least some of her present suffering. His awareness of this enables him to treat her as a whole person, respectfully, avoiding being paternalistic or oversolicitous, while at the same time being alert to themes of existential vulnerability and mortality.

Terence, Redux

Terence ushered Elaine to a seat on the couch in his office. He waited respectfully while Elaine stowed her cane under the sofa. Then, drawing his rolling executive chair out from behind his large desk, he sat at a comfortable distance opposite Elaine and indicated the box of tissues on the polished mahogany side table next to her left elbow. "How can I be of help, Elaine?" he asked in a gentle voice. Elaine began to speak and then bent over and broke into heavy sobs, her tears falling on her knees. "It's OK," Terence said. As Elaine continued to sob, he said, "Elaine, it's fine to cry. But I'd really like to know what's bothering you. When you're ready, can you try to speak? Let's take a deep breath and count to ten, OK?"

Elaine nodded, took a shuddering breath, and sat up.

Terence smiled gently. "OK. Can you tell me what's happened?"

Feeling more composed, Elaine began to speak. "After hearing your sermon Sunday, Terry, I knew I had to come talk with you. Jim still denies that he's having an affair, but there's just too much evidence. I . . . I find things. In his car, in the laundry. You know, all the usual stuff, lipstick stains, a receipt from the jewelry store for something I've certainly never received from him . . . And what's really killing me is that I think the kids are starting to suspect, too. In fact, knowing Emily and Peter, they probably knew before I did." She smiled ruefully. "It's all so trite I hate myself for even telling you any of this. It's like right out of a soap opera!"

"But it hurts, doesn't it?" Terence said, feeling the depth of her distress with genuine compassion. She nodded, and new tears sprang to her eyes. Terence leaned back slightly, looking at Elaine directly. "The question is," he said, conveying respect for her opinion, "what do you want your life to be about? How do you want to live? How do you think *God* wants you and Jim and the kids to live?"

She shook her head. "I knew you would know what to say," she said, already feeling that things might not be as out of control as they had felt. "You always know what to say."

"God wants *each* of you to have the love you deserve," Terence said, becoming aware of Elaine's idealization of him. Trying not to judge himself for the fleeting feeling of enjoyment of Elaine's admiring gaze, Terence sat up a bit straighter and ran his finger under his clerical collar. "Remember, Elaine, Jesus said, 'I came that they might have *life* and have it abundantly'! And that applies to *all* of you."

"I wish I could really believe that, Terry. But, you know, I don't think Jim has, you know, really *wanted* me for a long time, since my lupus got worse and I started to limp. I mean, who could blame him?" Elaine felt her face flush.

Terence felt his own face flush slightly in response and became aware of a warm, erotic feeling toward Elaine. "Get a grip, Terry," he thought to himself. He conjured Jane's face in his mind, the faces of his kids, the therapist he consulted for ongoing supervision, even the face of his bishop. Giving in to this feeling would damage all he had been working toward and would also hurt

Elaine. "Use this feeling as information," he thought to himself. "It's not about *you*, so don't get carried away here! It's about God, and about life."

Taking a deep breath, he sat more squarely in his chair and said matter-of-factly, "You can believe Jesus' promise, Elaine, for *all* of you. You just have to claim it. I know you can't speak for Jim here, or for the kids. You can only really change yourself, as I know you know. But sometimes when one person changes in a really healthy way, the others in the family make important changes, too."

Elaine nodded. "Yeah, that makes sense. I believe that."

"OK, so then the question is, What is a constructive way to make positive change happen? For example, if you woke up tomorrow, and everything was better, what would need to change?"[68]

"Well, for one thing, I wouldn't have lupus!" Elaine said, her face flushing. "But that's not something I can do much about, other than following doctor's orders—which I am . . ." Her voice trailed off, and her shoulders slumped.

"You seem discouraged."

"I am. Sometimes I think I've just become my disease. Like there's nothing else left to me."

Terence pondered this. He stopped himself from his habitual tendency to want to fix or prematurely reassure his parishioner. "Lupus is a rough thing to deal with," he acknowledged. They sat in silence for a moment, and one tear slid down Elaine's cheek.

Finally, Elaine broke the silence. "I do wish I could believe in that abundant-life idea."

Terence said, "You know, Elaine, maybe that saying of Jesus can be of some help to you, too, even with the lupus. Do you think the abundant life doesn't apply to you anymore?"

Elaine took another deep breath. "I guess I've felt pretty abandoned by God. Or punished, even."

Terence engaged Elaine for a while in conversation about this. Elaine did not exhibit clinical symptoms of depression—change of appetite, loss of sleep, fatigue, lack of enjoyment, disproportionate sadness almost every day, suicidal feelings, or preoccupation with death. Her fears and sadnesses about her body were objective, related to her diagnosis, and she still had energy to try to address her problems.[69] Terence helped Elaine to consider her own beliefs about God, God's love, and what God wanted for her life. Elaine became a bit more animated again, as she said, "No, I don't rationally have any reason to believe God is punishing me or that that's the kind of God I can believe in anyway. I guess it's possible that God wants me to have an abundant life, even with the lupus. And if I stop trying to pretend I can make everything go back to the way it was before I got diagnosed, maybe I can find it. Maybe God can help show it to me."

"Yes. I really do believe that, Elaine. Try praying about that, and I will pray for you, too." Terence felt some of the strain that had been present in the room begin to lift, as Elaine's shoulders relaxed and her face brightened ever so slightly.

"So, then, about Jim . . . ?" she asked.

"Yes, so, then, what about Jim?" Terence replied.

"Well, I've kept telling myself I have to let Jim know that I'm not fooled anymore by his lies and his empty words about how he still loves me 'more than ever.' I need to stand up to him and tell him that either he stops this, or I'm going to see a lawyer. I'm going to get a divorce, Terry. I know it will be hell on the kids and me, but it's the right thing to do."

"Whoa, hold on a minute," Terence said. "You've really said two things. The first is having an honest conversation with Jim. I agree with that, and I think maybe you do need to stand up for yourself, not deny what you feel is true. But it's quite a leap from there to the divorce lawyer. Is it possible that part of the problem is that you and Jim haven't been able to have an honest conversation about your relationship? It sounds like that hasn't been happening in quite a while, at least not from your point of view."

Elaine pulled back, suddenly aware of feeling an exciting, wishful desire for Terence. She caught herself in a fleeting fantasy of herself divorcing Jim, Terence divorcing Jane, and the two of them getting together. "No, it hasn't," she said, feeling inwardly chastened. "Now I'm embarrassed all over again. Maybe I'm imagining all kinds of things—with Jim, too. Maybe it's me who's really just not in love with Jim anymore."

"Well, these are some important questions you're raising here. I don't think either one of you know that yet. It sounds like emotions have been running high lately, and the lupus has been a big factor in all of this. The one thing I'm pretty sure I'm hearing is that there hasn't been enough communication between you and Jim, maybe for quite a long time. What would you think of the idea of doing some couple's counseling with Jim?"

Elaine agreed, feeling some relief that there might be another solution. But then she hesitated. "I don't know, though," she said. "I did suggest counseling once a couple of years ago, and all Jim said was that some radio talk-show guy called counseling the 'last stop on the road to divorce.'"

"Well, maybe it's time to try again. Do you think it would help for the two of you to come in here, and we could talk together about finding the right referral? I know some really good people who have helped some other couples' relationships get a lot stronger."

"OK, I'll give it a try. Would you call Jim and suggest this?"

Terence pondered Elaine's request. She looked so vulnerable and lost. He felt his desire to protect and bond with her rising again like a warm tide in his chest. "Red flag," he thought, this time smiling slightly at his repeated attempts to outfox himself.

"I appreciate your trust, Elaine. But I think this is something that will go best if you broach it yourself. It won't help if Jim thinks this is just me pushing some kind of touchy-feely agenda here. Tell him what you've told me this morning, how vulnerable you feel, and see if he won't meet you halfway. I could meet with you both on Thursday late afternoon, or we can try to find another time that works better. In the meantime, here's a card for a good pastoral counselor who specializes in couples. Maybe Jim will just want to go ahead and start counseling directly."

Elaine retrieved her cane and stood, wobbling slightly as the pain shot up her left leg. "Thanks, Terence," she said. Regaining her balance, Elaine stood taller and walked to the door. "I'll talk with Jim about all this. I do feel a little more hopeful—for both Jim and me."

The Shifting Paradigm for Pastoral Care

Both Gary and Terence were trained in the traditional model of pastoral care as a largely one-on-one, heroic, and even self-sacrificial enterprise. The operant metaphor for this model of pastoral caregiver has been the shepherd—the actual meaning of the word *pastor*. One of the great articulators of pastoral theology of the mid-twentieth century, Seward Hiltner,[70] first described the three primary functions of the shepherd-pastor as healing, sustaining, and guiding. This helped to differentiate pastoral care and counseling in the 1950s from the hegemony of psychiatry, and to restore a biblical, theological, and historically grounded paradigm to the work of pastoral caregivers, who were struggling to find their own distinctive identity as professionals. But it also participated in a paternalistic paradigm that was then common. The shepherd tends the flock, feeds and guides the sheep, protects them from wolves and marauders, and generally steers them in the direction they are to go. And, drawing on Christ's own words, the shepherd "lays down his life for the sheep" (John 10:11).

This model was taken seriously by generations of pastors who felt a call to sacrificial love of their flock and the task of moral and spiritual guidance. But herein lies a serious pitfall, that is, the tendency to see self-sacrifice as a defining image of ministry. While some sacrifice is probably always necessary in ministry, or, for that matter, in any devoted Christian life, the dominance of a sacrificial image has caused numerous problems. In particular, it can lead to taking oneself so seriously that one might view one's own pastoral ministry as so uniquely indispensable that one's own needs as a caregiver can be neglected indefinitely. If the pastor or the pastor's family should suffer for this, it is all within the framework of the self-sacrificial love of the shepherd.

This paradigm is now shifting. In large part, this is due to the influence of two very important and interrelated strands of theological thinking and pastoral praxis: (1) the growing presence of women in both lay and ordained leadership in many mainline denominations, and (2) the emergence, in part through liberation theology, of voices of the developing world in theology and of at least slight growth in diversity of racial and class leadership in our churches. Both of these influences have brought critiques from their own social location and theological perspective to the shepherd paradigm. No one, it should be noted, is trying to throw the baby (or the shepherd?) out with the bathwater. But there is an increasing awareness of the limitations of this individualistic, heroic model and a wonderful opening up of possibilities for a much wider horizon for pastoral care and pastoral theology. This opening or widening process may be seen in four dimensions: *contextualization, diversification, balance,* and *Christ-centered ministry.*

Contextualization

First, contextualization: Carroll Watkins Ali, a pastoral psychologist in Denver, tells the story of a pastoral counseling client named "Lemonine," whose only diagnosis was coping with the enormous external pressures of her social and economic situation. Lemonine paid for her fragile professional success in untold stress and constant fear, and eventually died at the age of forty-two. Watkins Ali writes:

> Truly, life was Lemonine's presenting problem. There are no other diagnoses in the traditional sense. Lemonine was basically suffering from being overcome by her own personal life, while trying to cope with all the external social realities that affected each age group of her family members. In essence, each weekly session during our relationship served mainly to build Lemonine up enough so that she could go back out to face a hostile world for another week. A major issue that came up often in our sessions was the racism Lemonine experienced in her workplace . . . The glass ceiling barred heavily against her advancement before she could even get her foot in the door because she was both Black and female . . . In retrospect, it now seems that therapy was Lemonine's last effort to find a way to overcome the many problems of her world . . . I have searched my mind time and again trying to think of what more I could have done or what I could have done differently to help Lemonine. The truth is that I did all I could possibly do within my professional

capacity as a pastoral counselor. What I was able to do as an individual was limited. It is very clear to me that a communal strategy of a network of care and resources was required to meet Lemonine's needs.[71]

As described in chapter 4, pastoral care based on the individualistic medical model, tended to operate one on one, seeking to effect healing intrapsychically, or, at most, due to the influence of family systems theory, within the family. This model tended not to recognize the powerful impact of social, political, economic, racial, ethnic, and cultural context of both individual and family development. The shift from "relational humanness to relational justice"[72] means that pastoral care can no longer focus on the individual in isolation from the wider context. This takes pastoral care and counseling out into the arena of advocacy as well as individual care. It also calls for an expanded awareness, in which our own openness as caregivers to the reality and the wisdom of those for whom we care can model the kind of mutuality and correct for the kind of top-down, power-over expert role that once held sway. We are also called to hold in our awareness the wider contextual realities in which individuals struggle to live, and to refrain from "diagnosing" as individual psychological or spiritual problems what are, in fact, outcomes of societal rather than individual illness and spiritual malaise.

This means that the arena of care is broadened. No longer confined only to the pastor's study, pastoral care may be understood as the preaching of sermons that call for personal empowerment and liberation of persons; offering small groups for support, Bible study, and discipleship aimed toward changing realities that stifle and oppress individuals' lives in the community; and getting out in the community, exercising the ancient Augustinian call of the church to stand as a witness to and a critiquing partner with the social and political institutions in our communities[73] and join with others who are working for social change that undergirds the possibility for personal change. To use an example from my years in specialized ministry with battered women, it would mean the difference between individual counseling only and counseling plus advocacy in the wider community. This broader approach would seek to empower this woman to identify her own strengths and options, while also preaching, teaching, working collaboratively with battered women's shelters and agencies for men who batter, and advocating with others in the community for the eradication of violence against women and the social structures that reinforce it.

Diversification

This contextualization of pastoral care, with its commitment to relational justice, leads to the second aspect of change in pastoral care: diversification. This refers to diversification of both caregivers and the resources made available to those seeking pastoral help. Not all pastoral care has ever been dispensed in the one-on-one setting of a professional office with a fixed appointment, nor has all pastoral care ever been dispensed solely by the clergy. The one-on-one model has all too often perpetuated a one-up expert role that tends subtly to "fix" rather than empower the one coming for help. However, there is now a growing respect for the wide variety of resources available for pastoral care and for the clergy-person as one resource—albeit an important one with particular gifts—among many. Pastoral theologians, using a phrase from Bonnie Miller-McLemore,[74] are now reconceiving pastors as "facilitators of networks of care," rather than sole caregivers. Margaret Kornfeld[75] has similarly written recently about pastoral care as a paradigm of cultivating wholeness, in which a variety of counselors with a variety of expertise collaborate in the facilitation of spiritual growth and healing of both individuals and communities.

Bonnie Miller-McLemore has revised another paradigm that was widely circulated from the mid-twentieth century, Anton Boisen's idea of the "living human document."[76] In his time, Boisen was concerned that pastoral caregivers turn from an overreliance on theory and texts to a more existential respect for the life of individuals in all their uniqueness. He called for "the study of living human documents rather than books," and this phrase *living human documents* struck a resonant cord in pastoral caregivers who sought, legitimately, to get closer to the lived inner experience of their helpees. However, this paradigm, too, was limited by its individualistic bent. Miller-McLemore has proposed replacing the "living human document" with the "living human web" as the "appropriate subject for investigation, interpretation, and transformation."[77] She advocates "a shift toward context, collaboration, and diversity," in which the work of caregiving includes both individual and communal care, respecting the complexity and multiple contextual realities of people's lives.

In practical terms, this means that the notion of "care" expands from that lone pastor in the study with a lone parishioner or couple or even family to a web of resources gathered collaboratively to address the complex, layered needs and struggles of the helpee. It means having a well-thumbed Rolodex (or Palm Pilot!), in which there are entries representing a wide variety of *personally known and trusted* helpers in the community with various expertise, including spiritual directors, therapists, social workers, school officials and educators, medical professionals, public agency workers, and community organizers. It means sharing the responsibility and authority for pastoral care with trained and empowered lay caregivers, such as Lay Eucharistic Ministers, small-group leaders, Stephen Ministers, parish nurses, and pastoral care teams. It means hitting the pavement to identify and join with others who are working in the community to change the conditions that perpetuate suffering, and bringing those individuals back into our congregations as witnesses to the wider needs of the community.

It also means seeking consultation. Even in one's own individual caregiving, one need not rely on one's own wisdom and experience, but can be supported by the accumulated wisdom and experience of many peers and senior colleagues, both in pastoral care and secular psychotherapy, and in other allied disciplines represented throughout the wider community.

There is a hidden benefit to this community-based approach, because, although it sounds like a lot, in one way it's actually less taxing than the old paradigm. The pastor no longer needs to be seen as having sole responsibility for the welfare of the "flock." This becomes a shared responsibility and a collaboration of the whole body of Christ by virtue of our baptismal covenant, shared also with the wider community.

Balance

This diversification of caring resources leads to the third aspect of change in the pastoral paradigm, that of balance. A collaborative model of pastoral care replaces the old self-sacrificing model of the shepherd with a model of balance—exemplified in care for self as well as others, and a respect for boundaries as a positive good. The image of the oxygen mask on an airplane is a familiar but true analogy. The safety announcement on every airliner instructs passengers in case of an emergency to put on their own oxygen mask first, before assisting another person. If we exhaust ourselves in giving without taking time to replenish, if we burn out, we soon are no use to anyone. We also are not much use to ourselves, and our relationship with others, and ultimately even with God, suffers. The *eros*, the life force of God, is meant for us to enjoy as caregivers as well. We, too, are intended to "have life and have it abundantly"! When we overextend ourselves on behalf of others, we are prone to falling into the trap of the self-aggrandizement of the martyr—"I'm indispensable, I'm so important, everyone needs me." We don't have time to refuel as we should in prayer and rest, in spiritual direction, in personal psychotherapy as needed, in self-nurturing activities and fun. We begin to derive our sense of satisfaction and self-worth from those we are helping, rather than from the resources of our own personal lives—and most importantly, rather than from our own nourishing relationship with God.

Jeanne Stevenson Moessner has held up the biblical image of the Good Samaritan as an alternative to the shepherd paradigm.[78] The Good Samaritan helped the man whom he found on the side of the road, half dead, stripped, and beaten. But he also went on with his own journey. He did not give up his life for the stranger, but rather shared life with him. Further, he solicited the help of another helper, the innkeeper—pledging resources and support, and pledging to return, but also keeping the other commitments of his life. This story, in fact, is a useful example of the power of a good, timely referral to a trusted resource. Nor did the Samaritan "refer and run," but rather, promised ongoing support for the referral. All this he accomplished without sacrificing his own plans and without becoming entangled in an enmeshed relationship inappropriate to the task of care. The message of the Samaritan is simple but poses a healthy alternative to some traditional models of care: share the caring task with other helpers, stay connected but not overinvolved, and stay whole yourself.

Moessner uses the Samaritan story also to illustrate Christ's summary of the law: love your neighbor as *yourself*.[79] The failure to care for self as well as for others can lead to a further peril beyond burnout: it is a very small step from deriving our self-worth from those we are helping to beginning to use them to gratify other needs of ours as well—emotional, even sexual. In this way, attention to keeping good boundaries is not withholding love and care, but rather, safeguarding that love and care within a container of trust, respect, and safety.[80] When we begin to overvalue our own importance in tending the needs of others, and begin to overidentify and confuse ourselves with our role or, worse, with the Savior, very bad things can happen.

Christ-Centered Ministry

Finally, it is Christ who is the great shepherd of the sheep, not ourselves. When we cling too hard to the shepherd paradigm, we may run the risk of confusing ourselves with the Savior—a temporarily gratifying, but ultimately soul-killing proposition for us and for all whom we serve. Dorothy McRae-McMahon,[81] pastor of Pitt Street Uniting Church, Sydney, Australia, in her book *Being Clergy, Staying Human,* calls for self-awareness, a certain lightness of being, and a daily vocation based in gratitude toward God and profound respect toward every other person. She writes, "Underpinning all that I do pastorally is the absolute conviction that God is at the bottom of every abyss, is the oasis in the desert, the light in the darkness that is never extinguished, and the waiting meaning in the nothingness."[82] She tells of her experience of realizing that the power of her ministry was not hers at all, but rather, God's acting through her:

> In our hands lie the bread and the wine and the water of the grace of baptism. When these precious elements were placed in my hands on the day of my ordination, I wondered if I would ever be worthy of carrying them. But as I broke the bread and offered the wine, I realized that the life I held would never be dependent on me or the strength or worthiness of my hands. A

presence was always there in once-offered grace and freedom; it was simply named by me and claimed in thanksgiving by the people of God.[83]

Jesus sent the disciples out two by two (Luke 10:1). He did not send individuals, but partners. And when those partners went forth, he foretold that they would be empowered to do great healing works in his name. This is the image that for me replaces the paradigm of the shepherd: the image of the disciples, going out as partners, without lots of extra provisions but with the confidence of the Gospel and the reliance on the hospitality of strangers that would make their mission complete. In this paradigm, we become companions to one another on the journey, and as we go, we may find, as did the disciples on the Emmaus road, that we even end up, without realizing it, walking side by side with Christ himself (Luke 24:13-35).

Conclusion: Recommendations for the Use of the Self in Pastoral Care

As shown in the vignettes in this book, effective pastoral care includes giving close attention to one's own thoughts, feelings, fantasies, and behaviors. This "use of the self" is not a matter of self-preoccupation but, on the contrary, a healthy utilization of one's own responses to enhance the quality of pastoral care. Appreciation of the complex, affect-laden nature of the intersubjective relationship between helper and helpee can deepen understanding, strengthen empathy, and increase the mutuality of respect, even as it enhances the creation of a safe space with healthy boundaries.

In summary, this deep use of the self as a pastoral caregiver relates to four specific recommendations for parish-based pastoral care, professional chaplaincy, and ministry in other pastoral care settings:

1. Caregivers should make intentional, thoughtful use of their own countertransference to recognize the level and nature of the needs present in the pastoral relationship. This includes awareness, as in classical countertransference, of one's own unresolved issues, feelings, and needs as they are stimulated by the pastoral care situation. It further includes openness, as in contemporary understandings of the countertransference, to clues about the deep needs of the person receiving pastoral care—especially needs that may not be fully conscious or clearly articulated in words. It is sometimes possible, as shown in the vignettes in this book, to dip into the pool of shared but as yet unarticulated knowledge in the "between" of the intersubjective relationship—the potential space in which new insights can emerge through the shared exploration of meaning. It will always be up to the recipient of care to decide finally what his or her needs may be. One should never impose interpre-

tations or state another's need for him or her. But the empathic exercise of vicarious imagination that can arise from an examination of one's own feelings in the countertransference can open a space for deeper exploration and, in particular, deeper, more receptive listening to all the levels of communication present in the pastoral dynamic.

2. All this must take place with a continual reminder to oneself to attend to issues of context. Race, gender, class, sexual orientation, physical ability, age, and other demographic factors that spell oppression for some and privilege for others must be considered in any empathic understanding of another's life situation. Stresses, conflicts, dilemmas, and pain are not only intrapsychically generated, nor are they necessarily signs of endogenous pathology. A consideration of the intersubjective relationship must include sensitivity to the social location of the other, with a profound respect for difference. This approach goes far beyond "tolerance" toward a genuine appreciation for difference and openness to learning from the other. Genuine empathy does not only operate out of commonality, but out of a capacity to vicariously imagine oneself into the different perspective of the other, with reverence. The proper stance of pastoral care is always "take off your shoes; you stand on holy ground." The intersubjective space created between two persons in the pastoral relationship is sacred space. We enter with awe, with fear and trembling.

3. This leads to a stance of humility. We cannot know everything or do everything for another. Empowerment means standing ready to accompany and facilitate the empowerment of the other, rather than being a heroic rescuer. An empowering approach builds on the strength of the other, while a rescuing or heroic approach, however other-oriented it may appear, actually builds up the strength and the status of oneself. In practical terms, this means knowing one's own limits objectively, without embarrassment or shame, and having a commitment to utilizing the full network of care that is available in the wider community. This includes resources both within and outside the parish or other immediate context of ministry. Outside the parish, one makes vigorous use of the well-thumbed Rolodex and continues to nurture collegial relationships with service providers and other professionals who may be of help in future situations of need. Within the parish, part of the work of pastoral care is to equip and empower the whole body of Christ, as represented in that particular place, to be caregivers, each member living out his or her baptismal vocation. This does not mean recruiting volunteers to fill needed ministry slots but, rather, supporting each member in discerning his or her own unique calling to ministry and then facilitating the development of this vocation in whatever form is most true to that particular call-

ing. In my experience, in such an approach to community ministry, needed "jobs" do not go unfilled—the Holy Spirit does get involved!—but people are free to learn and grow in ways that a volunteer recruitment model can never fulfill.

4. Finally, attention to the wisdom of one's own experience in the countertransference leads to a renewed attention to self-care. As discussed in the vignettes in this book, this involves the utilization of a variety of resources in the community for oneself: personal psychotherapy, spiritual direction, and professional consultation. The use of the imagination and the associative process of theological reflection outlined in this book also demand time to oneself, to read a wide range of literature; maintain one's "cultural literacy" through film, theater, and the arts; and perhaps write a journal to keep one's own creativity flowing and alive. Last but not least, self-care involves a commitment to a regular discipline of prayer and the intentional devotion of time to one's own spiritual growth. This is the ground, finally, from which all genuine pastoral care springs. It is God/Christ/Spirit, and not ourselves, who is the Shepherd and the Healer. Our job is not to make the healing happen, but our own role in helping will be strengthened by making ourselves available through daily prayer to the promptings of the Holy Spirit. We are renewed and refreshed as caregivers and as people ourselves in need of God's healing care. Prayer is not about controlling anything. It is about "showing up" and becoming aware of all the ways in which God's healing power is already at work in us and in the world. By simply showing up, by listening to God and sharing our deepest concerns in prayer, we can experience how God is moving in us, surprising us, and strengthening us each day. Daily renewing one's relationship to the Holy One puts one back in touch with the sacred foundation of all healing, all care. This, in turn, prepares us, again and again, for a use of the self in pastoral care that can be a channel of grace for both participants in the caring relationship.

> *I pray that the God of our Lord Jesus Christ, the God of Glory, may give you a spirit of wisdom and revelation as you come to know him, so that, with the eyes of your heart enlightened, you may know what is the hope to which you have been called, what are the riches of God's glorious inheritance among the saints, and what is the immeasurable greatness of God's power for us who believe, according to the working of God's great power.*
> —Ephesians 1:17-19

CHAPTER SIX

The Relational Paradigm in Pastoral Psychotherapy

THE PRECEDING CASE STUDIES of Linda, Gary, and Terence were examples of the use of the self in the practice of pastoral care, both in the parish and in chaplaincy. This chapter continues with one more case, in order to address the application of the same method of pastoral reflection to the practice of pastoral psychotherapy. Sara is a psychoanalytically oriented pastoral counselor doing individual psychotherapy. However, the discussion and recommendations that follow pertaining to Sara's case do not apply only to psychodynamically oriented therapists but can be usefully adapted by family systems and cognitive-oriented therapists as well.

Pastoral Counseling and Psychotherapy: Some Definitions

For the purposes of this book, the terms *pastoral counseling* and *pastoral psychotherapy* are used interchangeably. Pastoral counseling, or psychotherapy, is defined as a distinctive form of counseling in which the full resources, theoretical knowledge, and clinical methods of secular psychology and psychotherapy are brought together with pastoral theological method and practice to provide a holistic approach to psychotherapy that honors and integrates the spiritual dimension of each patient's life and experience. While parish-based pastoral care and chaplaincy may include at most brief, cognitive, or "solution-focused" pastoral counseling methods for up to a maximum of five or six sessions, the focus of pastoral care is primarily on pastoral support, spiritual direction, and guidance. In pastoral care situations involving more complex relational issues or long-standing patterns of conflict or emotional illness, the focus shifts to competent pastoral assessment and referral—while supporting the referral with appropriately boundaried spiritual support.

Pastoral psychotherapy, in contrast, participates fully in the range of counseling methods available to the psychotherapeutic disciplines, from brief therapy to cognitive-behavioral counseling to longer-term depth psychotherapy. Pastoral counselors as professionals adhere to a number of theoretical orientations and methodologies, including psychodynamic/psychoanalytic, family systems, cognitive-behavioral, humanistic-existential, and an eclectic approach using a variety of methods. In my own recent research on pastoral counselors' attitudes and uses of countertransference,[1] most identified as psychodynamic (about 42 percent) or eclectic (36 percent), with family systems (15 percent) making up most of the remaining 22 percent.[2] Nearly all pastoral counselors, then, work with unconscious as well as conscious dynamics in the therapeutic relationship, attempting to "make the unconscious conscious" in an effort to heal early-childhood wounds and unhealthy patterns of relationship that impede patients' quality of life and spiritual growth.

The respective domains of pastoral care and pastoral counseling/psychotherapy can be illustrated as shown in Figure 6, a diagram called the Johari window.[3] In this diagram, areas 1 and 3 are the usual domains of pastoral care. These are the realms of the helpee's conscious subjectivity. The helpee shares more from his or her private internal world as trust builds and and the helpee offers more private information for shared reflection. Domain 2 is also, on occasion, an area for pastoral care, as information that is observable but not wholly conscious on the part of the helpee is explored. This is an area of risk, because what is known to others but not known to self can be an arena of shame. Because exploration of nonverbal communication and behaviors can cause the helpee to feel exposed, such exploration requires tact and sensitivity. Unempathic exploration is likely to raise defensiveness and harm trust. Therefore, while Domain 2 is occasionally in the realm of pastoral care when gentle confrontation is required,[4] it is more the purview of pastoral counseling and psychotherapy.

The fourth quadrant is the realm of pastoral psychotherapy and not pastoral care. It represents the realm of the unconscious. Here, the unconscious relationship of helper and helpee will be manifested primarily through transference-countertransference dynamics. An understanding of the intersubjective nature of unconscious communication allows the therapist to dive more deeply with the helpee into the unknown, allowing the unconscious to become conscious over time, as meanings are coconstructed, revised, and shared through empathic exploration.

Sara

Sara returned to her office after the weekend and reviewed her appointments for the day. Seeing Miranda's name last on the schedule, she felt a resurgence of concern and anxiety. She was was grateful for the feeling of warmth and safety

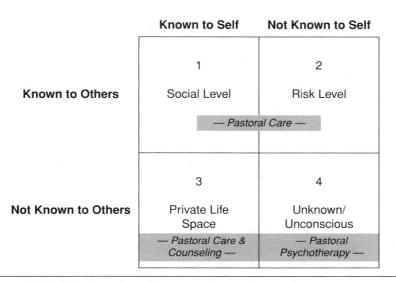

Figure 6. Johari Window, adapted for pastoral care and counseling

of her office, and she relaxed for a moment in her appreciation for her sense of collaboration and embeddedness in the Latino community, which had worked so hard to create this place of welcome.[5]

That afternoon, as Miranda's three o'clock appointment time came and went, Sara found herself watching the clock with growing anxiety. Three-twelve, three-thirteen, three-fourteen, and Miranda still failed to appear. Finally, as the minute hand clicked to three-fifteen, Sara picked up the phone and dialed Miranda's number. "My instincts were correct," she thought. "Miranda did need to meet in a safer place." Would any office, even this one, be soothing enough? Perhaps she really should suggest moving their sessions to her own home. She dialed Miranda's number with a new sense of resolve. A child's voice answered, "Hello?" on the tenth ring, just as Sara was about to hang up.

"Hello, is Miranda there?" Sara asked, wondering who the child was, since, unlike most of her other Latina clients, Miranda had no children and lived alone.

The child's voice replied, "Sara, is that you?"

Disconcerted, Sara said, "Yes. Who's this?"

"Sara," the child said, ignoring her question, "I'm so scared. I'm so, so scared." Then the child began to cry. "Can you help me?" she sobbed.

Sara froze, a feeling of panic rising in her throat. Something was horribly wrong, but she could not make any sense out of what she was hearing. "Miranda?" she asked again, realizing this child *was* Miranda.

"Help me, Sara!" the childlike voice sobbed again. "I'm so scared." Sara felt the hairs on the back of her neck stand up. Then, suddenly, Miranda hung up.

Sara stood, feeling paralyzed, still holding the phone to her ear as a recorded voice came on and intoned, "If you'd like to make a call, please hang up and try again . . . if you'd like to make a call . . ." Putting the phone down on her desk, she recalled again the last ten minutes of their last session. Something deep was happening, but she knew that unless she saw Miranda, they would not be able to process it further. Driven by both curiosity and fear, Sara decided to visit Miranda's apartment and find out what was going on. Miranda was the last patient of the day, so Sara knew she would have plenty of time to confront whatever it was that was happening. Grabbing her coat, she half walked, half ran out to her car and drove a short mile to Miranda's apartment building.

When Sara rang the bell, a woman's muffled voice spoke through the intercom, "Who is it?"

"It's me, Sara. I—I thought it might be good if we talked, Miranda. I spoke to the child who answered the phone, and I want to help. Do you want to let me in?"

"*No!*" the adult voice shouted, causing the intercom to buzz furiously. "Go away!"

Sara felt tears spring to her eyes at the unexpected rebuff. Her panic rising again, she pressed the Speak button on the intercom again. "Please, Miranda," she said. Her own voice sounded tinny and hollow as echoed back to her from the intercom mike. "I think you may need help."

There was no reply. Shocked, and confused, Sara waited seven long minutes, pacing the small vestibule of the building. Finally, feeling defeated and slightly hurt, she turned and walked back down the steps to her car.

Returning home to her own apartment, she saw her answering machine light blinking, ten rapid flashes. All the messages had come in during the half-hour drive from Miranda's building: two hang-ups, a call from her friend Mary suggesting dinner, four more hang-ups, someone—a woman?—breathing and clearing her throat, another hang-up, and finally Miranda's professional adult voice, loud and clear:

"I know I shouldn't call you at home, Sara, but how dare you, how *dare* you come to my apartment?! This is *my safe space*, and no one, *no one*, gets to come here. I have just written you a letter and an e-mail, and I am thinking about reporting you to your licensing board or whatever it is . . . *You have no right!* And you should know that I have the worst migraine I have ever had in years, and it's all because of *you! And don't call me!*"

～ ～ ～ ～

We leave Sara at a point in this vignette where she is wondering how things could have gone so horribly wrong. The case seems to have unraveled precipitously, in spite of Sara's deepening concern for Miranda and her efforts to increase her involvement. What Sara has not yet been able to perceive is that this very concern and involvement are what have led her, in spite of her best conscious intentions, to intervene untherapeutically. Perhaps especially for pastoral psychotherapists, whose training almost always begins out of a desire to care deeply for others, it may seem counterintuitive that actions prompted by compassion can run counter to the therapeutic task. But a more careful examination of the intersubjective dynamic between Sara and Miranda, as with every therapist and patient, reveals some deeper wisdom about how to be more truly helpful. In particular, reflection about the insights available in Sara's countertransference, from both classical and contemporary perspectives, might have guided Sara to take a more restrained but ultimately much more helpful approach. Such reflection must, as in the pastoral care cases in the previous chapters, also take into consideration the deep impact of the social location of both therapist and patient.

Countertransference and the Play of Differences

Like the pastoral care case studies in the previous two chapters, the case in this chapter is a composite based on a number of individuals' experiences and fictionalized for the sake of anonymity. It was developed in particular to illuminate certain common transference-countertransference dynamics that arise in pastoral counseling/psychotherapy. As in the earlier pastoral cases, consideration must be given to social, economic, racial, gender, age, and other factors, because these will contribute significantly to the intersubjective relationship between therapist and patient. Unconscious social factors in particular will have a central, though often overlooked, influence upon the unconscious relationship in psychotherapy. Experiences of oppression and discrimination operate not only at the conscious level but internally, at the level of each individual's internalized object relations, sense of self, and socially constructed aspects of self-worth and ability.[6]

As Puerto Rican women in their early thirties, both living in the continental United States, Sara and Miranda relate to each other not only through their individual and intrafamilial experiences, but also through their past and ongoing experiences—both similar and different—based on each one's experiences of larger systemic, political, and economic realities, experiences of discrimination and inclusion, and particular social location.[7] Both women fought hard to gain the level of achievement and recognition that each one has, and each is aware of subtle and less subtle discounting of her worth and opinions in the still largely male and overwhelmingly white professions of banking and pastoral counseling.[8]

Miranda's particular experiences of trauma and her willingness to talk about these incidents even with a trusted counselor are also affected by dimensions of cultural identity, family loyalty, and racial oppression. The meaning she is able to make surrounding her abuse has been shaped internally, in some ways unique to herself as an individual, and in some other ways formed by the responses and attitudes of her family, her church, the Puerto Rican community, the wider, nationally diverse community of Hispanics and Latinos in her metropolitan area, and the quite different dominant white culture surrounding them all. Miranda, like many abuse survivors of color, feels torn. On the one hand is her need to give voice to her own experience for the sake of her own healing. On the other hand are feelings of secrecy based on not bringing shame to her family and her culture,[9] who, as she well knows, have already suffered enough degradation and social disdain. She knows that revealing the evil of her experience may even have direct economic consequences for herself and members of her extended family.[10]

Sara, on her part, needs to avoid the assumption that she "knows" what Miranda is going through because they are both Puerto Rican women of a similar age. She must remain conscious about how similarities may lead her to over-identify with Miranda's experience and psychological life. At the same time, she needs to be aware of how the differences in their backgrounds play into the dynamic between the two women. Sara needs to be alert to ways in which her own childhood, in which there was no abuse, cannot be used as a simple point of reference (or judgment) in relation to Miranda's. Sara's childhood environment, while not entirely free of conflict or disapproval toward Sara's independent ambitions, was nontraumatic, steeped in traditional values of love for home and centrality of family. It was protective and nurturing of children and characterized by warmth, religious devotion, and hospitality.[11] This very different upbringing can at times lead Sara to make faulty assumptions, to overdiagnose or pathologize Miranda, to fail even to see certain dynamics in Miranda's experience or unconsciously to avoid facing some of Miranda's more terrifying and painful childhood realities.

Again, as in the earlier pastoral care cases, it is important to be mindful of how race, culture, class, and other factors become internalized and operate as an intrinsic part of the transference-countertransference dynamic of the therapeutic relationship. The reader is therefore invited again to "play with difference"[12] and to ask, "How might this case work itself out differently if each individual in the narrative were [this race], [this sexual orientation], [this age], [this socioeconomic class], [this socio-geographical setting], etc.? Or if one or both participants were men?" Again, without resorting to stereotypes, how might the power dynamics shift—both externally and internally—with changes in social location of one or both participants in the therapeutic relationship? How might the pastoral counselor feel about his or her own identity and authority, both as therapist and as clergyperson? How might both therapist and patient feel, experience, or react differently? How might elements in the external environment beyond the safe space of the consulting room affect the therapy itself?

The case of Sara and Miranda will speak to each reader's own situation differently but, again, may provide one useful illustration of how the intersubjective dynamics of the transference-countertransference relationship can work in pastoral psychotherapy. Again, following Emmanuel Lartey, even across great cultural differences and social locations, each individual's experience will be like all others, like some others, and like none others.[13] Further, as great as the impact of all these factors will be in the unconscious dynamic of any pastoral care relationship, the effect will be heightened in the context of pastoral psychotherapy. This is precisely because in psychotherapy, unlike pastoral care and chaplaincy, the unconscious relationship is the focus of all deep therapeutic work. The use of the self in psychotherapy as a method for understanding the inner dynamic life of a patient is similar to its utilization in pastoral care as a tool for assessment. What differs between pastoral care and pastoral psychotherapy is the specific way in which that diagnostic understanding is then used to help the patient. Whereas the focus in pastoral care is either very brief, problem-solving counseling and/or referral to more in-depth counseling resources, the focus in longer-term pastoral psychotherapy *is* the transference-contertransference dynamic itself.

This intersubjective continuum of mutual impact and influence, especially when it is experienced at the level of nonverbal enactment, is the primary manifestation in the therapeutic setting of the patient's inner world. Nonverbal communication tends to arise from a reliving of the patient's habitual relational patterns, contained within the safety of the therapeutic relationship. Thus, a careful examination of the countertransference, as the therapist's own immediate experience of the patient's both conscious and unconscious communications, is not only one important aspect of any depth-psychotherapeutic practice but, as contemporary psychoanalytic writers have argued, perhaps the *most* important channel of information. As such, the countertransference serves as a crucial guide to one's therapeutic interventions.

Classical Countertransference and Pastoral Assessment

What, then, can be learned about the beneficial use of the therapist's self from this painful rupture in Sara and Miranda's therapeutic relationship? First, as in the pastoral care cases in chapters 4 and 5, it is important to examine the countertransference that is operative in the classical sense—that is, what unresolved issues, particularly at the unconscious level, may be affecting Sara's empathic capacity to understand Miranda's communications, both verbal and nonverbal?

Beginning with the dramatic enactment at the end of the previous therapy hour, what unfinished business may be interfering with Sara's ability to read Miranda's current feelings and behaviors accurately and to respond with appropriate interventions? These questions already constitute an important aspect of reflection that Sara, in spite of adequate classical training in pastoral counseling, failed to take the time to do when her own feelings began to well up in response to Sara's silently clinging to her legs.

How did Sara's own unconscious motives and needs, her own unresolved issues perhaps influence her responses to Miranda in recent sessions? An understanding of Sara's countertransference in this classical sense can help identify when and how the course of therapy began to slide toward being countertherapeutic for Miranda.

Similarities in Sara's and Miranda's backgrounds, ages, and current life situations made it easy for Sara to identify—or overidentify—with Miranda and at times to respond with an almost sisterly affection to Miranda's communications.[14] There has been, in self psychological terminology, a "twinship" transference[15]—that is, a benign selfobject transference in which Miranda has been able to draw unconsciously on similarities in Sara's experiences, outlook, and affect to feel normal, safe, and confirmed in her own perceptions of the world. At times, Miranda has felt this as reassuring and fortifying. It helped her to feel less alone. Sara, as her therapist, seemed neither overly threatening nor incapable of understanding the particular cultural and social experiences and pressures of being a Puerto Rican woman pursuing a career in a largely white, male-dominated profession. This transference, as frequently happens, also blended with an idealizing transference in which Miranda would unconsciously seek confirmation, strength, and hope in Sara's perceived success and competence.

Both women had broken from their families' traditional women's roles by going to college, remaining unmarried into their thirties, and pursuing highly demanding professional work.[16] This common experience had a mixed effect on Sara's countertransference toward Miranda. Sara was inclined to encourage and applaud Miranda's successes but also at times failed to attend to less positive feelings of ambivalence, fear, or failure. Because Sara's own motto to survive was "I must be strong,"[17] it was more difficult for her to stay with her patient's feelings of vulnerability, smallness, or weakness. In particular, stemming from some of her own unresolved conflicts about stepping outside a traditional woman's role and her own family's ambivalent responses to her break with tradition, Sara was also somewhat less able or willing to explore feelings of loss surrounding the path not taken: feelings of regret and loneliness surrounding her sexual and role identity as a woman, the tug between professional duties and involvement in extended-family activities, and her relationship to traditional womanly roles regarding marriage, children, and care for older and younger generations.

Rewind to the very end of Miranda's last therapy session. Some amount of enactment in psychotherapy is inevitable,[18] and certain patient behaviors are so sudden as to be unpreventable. However, Sara let things get out of hand. Miranda had already curled up on the floor more than once, and in the last session, Sara responded impulsively by reaching down and touching Miranda's hair. While consciously thinking her own nonverbal gesture was one of nurture and support, Sara in fact failed to work therapeutically, in two ways. First, she neglected to reflect on how the developing nonverbal interaction might be conveying information about her patient's inner experience, especially considering the multiple meanings such enactments might have for her patient, negative as well as positive. Second, when the first instance of Miranda curling up on the floor occurred, she allowed it to continue in subsequent sessions, without attempting to help Miranda explore what this behavior meant. In both these respects, Sara, with the best of supportive intentions, fell out of words into action with Miranda.

While this might be acceptable, even exciting in a personal intimate relationship, it is countertherapeutic in a pastoral counseling relationship, because the effect of psychotherapy depends upon making the unconscious conscious through the medium of verbal meaning. At times, whatever is seeking expression is either too deep in the unconscious or too firmly walled off through dissociation to be able to become accessible directly in narrative or verbal form. In such cases, patients are encouraged to describe what they experience in their bodily sensations, dreams, or mental images until their experiences can be processed through symbolization to verbalization. But in every case, in psychotherapy, it is finally the verbal realm, not the nonverbal, in which understanding and healing can take place. This is not to discount certain forms of drama, dance, or movement therapy, in which body movement is a part of the process of bringing unconscious material to awareness. However, mere participation by a therapist in nonverbal enactments, without an effort to explore what these mean, both silently to oneself during and after a therapy session and also aloud in collaboration with the patient, ceases to be therapy and starts down the "slippery slope"[19] toward an unboundaried and undefined intimate relationship.

How could Sara have worked with the recent, dramatic developments in Miranda's therapy in a way that would have constructively used Miranda's nonverbal communications and her own response as therapist? Ideally, the first session in which Miranda curled up on the floor close to Sara's knees would have been the moment in which Sara would have recognized that something profound needed exploration. Sara's reflections needed to begin with this first significant break in the usual framework of the patient sitting on the couch opposite her. Even if Sara had been too overwhelmed by her countertransference reactions to know exactly what to do in the moment, immediately after the session Sara would need to process what happened during this moment, attempting to understand the moment in terms of numerous possible transference and countertransference implications.

First, she needed to understand her own classical countertransference reactions. The first time Miranda slid to the floor, Sara was astounded. She watched Miranda's usual stiff, professional self melt and give way to something altogether more soft, small, and fragile. Miranda's childlike voice and fetal position conveyed a combination of profound sorrow and fear. Although Sara is not a mother herself, she grew up in a family with many children and from an early age had comforted one small sibling or cousin after another. She felt a strong maternal pull toward the suddenly vulnerable Miranda, longing to somehow take her onto her lap and cradle her. She knew that this was not an acceptable response but could not think in the moment what else to do. She found herself instead murmuring reassuring words and allowing Miranda to remain there until the end of the session.

Optimally, Sara would have helped Miranda by at first allowing the silence and the crying and by eventually suggesting to Miranda that she try to notice what she was feeling and seeing if she could begin to verbalize it. At some point not too long into the enactment on the floor, it would be important for Sara to suggest that Miranda sit back on the couch. This response would convey to Miranda that even though she was experiencing herself moving into an unaccustomed, vulnerable affect state, Sara would not let it become unbounded and unsafe. Miranda was experiencing a dissociated state. Such states can be full of deep import, but even in forms of therapy that work intensely with such states for cathartic effect, dissociation should not be allowed to continue for too long, or both participants may feel unmoored and even frightened.

No matter how late in the session this enactment first occurred, it would be incumbent on Sara as the therapist to attend carefully to the passage of the hour and help Miranda actively regain her adult composure at least five or ideally ten minutes before the end of the session. In this way, Sara would ensure at least a brief moment to move what happened from the experiential realm back to the realm of shared reflection. This would facilitate Miranda's transition from the dissociated affect state she accessed during the session to her normal adult state upon leaving the session. Moreover, it would also safely open the door for further exploration of the enactment at the beginning of the next session.

Having thus provided safe containment at the appearance of this first dramatic enactment, Sara would have time between sessions to examine her coun-

tertransference, in both classical and contemporary senses, to reflect theologically on the latest development in the case, and then to revise and deepen her
therapeutic assessment of Miranda's needs.

Sara's examination of her countertransference in the classical sense should
draw her attention to her maternal feelings toward Miranda. Although Sara
did not act impulsively on her inward desire to gather Miranda onto her lap,
her desire to reassure Miranda came out of the same countertransference feeling. Once Sara can identify her feelings as maternal, she can separate out her
habitual response to the children in her life from this "child," who is in reality
also an adult who longs to be empowered to care for and stand up for herself.
Safety and a commitment to understanding Miranda's subjective state in any
given moment are more therapeutic for Miranda in the long run than simple
reassurance, although this does not by any means preclude responding initially
to Miranda's tears with compassion.

A kindly spoken mirroring response, such as "It sounds like you've touched
something really painful and deep" is actually more facilitative to Miranda than a
soothing statement like "There, there, everything is going to be OK." Miranda
does not know that everything is going to be OK, nor does Sara. Miranda may
experience much more pain as the memories of her traumatic experience emerge,
and it is important not to give false promises of comfort. On the other hand,
Sara can truthfully let Miranda know that people do survive such pain, that she
will be with Miranda as she goes forward on her journey of deepening understanding, and that this is how healing ultimately happens—through understanding and exploration of meaning.

Once Sara has identified and contained her impulse to respond to Miranda
maternally, she might be able to recognize a less accessible and less ego-syntonic
motivation for her impulse to reassure Miranda as well. Maternal feelings would
resonate well with Miranda's overall sense of herself and would be reinforced
by her family and culture of origin. However, if she is honest with herself and
able to access issues worked through in her own psychotherapy, she may now
also be able to recognize some of the less flattering or desirable aspects of her
urge to reassure.

A split might become apparent to her in the dynamic between Miranda and
herself. Miranda, as has become increasingly apparent over the course of two
years in in-depth psychotherapy, suffered severe sexual abuse in her early childhood years. While Miranda's memories of abuse are just beginning to surface,[20]
the details that have become accessible, together with the pattern of post-
traumatic behaviors in Miranda's relationships over the years, have begun to
draw a picture of serial molestation by her paternal uncle and her older brother
(twelve years her senior and often functioning in the household like another

parental figure to Miranda). The family moved to the northeastern United States when Miranda was ten years old, first to a large city and then to an older established suburban neighborhood just outside the city limits. Within the first year, the older brother, preferring to stay in the city, moved out of the house into his own apartment. Miranda felt safe for the first time at the age of eleven. She quickly put her earlier terrors out of her mind, busying herself with school-work, making new friends, and coping for the first time with a mixed-ethnic neighborhood, classroom, and church setting. For Miranda, the experience of her first home in Puerto Rico and the first year in the States was like a bad dream. She did not share her parents' wistful reminiscences of their old neigh-borhood, *el barrio de Cabo Rojo,* and adopted a white, middle-class Horatio Alger work ethic as her ideal. Consciously and unconsciously, she worked to distance herself from all the pain that she left behind in the shadows of her early-childhood homes, although she continued to share, more abstractly and at a distance, the pride of her Puerto Rican heritage.

Sara, in contrast, grew up in a large, supportive family who lived among many cousins, aunts, and uncles scattered within a twenty-mile radius in a res-idential urban setting. Her family brought her to the Northeast when she was two years old. Her childhood was punctuated by long letters, brief phone calls, and yearly trips back "home" to San Juan. Puerto Rico represented to her an idealized vision of the perfect home, *"Borinquén,"* the beloved island—as long as she was also able to take advantage of the opportunities presented to her as a young woman on the continent. She learned Puerto Rican cooking from the many women in her grandmother's generation who gathered in the family kitchen every weekend. She maintained impeccable Spanish and together with her fam-ily attended a liberal Christian congregation, mostly white but with a signifi-cant proportion of Hispanic members. Her desire to be ordained as a minister and then to become a pastoral counselor was supported and encouraged by this congregation and also by her desire to work with more disadvantaged Latino children and families. Her therapy training had further excited her about the possibility of offering herself to the community as a much-needed psychother-apist who could work fluently in Spanish.

It was always somewhat difficult, therefore, in spite of many years of experi-ence working with various types of abuse and trauma in her practice, to com-prehend or fully empathize with victims of abuse in a Puerto Rican home. Although her head understood the statistics showing that no cultural or ethnic group is either more or less likely to experience domestic violence or child abuse, and she knew that the image of a higher percentage of abuse among Latino families was a myth,[21] the reality of abuse hit home much more painfully when a patient was a member of her own cultural and ethnic group. She felt caught between loyalty toward her patient's reality and loyalty to her culture and her own experience in not wanting such abuse ever to be true. This, in combination with her own drive to achieve as a Latina professional and her personal motto to be strong, lay beneath her hasty desire to reassure Miranda and perhaps even try to get Miranda to cheer up.

Sara's urge to reassure Miranda, therefore, was not only out of a conscious desire to be warm and caring. As is often the case, Sara unconsciously hoped that if she reassured Miranda that everything would be OK, then it really would be OK—the abuse would disappear altogether. Sara's unconscious wish was that Miranda could feel better so that she could feel better and they both could return to the state in which Miranda's abuse could be comfortably denied or erased. This feeling would also join powerfully with one or more affect states within Miranda, in which she herself either did not carry the knowledge of the abuse or had been brainwashed into believing it was not abuse or it didn't happen. At its most destructive, therefore, Sara's apparently caring reassurance may even have the effect of joining with one of Miranda's internalized perpetrators by minimizing and denying the pain of the abuse and attempting to shush Miranda back into a state of silent compliance with pseudo-normality. Rather than helping Miranda integrate the dissociated child affect state through coming to understand it as her adult self, Sara's reassurance also paradoxically keeps the child state split off from Miranda's whole awareness by muting it with uninterpreted comfort.

At this point, Sara may be able to recognize one further, common impulse in her desire to reassure and comfort Miranda. If she is able to review her own feelings and behaviors calmly, without judgment or self-condemnation, she may identify within herself the tender spot of vulnerability that is common among many therapists: the need to be needed. There was something covertly thrilling for Sara about Miranda's "breakthrough" to a more vulnerable, early aspect of her self. Sara's role in her own family, in spite of some inability on their part to understand her, has been one of the admired, competent caregiver. She carries this "assignment" into the world and into her consulting room as well. There is a fine line for Sara between job fulfillment and genuine call, on the one hand, and, on the other, a secret, preconscious vision of herself as a kind of Mother Teresa or Sor Juana Inés de la Cruz,[22] caring for the poor, the downtrodden, and the sick. When Miranda's usually cool, brittle demeanor melted, Sara not only felt her heart go out in compassion to her patient, but felt somewhat a sense of inflation of her own importance in Miranda's healing. The desire to bring Miranda into her home, touch her hair, and murmur soothing words all tapped into her desire to bind Miranda to herself as Miranda's special healer. Unfortunately, this reinforced a view of Miranda as weak and needy and tended to split off Miranda's own capable, strong side.

Motives for ministry are always mixed. This is not to say that there is never a genuine guiding sense of vocation and compassion. But even a genuine call will often have some of its origins in a family role induction as "the caretaker" or "the sensitive one." Sometimes this can in itself be an act of self-preservation, as in the case of children of alcoholics or abusive parents who must keep their antennas up at all times to avoid harm. Sometimes there is simply the lure of what appears to be the glamour of ministry, idealized and inflated as a saintly vocation or at least a path to personal fame and glory. Later, this chapter will further explore the impulse to be the special carer.

Sara must become aware of the many-layered motives beneath her desire to comfort Miranda without moving toward a more containing and exploratory stance. Only then can she think more clearly about Miranda's emerging needs from a traditional diagnostic standpoint.

Pastoral Therapeutic Assessment

Sara is now in a position to recognize that what Miranda needs is to be seen and acknowledged, not just as a cool, competent professional woman, but in all her many complex parts and aspects. Miranda needs to know that if she shows Sara the small, vulnerable, frightened childlike side of herself, this in no way erases the strong, competent side. At the same time, she needs to know that if she becomes angry, defensive, or enraged, this also can be contained and understood within the context of her healing from abuse. On one level, Miranda needs what every patient in therapy (and indeed, every child, every adult) needs. She needs to know that her therapist, and those closest to her, will be able to see her for all the parts of who she is—frightened, strong, angry, happy, anxious, calm—and stay close. She needs to know that if she allows the most hidden inner parts of herself to emerge, her therapist will neither flee nor punish her. Neither abandoned nor retaliated against, she can then begin to allow more and more parts of her self—more memories, more feelings, more experiences—to be brought into the light of consciousness and understood.

This is the process of healing in psychotherapy: the process of bringing formerly fragmented and split off parts of the self and one's own experience back into consciousness, where they can be integrated, made whole. This is true not only in cases of severe trauma, as with Miranda. This process is the work of all psychotherapy. Following the concept of the human psyche described in chapter 3 as more multiple, fluid, and dynamic than conceived in earlier classical models of mind, all human beings share to varying degrees this tendency to multiple self-states. All healing, indeed, all healthy growth, is based upon increasing awareness and integration of all one's disparate parts, including internalized experiences, objects, and self-states, until a mature self-acceptance and self-knowledge is attained. This is normally the work of a lifetime, culminating at best in a level of compassion for both self and others that might be said to characterize the human being's fullest psychological and spiritual development.

In psychotherapy, the therapist helps the patient to access formerly repressed, dissociated, or disavowed parts of the self, so the patient can recognize, befriend, even accept and love these as parts of the patient's self. Apparent inconsistencies can be understood as part of a larger complex unity of the whole person. Healing is not, then, a process of homogenization, but rather a process that builds a more energetic, spiritually healthy internal web of relationships among all the parts that make up the uniqueness of the person—not unlike the relational wholeness of the Holy Trinity.

The first step is beginning to happen in Miranda's therapy, as Miranda has allowed her frightened, abused child-self to make an appearance in the consulting room. Sara's capacity to see, come to know, and accept this aspect of Miranda is in and of itself therapeutic. She will not help the process, and will likely harm it, by jumping to reassure Miranda and thus denying Miranda's emerging knowledge of her past suffering and fear. At the same time, when Miranda begins to submerge in the waters of her dissociative experience, it is important for Sara to go with her, but only so far. Sara must "keep one hand on the side of the pool" at all times, so that both participants in the therapy are anchored in the present reality as well as swimming in the dissociated past. If Sara empathically dives into Miranda's experience so deeply that she loses her own mooring, both participants may find themselves psychically floundering, even drowning. Sara's work is to dip empathically into Miranda's experience but without losing herself (a capacity sometimes referred to as "regression in the service of the ego").[23]

This is the discipline of therapy and part of what makes it different from other close relationships. It is the therapist's work to hold on to her capacity to evaluate her own responses, to consider what her countertransference is telling her, as well as what in the intersubjective relationship is being communicated about the patient's own experiences and needs from moment to moment. By using her "free-floating attention" to attend to all these levels of knowledge, Sara will be in the best position to safely contain this experience so that it is therapeutic for Miranda, rather than retraumatizing.

If Sara can apprehend all the various parts of Miranda, even when Miranda seems lost in just one aspect of herself, she can also help to empower Miranda to remember her own capacities. By helping Miranda to discover ways to dip in and climb back out of the pool of dissociated experience, rather than simply soothing her, Sara can facilitate Miranda's integration of her own inner resources. Miranda may, in time, discover new powers in the parts of herself she had split off or disavowed. Eventually, the brittle character structure that has held her up for so long may become modified as other, more complex and vulnerable affect states become more consistently available to her. Miranda may even eventually find strength and blessing in those parts of herself she once feared as weak or damaged: "strong at the broken places."[24]

Totalist Countertransference and Pastoral Therapeutic Assessment

As in the pastoral care cases in chapters 4 and 5, Sara's reflections will not be complete if she leaves them at the classical understanding of countertransference and a traditional diagnosis reevaluation. These are important first steps. However, a further exploration of her countertransference in the contemporary sense, as information about her patient's own dynamics, will greatly enhance her understanding of Miranda's needs. Any insight she may gain through her own reflections must remain provisional until she has an opportunity to explore the meaning of the enactment in greater detail together with Miranda. Even so, such introspective work is essential to being open to what is beginning to unfold in the intersubjective space between therapist and patient, as well as the dynamics that are developing in the unconscious relationship.

Sara needs to ask herself as soon as possible after the first session in which Miranda curled up on the floor, "What might all this be conveying to me about what Miranda needs?" In particular, she needs to reflect on how her own responses not only gave her clues about her own unresolved issues but also may have been signaling important unexplored information, both about Miranda's inner state and about what is happening in the transference and in the unconscious relationship between them.

To do this, Sara must try to go back and re-create as vividly as possible what was happening and what both participants were feeling at the *exact moment* Miranda first slipped to the floor holding the teddy bear to her chest. Until she is able to ask Miranda to go back and try to recall what was happening at that precise moment, she cannot fully grasp what caused Miranda to shift into this dramatically different affect state. But she can attempt to recall what was happening as clearly as possible from her own perspective and try to recapture what she was feeling in the moment. Was there, in fact, something that was said or done that precipitated Miranda's shift in affect and behavior? What were they talking about just before Miranda became so overtly childlike?

Sara must try to reconstruct the sequence of events, much as she did in writing process notes for clinical supervision. Thinking back in minute detail, she recalls the following: Early in the session, Miranda had come in looking even more brittle than her usual presentation. She reported that things had been difficult at work. She had a young male trainee, Mark, who was behaving belligerently toward her and refusing to accept her supervision. That morning he had told her that she had never asked him to do something she had in fact repeatedly asked him to do. In a not too subtle manner, he had suggested that if she couldn't "get her facts straight," he would have to complain to Ted, her senior manager. Miranda had also caught Mark staring at her several times when he thought she wasn't looking. She experienced his gaze as intrusive and vaguely sexually insinuating. Miranda also found herself floundering to analyze what she perceived to be complex gender and power politics: Mark had a few times muttered comments about needing "affirmative action for white males" and always seemed to be barely containing his rage at having a female supervisor of color. Mark frequently seemed to fluctuate between feelings of aggressive competitivness and of resentment-laden intimidation. Miranda was unsure how much Ted was aware of Mark's attitude and behavior, whether he even tacitly condoned it, and how much he would actually support her authority if Mark went to him.

As Miranda and Sara explored together the impact this interaction was having on Miranda, they began to understand how Miranda felt the office dynamic in many ways to be replicating the dynamics of her childhood abuse. As a child, Miranda had been told numerous times that the abuse she was experiencing was, in fact, love and care, and if she cried out or complained, it was suggested that she was confused or crazy. Miranda was also warned that if she became uncooperative, her mother would be told that she had been a bad girl. She understood, but only vaguely as a child, that there were complicated but largely unspoken rivalries and conflicts among her father and the uncle and older brother who abused her, and that figuring out these dynamics would possibly only make things worse for her. By trying to understand one of the men, she might be perceived as sympathizing or even siding with him. This, in turn, might trigger more abuse in the form of possessiveness by one or both of the other two males in the family. Neither her abusers nor her father would have admitted that they were aware of the abuse by the others, but it had also become apparent to Miranda in the course of her therapy that on some level everyone knew everything and had colluded in a conspiracy of silence in order to maintain the family's feeble equilibrium.

As Sara quietly listened, with minimal prompts, Miranda began to recognize and verbalize the parallels in her current work situation. The discounting of her perception of reality, the sense of being sexually invaded by Mark's intrusive gaze, the threat of being reported to someone with power over her, and the feeling of confusion over the complex, potentially competitive and threatening dynamics were all elements in her childhood experience as well. As Miranda began to articulate these parallels, the walls between her usual capable, unemotional adult state and her childhood terror began to crack a little. Old, split-off feelings of pain, confusion, terror, and grief pulled her into a form of embodied flashback experience in which she suddenly found herself not just thinking about these childhood feelings but submerged in them. Simultaneously trusting and testing the safety of the consulting room, Miranda slid to the floor, immersed in her past. At that moment, Sara herself experienced a sharp upsurge of emotion, both excited and panicky.

Such dramatic enactments on the part of a patient, while frequently eliciting compassion and strong feelings from a therapist, are paradoxical in terms of what they usually signal for the patient's needs. Such powerful enactments are unusual in psychotherapy, but they are not unheard of. Contemporary psychoanalytic writers are beginning to bring these experiences to light in order to explore the impact and meaning of such occurrences, which in classical case studies were either denied or deliberately left out because they fell so far outside the paradigm of practice methodology.[25] This is not at all to say that such enactments are now to be encouraged and reciprocated nonverbally by the therapist. On the contrary, while such enactments may seem on the surface to call for greater physical and emotional closeness on the part of the therapist, such breaks in the usual therapeutic frame signal a fragility around boundaries and often also represent an unconscious or preconscious testing of the limits of safety of the "container" of the therapy. There is a mixed message that therapists find confusing: On the surface there is a demand for greater attachment—"I want to be closer to you." But less accessible to consciousness, often, and especially with a patient who has been traumatized in the past, is an unconscious query: "If I drop my vigilance about boundaries, will you also violate me?" This is not to discount one part of the message or the other. Often, both are true. There is a longing for greater connection and, at the same time, a testing of safety.

Sara reacted without pausing to reflect on the possible import of her own reactions and feelings. Stimulated by the drama of the moment and propelled by her anxiety, she let her caretaking impulse take over and touched Miranda's hair. However, this was not the response Miranda needed. Sara had missed Miranda's actual communication. Sara needed to quiet her strong rush of feelings and *use* them—to use her *self*—to comprehend more accurately what was occurring and what Sara was really trying to convey to her about her own inner state.

If Sara had stopped to consider what her strong emotional responses might have been telling her, not only about her own unresolved issues but about

Miranda's feeings, she might have recognized that both a desire for closeness and a panic associated with that desire were present in Miranda in that moment. The desire for closeness was more apparent in Miranda's overt behavior, but Sara's own panic was reflecting Miranda's own terror at a less manifest, hence even deeper, level. The intimacy desired, therefore, could not be best met by a nonverbal response that perpetuated a level of uninterpreted physical interaction. On the contrary, Miranda needed help in articulating what she was feeling and in reflecting on why letting down her usual adult guard was both so stimulating and so frightening at the same time. Such exploration could have led to a significant deepening of the work around Miranda's traumatic experiences and the way those experiences were still directly affecting her life and her relationships in the present. In the full scenario given, Sara's gesture of reaching down and touching Miranda's hair was, in fact, countertherapeutic and deeply disturbing to Miranda. Given Miranda's history of multiple abuses, such a gesture would likely be experienced as a confusing blend of nurture and erotic violation. The confusion itself would then have further replicated certain aspects of her abuse.

Most likely, then, it was Sara's touch itself that triggered Miranda's further action of grabbing Sara's knees and hugging her legs for the next ten minutes. Miranda was dissociating, frozen as if under the spell of the same paralyzing mix of feelings she had experienced during her abuse in childhood. Then, at the end of the session, her efficient adult self "woke up" to find herself shamefully locked in an unfamiliar posture and feeling state. Horrified but unable to express feelings in her usual adult state, Miranda then stalked out without a word, leaving Sara with all the anxiety and confusion bordering on terror and shame that Miranda could no longer feel for herself. This, more than any other element in the session, is what caused Miranda to miss the next session, feeling intensely confused and unsafe.

Being an unconscious recipient of Miranda's anxiety, combined with her own inner anxiety issues, threw Sara, in turn, into a heightened state of fear and impulsivity mirroring Miranda's earlier behavior. Sara's impulsive fantasy of calling Miranda to offer her a session at Sara's own home was motivated not by a carefully considered plan to increase Miranda's sense of safety. Her sense that she was following her "instincts" about Miranda's needs was actually misguided, given the lack of any careful reflection. Such an offer would have been an unconscious continuation of the unboundaried, anxious state of confusion with which she was left at the end of the session. What Miranda needed from Sara was not an offer of more nontherapeutic closeness, but for Sara to take the time to pause and think as a trained professional. Sara could best benefit Miranda not by acting, but by pondering what her own reactions and impulses might mean, both about her own unresolved issues and about Miranda's subjective state at the end of the hour.

Sara's further intrusions into Miranda's space, first by calling and then by going to her apartment, triggered a chain reaction in Miranda of further dissociation into her childhood panic, and then a reactive rage, as she attempted without Sara's help to regain her adult state of self-control. In her state of rage, Miranda also tapped into both her own suppressed childhood rage at the abuse and the now-internalized, ever-present threats and rage of her abusers. Even more destabilizing for Miranda, all this was carried outside the contained context of the supposedly safe consulting room. This put Miranda into a very dangerous situation, in which unmanaged dissociation, unconscious identification with her abusers, panic, and rage could have triggered violence. Most likely, given her long brainwashing to believe herself to be bad and at fault, this would have been directed toward herself, either as self-punishment, directed by persecutory aspects of her self, internalized from her perpetrators in childhood.

If this sequence of events actually played out fully, as in the vignette, Sara would need to seek consultation immediately, now with a view not only of helping Miranda but toward reestablishing safety and determining whether the treatment was so compromised that Sara would need to refer Miranda to another therapist. Without access to further communication with Miranda, it would be virtually impossible for Sara at this point to reestablish an exploratory stance in the psychotherapy. Her best hope at this point might be, in spite of Miranda's request not to contact her, to make a last effort at communication, perhaps by sending a note. If given the chance, Sara must acknowledge that Miranda experienced her interventions as an empathic rupture and must offer to be available to listen and try to understand what Miranda thought and felt, and what she needs now. It would be up to Miranda to determine whether she felt safe enough to go forward with the therapy or even to respond to Sara's attempt at repairing the relationship.

After such a breach as going to a patient's home, damage control is perhaps the best that could be expected for a long time in the therapy. Any enactment that takes the therapist outside the bounds of the consulting room is considered unethical and threatens one of the central reasons why therapy is considered a safe space for exploration of disturbing inner material—because it is set apart from the patient's day-to-day environment and relationships. Even purely accidental meetings on the street or encounters with a patient with either one's own or the patient's friends or family members present can provoke intense emotions, even disturbances. To the degree that the patient experiences such an encounter as a jarring collision of private and public, inner and outer worlds, this can be disruptive to the therapeutic relationship. While such accidental meetings may eventually be useful to the patient if the patient and therapist together explore their meaning sufficiently, planned incursions into the patient's private space almost always do more harm than good.

There were a number of possible footholds along the "slippery slope" that Sara could have used to stop herself, using her own reactions to gain helpful information on how to be genuinely useful to Miranda, all before reaching the point of actually going to Miranda's apartment. After the first session in which Miranda sat on the floor, with sufficient reflection between sessions, Sara could have initiated a process of shared exploration that would have lessened the likelihood of Miranda's doing so again. Or if it did happen again, there would have been a process already set in place to help Miranda quickly and safely move back to a place of verbal rather than nonverbal expression.

As already discussed, Sara should have refrained entirely from reaching down to touch Sara's hair. If Miranda had hugged Sara's legs anyway, Sara could have gently extricated herself. While it would have been very important for Sara to be careful not to shame Miranda for her behavior, she could have kindly directed Miranda back to a seated position across from her. At this point, utilizing careful countertransference reflection, Sara could have stopped herself from contributing further to un-thought-out enactments. If she could have identified all the classical countertransference elements already described and, further, recognized that some of her anxiety and confusion was not only stemming from her own unresolved issues but also reflecting Miranda's own anxiety and confusion as she came into unaccustomed contact with the part of herself that held more of her experience of trauma, Sara could have reestablished, at least within herself, a more circumspect, boundaried response to Miranda.

If Miranda failed anyway to appear for her next appointment, Sara then could have taken a much less anxiety-driven approach. While therapists differ on whether or when to call a patient who is a no-show, in this situation, it might have been preferable for Sara not to call Miranda or, at least, not to call her fifteen minutes into the missed hour. Unless Sara had concrete evidence to believe that Miranda was an immediate danger to herself or others (in which case she would call paramedics), it would be reasonable for Sara to wait out the hour and perhaps call to check whether they had somehow crossed signals about the next appointment time. Sara should be alert to the likelihood that Miranda's missing a session is another nonverbal communication. But this is best explored in session, not over the phone, except as a last resort should Miranda refuse to come back at all. Even if Sara's custom were to call patients after fifteen minutes, this should be done as a normal routine, not out of a sense of anxiety.

Miranda's dissociated childlike response was not necessarily a reaction to the fact of Sara's phone call per se. Miranda might have been able to respond from her rational, adult self-state if Sara's call had conveyed simply a nonanxious, routine schedule concern. It was Sara's panicked and stimulated tone, not the fact of calling in and of itself, which in effect handed back to Miranda the very sense of fear that Miranda had unconsciously left behind when she left Sara's office. This, combined with a sense of confusion about inner and outer worlds that any unplanned contact with the therapist could provoke, and the autonomic flooding of shame from feeling thus exposed in one's home environment (even over the phone), threw Miranda back into dissociation. This further escalated Sara's reactivity, already at a fairly high level, into an uncontrolled, impulsive panic, resulting in Sara's going to Miranda's home and, with only the best of conscious intentions, actually retraumatizing her.

This analysis of the step-by-step unfolding of the dynamics that led to Sara's going to Miranda's home shows how swiftly one unprocessed enactment can lead to another if the therapist is not careful about continuously maintaining a reflective stance. Even actions that seem motivated by the most obvious care and support can be experienced very differently by a patient, especially where there is a history of prior boundary violations. Both the therapist and the patient must desire to connect at some deep level if the therapy is to be successful and lasting healing for the patient is to occur. Paradoxically, it will be the therapist's genuine desire to understand what has occurred and offer deep empathic connection through the medium of verbal exploration, not an intensification of physical closeness or touch, that will both meet the desire for greater connection and at the same time reassure the patient that the boundaries are secure.

Miranda needed *empathy*, not *sympathy*—that is, she needed to be seen and understood in multiple, complex, and even contradictory ways. She did not need to be smothered, touched, pitied, or intruded upon by a therapist who needs to cheer her up with false optimism, needs to see herself being helpful— or, worse, needs to be needed! By helping a patient return to the level of verbal reflection, the therapist conveys his or her desire that the patient be understood, not violated. Caring is, finally, best expressed not through uncritical physical touch or reassurance, but through deep understanding. More will be said about this in the discussion of psychotherapy research later in this chapter.

Theological Reflection

As in the practice of pastoral care, pastoral psychotherapists should engage in a disciplined, regular practice of theological reflection about their patients. Largely due to the predominance of the medical model of psychotherapy in pastoral counseling training in the last two to three decades, as described in chapter 2, theological reflection has too often been neglected or treated as a kind of appendix, tacked onto case presentations to legitimate one's pastoral credentials.

But theological reflection is not incidental to the work of pastoral diagnosis and treatment. As demonstrated in the pastoral care cases in chapter 4, the theological reflection itself provides important clinical as well as spiritual clues to the patient's innermost formative experiences, sufferings, and desires. In fact, the distinction between "clinical" or "psychological" and "spiritual" breaks down altogether in light of the holistic evidence of the therapist's countertransference reflections. The unity of psychological and spiritual, reflected in the actual meaning of the word *psyche* itself as soul or spirit, can be subjectively accessed through the affective, imaginal, and cognitive experience of the knowledge that becomes available in the intersubjective space between therapist and patient, at both conscious and unconscious levels. The theological method recommended in this book, further, utilizes the unconscious and psychological dimensions of the process of free association to arrive at a tentative theological understanding of the patient's deepest hurts and needs.

Let us assume that Sara has caught herself early enough to think before acting inappropriately, and the therapy is still safely in progress. Drawing together all the insights from her reflections on her countertransference and Miranda's needs, Sara is now in a position to reflect theologically on Miranda's situation. This last step may generate some deeper insights into what may be happening in the unconscious relationship between them and help Sara to be more open to Miranda's deepest spiritual and psychological needs. Sara sits with the question "What theological, spiritual, religious themes come into my awareness as I simply sit with Miranda in mind?"

Visual images begin to float into her awareness, like a dream. She sees moving pictures of Miranda and herself swimming. At first, the images seem peaceful, and the women seem to be taking turns, diving down, looking for something. But then the waters become turbulent. She feels a sudden burst of fear in her heart as she visualizes a menacing wave of green water break over her own head, and she momentarily loses sight of Miranda. "Help, Lord!" she prays, and pictures herself bobbing back up to the surface. Miranda is there, too. She visualizes Jesus walking across the waves to them, holding out his hand. And suddenly, she sees that there is a boat, and it has been there all along. Jesus says, "Take heart, it is I, do not be afraid." And Jesus helps them into the boat.

Bringing herself back from this reverie to a more analytical thinking mode, Sara immediately connects this dreamlike sequence with the story of Jesus walking across the water to Peter and the disciples in Matthew 14:22-33. Peter attempted to walk on the water, but at the point his fear overtook him, he lost sight of his faith and began to sink. Jesus reached out his hand and caught him, and they all were amazed. She also recalls the story of Jesus calming the storm in Mark 4:35-41 (also Luke 8:22-25). Sara recognizes a lesson for herself in these

Bible stories that will help her to stay conscious of her own grandiose or maternal impulses and stay open to the meaning of Miranda's fear. She is reminded that both she and Miranda are held by God's grace and power. In the words of one of the favorite sayings of her grandmothers, *"El Señor siempre provee para todas nuestras necesidades."* (The Lord always provides for all our needs.) A favorite psalm, Psalm 125, often quoted by members of her church and family, comes to mind: *"Los que confían en Jehová, son como el monte de Síon, que no se mueve, sino que permanece para siempre. Como Jerusalén tiene montes alrededor de ella, así Jehová está alrededor de su pueblo."* (Those who trust in God are like Mount Zion, which cannot be moved, but abides forever. As the mountains surround Jerusalem, so God surrounds God's people.)[26]

Sara's theological reflection reminds her that it is God, that it is Jesus, who is the healer, not herself. Moving now into third-order theological reflection, Sara recognizes that she can help Miranda best by staying open to all that happens in the mysterious, deep waters of their relationship with a faithful heart, knowing that even the experience of fear is simply one more aspect of information, not a call to precipitous action. The worst has already happened to Miranda. What she is reliving now is painful, but the experience this time can be healing, not destructive. If Sara can keep sight of the boat when Miranda appears to be floundering, and regularly help Miranda climb back into the boat herself so she can better understand what is under the menacing waves, then Jesus will be there with both of them to comfort, heal, and finally commission them.

Sara then recalls another boat story from the Bible—the calling of the first disciples. Sara realizes that both Miranda's strength and her woundedness are a part of who she is, and all are valuable. Miranda's healing is not an end in itself, but a way of restoring her to the joy of her own unique calling, whatever that may be. Sara thinks of a hymn that has become a favorite in her bilingual congregation, *"Pescador de Hombres."*[27] She hears in the words of the song all her own needs and her own sense of call, not as an extraordinary saint, but simply as a faithful and willing disciple. And she hears how God is calling to all the parts of Miranda, her strength, her exhaustion, her hope, and her deepest yearning to be truly seen for all of who she is:

> *Tú has venido a la orilla;*
> *No has buscado ni a sabios, ni a ricos;*
> *Tan sólo quieres que yo te siga.*
> *(Estribillo:) Señor: me has mirado a los ojos;*
> *Sonriendo, has dicho mi nombre;*
> *En la arena he dejado mi barca;*
> *Junto a ti buscaré otro mar.*

Tú sabes bien lo que tengo:
En mi barca no hay oro no espadas;
Tan sólo redes y mi trabajo. —*Estribillo*

Tú necesitas mis manos,
Mi cansancio que a otros descanse,
Amor que quiera seguir amando. —*Estribillo*

Tú, Pescador de otros mares,
Ansia eterna de almas que esperan.
Amigo bueno, que así me llamas. —*Estribillo*

You have come down to the lakeshore
Seeking neither the wise nor the wealthy,
But only asking for me to follow.
(Refrain:) Sweet Lord, you have looked into my eyes;
Kindly smiling, you've called out my name.
On the sand I have abandoned my small boat;
Now with you, I will seek other seas.

You know full well what I have, Lord:
Neither treasure nor weapons for conquest,
Just these my fishnets and will for working. —Refrain

You need my hands, my exhaustion,
Working love for the rest of the weary—
A love that's willing to go on loving. —Refrain

You who have fished other waters;
You, the longing of souls that are yearning;
O loving Friend, you have come to call me. —Refrain

Findings from Empirical Research

In the case vignette about Sara, she has been pulled at several points toward nonverbal, impulsive actions rather than remaining in the realm of reflection and verbal exploration with her patient. Her impulses to act were further reinforced by her very desire to nurture and care for the other. This case study illustrates one fairly typical dynamic between a therapist and patient with a history of sexual trauma, but this dynamic also occurs in cases involving other issues including depression, anxiety, and suffering in interpersonal relationships. The therapist's impulse to care, and even to be a special carer, is a common and understandable trap for compassionate professionals. The intersubjective dynamic of every therapeutic relationship will have its own unique character and evolve in its own unique way. However, the impulse to care often intrudes in the therapeutic process, driven by unconscious determinants that are often sealed over by the therapist's own experience of familial and social approval for being kind and self-giving. What are real therapeutic relationships like? How do therapists handle enactments like the one in the case of Sara, and how should they?

To answer these questions, I began to do empirical research in the area of countertransference and the use of the self in psychotherapy. Very little research has actually been done in the pastoral counseling field, and almost none on pastoral counselors' actual practices.[28] It is my hope that the data from this research about pastoral counselors' self-knowledge and experience may offer new insights for both practice and training and may help illuminate some of the ethical boundary struggles currently being experienced in the pastoral counseling field. In a fairly large empirical research survey, completed in 2000,[29] I attempted to address the overarching question, How do pastoral psychotherapists conceptualize their countertransference (their responses, thoughts, feelings, fantasies, and sensations in relation to the patient), and how do they make use of these conceptualizations and attitudes in their actual practice with patients?

Research Design

For this research, I used a combination of quantitative (that is, statistically measurable) and qualitative (ethnographic and content analysis) methodology in the form of an anonymous questionnaire[30] sent to 125 randomly selected Fellows and Diplomates in the American Association of Pastoral Counselors. Questionnaires were also sent to a comparison group of 125 nonreligiously trained Board-Certified Diplomates in Clinical Social Work.[31] A total of 55 valid questionnaires were returned by pastoral counselors for a response rate of 44 percent, and 28 by clinical social workers for a response rate of 24 percent. The combined response rate for both groups was 34 percent. For every question, pastoral counselors' responses were compared with the comparably experienced group of nonreligious therapists, in order to generate a clearer picture of the distinctiveness of pastoral counselors' attitudes, theories, and practices.

The survey itself comprised two instruments: the psychoanalytically informed Attitudes Toward Countertransference (ATC)[32] and an instrument developed specifically for this study, the Therapeutic Relationship Questionnaire (TRQ). The survey also collected demographic data and professional practice information for purposes of comparison.

The survey was designed to address the overall question of how pastoral counselors conceptualize and utilize the countertransference in their therapeutic work. This central question generated many more areas for investigation, including these questions:

- What are therapists' working definitions, attitudes, and beliefs about countertransference and the therapeutic relationship?
- How and to what extent do the therapists in each discipline recognize and attend a level of unconscious relationship?
- What do therapists report as their levels of awareness of countertransference affect states in their actual clinical work?
- What is the relative experience of pastoral counselors and clinical social workers of sexual, aggressive, and other feelings in the transference/countertransference?
- To what degree do therapists disclose these countertransference affects and experiences to clients?
- How are "enactments"—nonverbal behaviors that occur in the context of treatment and may function as nonverbal communication of transference or countertransference—understood and handled therapeutically?
- What, if any, is the role of ritual in the therapeutic process?
- How prevalent are unethical enactments, and do these correlate in any way with therapists' beliefs about countertransference, attitudes about how to utilize countertransference, reported levels of awareness of countertransference affect states, and disclosure of these to clients in their actual work?
- How do therapists rate the importance of awareness of the countertransference in preventing unethical behaviors?
- How do therapists endeavor to get back on track when feeling threatened or overwhelmed by powerful countertransference affects or experiences?
- Does religious training and identity appear to make a difference in how therapists approach these questions?

Enactments were investigated specifically using two lists of behaviors on the TRQ, called the Client Enactment Subscale and the Therapist Enactment Subscale. These subscales asked participants to indicate on a scale of 1 to 7 the frequency in their experience of specific nonverbal behaviors/enactments, 31 by clients and 35 by the therapists themselves. Items on the Client Enactment Subscale included such enactments as calling the therapist at home, deferring payment, attempting to hug and hugging the therapist, sitting on the therapist's lap, engaging in sexual touching, hitting the therapist, swearing, slamming a door, and bringing a gift. Items on the Therapist Enactment Subscale included meeting a client outside the office; visiting a client in the hospital; offering tea, food, or a ride; holding a client's hand; hugging; kissing; sexual touching; sexual intercourse; hitting; swearing at a client; lending money; lending objects; praying for and with a client; and creating and performing rituals and/or formal religious rites for the client.

Specific enactments listed on the questionnaire were independently rated as ethical or unethical for the purpose of the study by an independent expert ethics panel, consisting of two senior clinical social workers and two directors of pastoral counseling centers. These senior clinicians were asked to review each item on the two enactment subscales and rate it as falling into one of three categories: (1) "clearly within ethical boundaries"; (2) "on the borderline of what is ethical or unethical, might depend on the context or the particular client's needs, diagnosis, etc."; and (3) "clearly *un*-ethical behavior on the part of the therapist, either to permit the client to do the behavior described, or to do the behavior described." Items were designated as clearly ethical or clearly unethical only if three of the four clinicians defined them as such.

In addition to the preceding research questions, the study tested several formal hypotheses. The two most important were as follows:[33] The first hypothesis was that there would be a statistically significant *difference between the two disciplines*—pastoral counselors and clinical social workers—in both their conceptualization and utilization of countertransference. The second was that there would be statistically significant *gender differences* in responses as well.[34]

Results of the Study

The study yielded a rich amount of data, which was analyzed using standard quantitative and qualitative methods.[35] Therapists of both disciplines subscribed more to a totalist than a classical view of countertransference as defined in the literature. Not surprisingly, pastoral counselors were statistically much more likely to use prayer and ritual in their practice of psychotherapy, and they claimed greater expertise in addressing clients' spiritual issues.

With regard to enactments, a substantial number of therapists from both disciplines reported having engaged at least once in a number of behaviors deemed unethical by an independent panel. A statistically significant association was found, especially among religiously ordained male therapists, between the report of experiencing erotic feelings in psychotherapy and nonerotic but unethical enactments. Enactments were most often justified by both male and female therapists under the rubric of rapport, genuineness, and the "real relationship."[36]

In light of these findings, a psychodynamic consideration of therapists' need to be seen as warm, caring, and special helpers led to three main recommendations for both pastoral psychotherapy and clinical social work:

1. A renewed clinical focus on verbal exploration of transference and counter-transference dynamics in the context of an intersubjective relationship operating at conscious and unconscious levels

2. Greater use by therapists of in-depth clinical consultation and supervision with particular focus on countertransference and the intersubjective relationship

3. A deromanticization of the term *empathy* and a recuperation of its diagnostic usefulness

The following discussion details these results.

Therapists from both disciplines, especially pastoral counselors, generally scored high on the ATC on totalist understandings of countertransference. They agreed that countertransference is the total emotional reaction of the therapist to the patient and essentially a valuable tool in psychotherapy. They endorsed the openness of therapists to their own inner thoughts, feelings, fantasies, impulses, and "pulls" from the patient as a potential source of information about patients' dynamics and as a guide to interventions. These views, contrary to some of the literature about "borderline" and psychotic patients, were held to be valid regardless of diagnostic category. Participants in the study endorsed the concept of therapist as cocreator of the transference.

In their own words, participants described the therapeutic relationship overwhelmingly in terms of a nonhierarchical, boundaried, but collaborative working relationship. They tended to depict the work of therapy in largely cognitive terms, focusing more on expanding awareness than on feeling or experience. The role of the therapist, in metaphorical terms drawn from the "world hypotheses" of philosopher Stephen C. Pepper,[37] appeared to be understood less often as a repairer of a mechanism, or even in organic terms as a healer of wounds, than as a companion in patients' efforts to tell the stories of their lives and to come to deeper contextual understandings of how these stories shape daily choices, relationships, and current behavior. The relationship itself was viewed by many as therapeutic—as in the words of existentialist therapist Irvin Yalom, "It is the relationship that heals."[38]

Actual Practices and Enactments

In reports of actual practices, therapists, especially clinical social workers, responded more conservatively on the ATC, with a number of responses falling into the classical range. They reported occasionally using their affective reactions and associations as a source of information, but for the most part reported actual experiences of affective responses occurring only infrequently. Pastoral counselors reported communicating their associations and affective reactions directly to patients "infrequently" (compared to social workers "very rarely").

Mean reports of actual enactments were low overall, with the most obviously unethical enactments (for example, kissing a patient on the mouth, engaging in sexual touching, having intercourse, or hitting a patient) reported as occurring "absolutely never" by all participants.

Pastoral counselors had slightly higher mean scores for therapist enactments, both ethical and unethical, although in overall mean scores, both disciplines scored low in the therapist enactments taken together (averaging "almost never"). Most departures appeared to be in keeping with their respective professions: pastoral counselors tended to blend parish and/or pastoral functions such as performing sacraments and inviting patients to worship or lectures, while social workers more often reported writing letters on behalf of patients, visiting patients in the hospital, and contacting other family members to activate a patient's support network in times of crisis. Pastoral counselors were overwhelmingly more likely to pray for and with patients, as well as to create or participate in rituals in therapy.

Although mean scores were low, *actual frequencies* of reports of specific enactments listed on the TRQ paint a somewhat different picture than either the mean scores or therapists' reports of practices on the ATC might suggest. Although there was some evidence that the participants were guarding their answers somewhat (in spite of an anonymous questionnaire), certain items determined by the independent ethics panel to be unethical did not show zero tolerance by practitioners of either profession or of either gender, even in their own self-reports. In a surprisingly large number of instances, therapists reported that their clients had on at least one occasion (that is, *not* "absolutely never") showed these therapists photographs of themselves naked, sat or laid their head in the therapist's lap, attempted to or in one instance actually did kiss the therapist on the mouth. Almost half the therapists had "held" patients, and therapists also met patients outside session, and kissed them on the cheek or forehead. Approximately one-fourth (mostly pastoral counselors) had invited patients to a lecture and/or worship, and nearly half of all the pastoral counselors had offered a formal religious rite or sacrament such as baptizing a child or performing a wedding. Regarding two more enactments frequently mentioned as ethically questionable in the literature, nearly one-third of the participants had had a patient sit next to them on the floor, and 41 percent had sat next to a patient on the couch.

The actual frequency of these unethical enactments, with a comparison of pastoral counselors and secular therapists, is shown in Table 3.

Correlations of Theoretical Beliefs and Practices
Turning to correlations between therapists' theoretical beliefs and practice (as reported on the ATC instrument) with *actual* enactments (reported on the

Table 3. Frequency of Unethical Enactments, by Discipline

	Discipline		
Enactment	All Practitioners N (%)	Pastoral Counselors N (%)	Social Workers N (%)
Client . . . showed naked photos*	8 (10%)	4 (7%)	4 (14%)
. . . sat on floor next to therapist	26 (31%)	18 (33%)	8 (29%)
. . . sat on couch next to therapist	34 (41%)	19 (34%)	15 (54%)
. . . sat in therapist's lap	4 (5%)	2 (4%)	2 (7%)
. . . laid head in therapist's lap	7 (8%)	5 (9%)	2 (7%)
. . . embraced therapist	18 (23%)	12 (22%)	6 (23%)
. . . attempted to kiss therapist on mouth	4 (5%)	3 (6%)	1 (4%)
. . . kissed therapist on mouth	1 (1%)	0 (0%)	1 (4%)
Therapist . . . met client outside session	23 (28%)	14 (25%)	8 (29%)
. . . held client	39 (47%)	28 (51%)	11 (39%)
. . . kissed client on cheek or forehead	11 (13%)	8 (15%)	3 (11%)
. . . invited client to lecture*	22 (27%)	19 (35%)	3 (11%)
. . . invited client to worship**	21 (25%)	19 (35%)	2 (7%)
. . . offered client sacrament**	23 (28%)	23 (42%)	0 (0%)

*Significant difference between means (*t*-test) of the two disciplines, $p \leq .05$.
**Significant difference between means (*t*-test) of the two disciplines, $p \leq .01$.

TRQ), an interesting pattern emerges.[39] Erotic feeling in the therapist was the affect that had the greatest number of correlations with enactments overall. Fairly high numbers of correlations with specific enactments were also found for anger, visual imagery, and physical sensations.

Of greater concern was the finding that fewer correlations involved *using* specific countertransference reactions as a source of *information* about the client's dynamics, although the experiencing of erotic feelings and dreams did appear to trigger some introspection. In general, the use of therapists' own higher thought process to examine the meaning of their own affective responses did not correlate positively with many enactments. In fact, it generated the most negative correlations with enactments. In other words, the more therapists engaged in private introspection about the meaning of their reactions, the less likely they were to engage in enactments.

On the other hand, therapists who reported experiencing and *communicating* their countertransference reactions to patients generated the most correlations with enactments. Communication of affects directly to patients actually may be considered in itself as a form of verbal enactment. This correlated most highly with enactments by clients and especially by therapists. There was also a high degree of intercorrelation among all the separate items involving the communication of affects to patients, suggesting that those therapists who tend to disclose any one affect would tend to disclose many.

How, then, were enactments handled by these therapists when they occurred in the course of therapy?

Exploring Enactments with Patients

In terms of handling enactments, secular therapists reported on average that they "sometimes" explored with patients the impact of enactments. Pastoral counselors reported doing so in a range spanning "sometimes," "often," and "always" (see Table 4).

When asked to give an example of a specific enactment in their own words, however, a slightly different picture emerged. Forty-two percent of all respondents, and nearly half of pastoral counselors, did report exploring with patients the meaning and impact of the specific examples of enactments for which they gave narrative examples in their own words. These explorations occurred both before and after the enactments took place. On another part of the questionnaire, such explorations also correlated statistically with using one's own countertransference reactions as a source of information about the patient's dynamics.

At the same time, however, a disturbing minor trend was observed in that over one-fourth of respondents reported *not exploring the enactments they chose as examples at all.* This was even slightly more true of pastoral counselors, 28 percent of whom did not choose to explore the enactments they described (see Table 5). This is all the more significant in that these enactments were important enough to be remembered by the participants in detail and recorded as examples of their experience with nonverbal behaviors in their therapy practice. This finding suggests that although many therapists are conscientiously exploring enactments at least some of the time, over one-fourth of pastoral counselors are not engaging at all in such exploratory understanding of the meaning of behaviors and nonverbal communications.

These findings were corroborated by the therapists' attitudes and beliefs about the nature of the therapeutic relationship itself and by their focus on conscious versus unconscious dynamics in their relationships with their patients.

Therapists' Thoughts about the Therapeutic Relationship Itself

While, in response to another question, therapists reported on average that they generally focus on the relationship itself "to a significant degree," their qualitative examples suggest that this focus is largely *interpersonal* and does not necessarily emphasize the unconscious relationship between them. This view is further supported by the finding that focus on the relationship itself

Table 4. Reported Frequency of Exploring Enactments, by Discipline

Explore Enactments...	Discipline	
	Pastoral Counselors	*Clinical Social Workers*
...never	0	2 (7%)
...infrequently/occasionally	10 (20%)	2 (7%)
...sometimes	13 (26%)	14 (52%)
...often	16 (32%)	7 (26%)
...always	11 (22%)	2 (7%)

Table 5. Frequency of Exploring Meaning and Impact of a *Specific* Enactment as Described in Therapists' Own Words, by Discipline

Explored Meaning and Impact of Enactment ...	Discipline	
	Pastoral Counselors	*Clinical Social Workers*
...not at all	15 (28%)	5 (23%)
...before the action took place	4 (7.5%)	1 (4.5%)
...after the action took place	8 (15%)	7 (32%)
...both before and after the action took place	26 (49%)	9 (41%)

correlated positively with reports of experiencing affects (on the ATC) but *not* with the actual use of these affects as a source of secondary process information about clients' dynamics (in spite of correlating with theoretical beliefs *about* such use of affect).

In their own words and in their choices of theoretical terminology, the therapists generally tended to be less focused on unconscious process than their predominant identification with psychoanalytic/psychodynamic theoretical orientation would suggest. Nearly all respondents chose *empathy* as a term that was important to their practice. However, based on the qualitative data, it appears that this was used less in the strictly psychoanalytic sense, as a tool to understand unconscious as well as conscious processes in the other,[40] and more in the Rogerian sense of understanding as compassion wedded to warmth, caring, and unconditional positive regard.[41] This interpretation of the term *empathy* is further corroborated by a finding that the eleven therapists who reported having kissed a client's forehead also showed a statistically very strong correlation[42] with the term *empathy*.

Thus, although nearly all the therapists in this study agreed that there is such a thing as an unconscious relationship and the majority endorsed totalist views about the importance of examining one's own internal countertransference responses and unconscious pulls, the data suggests that in their own definitions of the therapeutic relationship and actual reported practices vis-à-vis enactments, they have actually focused most on the conscious, interpersonal aspects of the relationship.

What further findings and implications did the results of the study have concerning actual sexual boundary violations?

Sexual Boundary Violations

When asked to estimate the current prevalence of sexual misconduct in their own respective professions, participants' mean responses were slightly higher than average estimates reported in previous literature: 14.5 percent for pastoral counselors and 12 percent for social workers. There was a wide range of responses for both disciplines, from 1 to 50 percent. When it came to having heard direct reports of sexual boundary violations from both colleagues and clients, the numbers were very high. Over one-third of all respondents had heard a colleague tell them of crossing a sexual boundary with a client. Approximately two-thirds had heard a client report another therapist crossing a sexual boundary with him or her (a mean of 2.6 incidents told with a range of 1 to 10). And 82 percent of all respondents had heard a client report of a clergyperson crossing a sexual boundary with him or her (a mean of over 4 incidents told and a range of 1 to 40). A very high majority of pastoral counselors, 89 percent, had heard a client report of a clergyperson crossing a sexual boundary, with a mean of over 5 incidents told per therapist.

When asked how best to prevent unethical behaviors, therapists in both disciplines considered self-awareness to be essential, including awareness both of one's own possible unconscious conflicts, and of *all* one's thoughts and feelings toward clients. Specific methods most favored by both disciplines for getting back on track after feeling overwhelmed by a patient were as follows: consultation with supervisors (the first preference of 100 percent of pastoral counselors), closely followed by consultation with peers (the preference of 89 percent of clinical social workers), and personal therapy (96 percent of pastoral counselors and 82 percent of clinical social workers).

This pattern of responses did not match, however, with therapists' self-reports about the impact on themselves of the specific enactments they had given as examples from their own practice. In particular, not one respondent disclosed an example of delving into his or her own intrapsychic material (even when supervision was mentioned). Even when supervision was utilized, the self-report indicated that this had focused on the therapist's conscious feelings about the external relationship with the patient. In addition, these conscious feelings, as reported, tended to be only positive.

One of the key questions of the research, further, was to determine whether the religious training and identity of pastoral counselors made a significant difference in their attitudes and practices regarding their use of the counter-transference in psychotherapy.

Did Religious Training Make a Difference?

Religious training did appear to make a statistically significant difference in therapists' understandings of their work with patients and of what heals. For pastoral counselors, the dimension of prayer and spirituality provided an additional central component to their self-understanding and to the understanding of the therapeutic process itself. Not only do pastoral counselors pray and perform rituals more often, they also overwhelmingly agreed that their religious beliefs support their understandings of health, growth, and healing, and that prayer strengthens not only their patients but themselves as caregivers. Practitioners in both disciplines report themselves to be well qualified to address existential questions of meaning, purpose, and identity, but pastoral counselors showed much greater confidence in this area[43] and also claimed much greater professional expertise and authority in addressing clients' spiritual issues and questions.[44] Detailed responses about therapists' religious beliefs and clinical practice are shown in Table 6.

Did Gender Make a Difference?

Gender also made a statistically significant difference.[45] The differences involving the largest numbers of respondents had to do with therapists' conceptualization of the therapeutic relationship itself. Women were more likely to define the therapeutic relationship using the language of the world of intimate, social relationships[46] and were also somewhat more likely to describe it in terms of its qualities rather than its structure. They described it more in terms of being than doing, and more often specifically including the word *empathy*. Male therapists tended to describe it much more often using language from the world of work, often using structural language and active terminology—doing rather than being.

When women reported slightly higher levels of enactment, these tended to involve actions on either the therapist's or the patient's part (such as hugging, showing photographs, giving and receiving symbolic gifts, and attending patients' important events) that were efforts at connection and empathy (understood as compassion), fitting with a view of the relationship as a "corrective emotional experience." In contrast, male therapists were more likely to experience aggressive enactments by patients.

Both men and women reported a number of *unethical* enactments having occurred at least once, and the only statistically significant difference was in the performing of a sacrament (due to more male ordained clergy than female).

Table 6. Responses to Statements about Religious Beliefs and Clinical Practice

	Discipline	
Statement	*Pastoral Counselors*	*Clinical Social Workers*
My religious beliefs support my belief in the value of clients' growth and healing.*	6.47 (strongly agree to very strongly agree)	4.41 (no opinion/ undecided, toward generally agree)
My religious beliefs provide me with a model for a healthy person.*	6.16 (strongly agree)	3.93 (no opinion/ undecided)
Attending public worship strengthens me to be an effective therapist.*	5.31 (generally agree)	3.39 (generally disagree)
Praying for my client(s) helps me be an effective therapist.*	5.49 (generally agree to strongly agree)	2.61 (strongly disagree to generally disagree)
Praying for my client(s) helps them to heal.*	5.37 (generally agree)	2.54 (strongly disagree to generally disagree)
I believe I am well qualified to address clients' spiritual issues and questions.*	6.08 (strongly agree)	3.54 (generally disagree to no opinion, undecided)
I believe I am well qualified to address questions of meaning, purpose, and identity.*	6.25 (strongly agree)	5.07 (generally agree)

*Significant difference between means (*t*-test) of the two disciplines, $p \leq .0001$.

Women's reports of practices classified as unethical tended to be those that might be viewed from a psychoanalytic perspective as relating to pre-oedipal or infantile erotic nurture or maternal comfort—for example, sitting next to a client on the floor (15 women, or 34 percent) or couch (21 women, or 48 percent), and having the client put his or her head in the therapist's lap (5 women, or 11 percent). Unethical enactments reported by men with greater frequency, in contrast, tended to carry more adult erotic overtones: being embraced by a client (10 men, or 26 percent), and having a client attempt to kiss the therapist on the mouth (3 men, or 8 percent).

Men, particularly ordained clergymen with both longer years' ordained experience and clinical experience, were the respondents most likely to have reported being aware of experiencing erotic feelings. Men were also twice as likely to have been told by a colleague of a sexual boundary violation (on average, three times more incidents reported), as well as hearing higher numbers of client reports of professional sexual abuse by therapists.

What Does the Data Mean?

When given theoretical statements saturated with psychoanalytic language and attention to nuances of the unconscious relationship between therapist and patient, therapists from both disciplines largely agreed with totalist statements about the meaning of pulls, enactments, and projective identification. However, therapists mostly scored as undecided or in the conservative classical range in their attitudes toward experiencing, using, and communicating unconscious material. This might simply cause us to think that therapists are more conservative in practice than in their beliefs. However, the therapists' self-reports of actual enactments in their own practices suggest a different interpretation. From the finding of a number of unethical enactments for which there was neither zero tolerance nor just one or two lone examples, it appears that something else is possibly going on.

The qualitative data, as well as quantitative data about the relative lack of focus on the therapeutic relationship itself, supplies clues about what might actually be occurring in the consulting rooms of pastoral counselors and other therapists. It appears, given the virtually unanimous lack of self-reports on inner feelings or unconscious dynamics, together with the finding that one-fourth of therapists did not ever explore with patients the enactments they chose to describe, that psychoanalytic theoretical ideas (totalist *or* classical) are not necessarily at the forefront of many of these therapists' thinking. Although these therapists are conversant with psychoanalytic concepts, they do not demonstrate that they are actually applying these concepts consistently in their practice—not to their patients, themselves, the relationship between them, or their choices of interventions and decisions when and how to be more active.[47] This finding was quite surprising, in light of the large percentage of therapists in the study who explicitly identified themselves as psychoanalytic/psychodynamic in orientation.

Moreover, as shown in the correlation of specific enactments reported on the TRQ with actual practices reported on the ATC, a higher level of enactments generally correlates positively with a higher level of experiencing of affects and with communicating them to patients—in itself a form of verbal enactment. However, a higher level of enactments also correlates negatively with the examination of what most of these affects might mean in terms of the client's internal dynamics. In this light, focusing on the relationship itself, or working "in the room" to a "significant degree," does not necessarily mean interpretation of the transference or exploration of unconscious dynamics. Rather, it could simply mean frequent communication about here-and-now feelings and actions, but only at a conscious, interpersonal level.

All of this would fit a profile of those practitioners who allow or do a number of enactments with the conscious intention of strengthening rapport or conveying genuine care and concern to the patient. They might be aware of their own affective experiences but not the way these have either given rise to the enactments or appeared in reaction to them. They might not therefore be accessing these affects through a process of self-examination in the service of guiding their interventions. This would fit with the larger pattern of many therapists only "sometimes" examining enactments with patients, and one-fourth of therapists "never" doing so. In fact, although no large generalizations may be made from one case, the one respondent who did report having a client kiss him on the mouth was a clinical social worker who identified himself as "cognitive-behavioral" in theoretical orientation. This respondent reported the impact on himself of enactments, including giving patients money for emergency food or transportation needs, as "feeling of job satisfaction."

The "Real Relationship"

A key issue, then, seemed to be that of the so-called real relationship. In their own words, therapists frequently explained or defended their examples of enactments by invoking the idea that the actions they took served to strengthen the rapport with the patient, enhance trust, "ground" a dissociating patient, or reinforce a message of genuine concern, care, and support, especially in a time of crisis or serious loss. The idea is one of a real human connection. In the words of the therapist who described herself as warm, modeling her choices after those of her own therapist, "I believe in a real component of the therapeutic relationship as a way for a person to feel real things." Values of warmth, empathy (in the sense of compassion), and unconditional positive regard appear to undergird this approach.

Evidence of attention to this "real component" of the relationship can be found in the psychoanalytic literature. Ralph Greenson's term *real relationship*[48] came into common usage in psychoanalysis to refer to something that might be understood as separate from the distortions and projective pulls of a classically understood transference dynamic. This idea of "reality" is also echoed in D. W. Winnicott's descriptions of momentary flashes of the real therapist breaking through the transference to momentarily destroy the patient's inner therapist-object and create a new experience, as when his patient "came across the professional white line" and hit him. Through his instantaneous, unpublishable reaction, Winnicott says, "she got a little bit of the *real me*" (emphasis added).[49]

Closely related to the "real relationship" is also Franz Alexander's concept of the "corrective emotional experience."[50] Although this concept has been largely repudiated in psychoanalysis, it remains a popular term in psychotherapy. The idea of the corrective emotional experience in some therapies even slides over into a notion of "reparenting" the client, confusing the necessary understanding and mourning of deficits or abuses experienced in early childhood (whether actually imposed by parents or experienced as such by the child) with a therapist's actively striving to supply in present time what was missing in the past. Participants in this study who stated that they were more likely to attend events or visit a patient in the hospital in the absence of significant others in the patient's life did appear at times to be attempting to step into this sort of substitutionary role, rather than preserving a more neutral space *apart* from the patient's daily life, in which the patient's inner experience and the transference-countertransference relationship could be safely explored.

Normative versus Good, and the Researcher's Countertransference

One might ask, at this juncture, "So what? Pastoral counselors and secular therapists are not psychoanalysts, even if they are psychodynamically oriented in their theoretical beliefs. Isn't it possible to conclude that these therapists' responses simply represent attitudes and behaviors that are both normative and appropriate for their respective disciplines?" The respondents in the study did write thoughtfully about the importance of respect and boundaries, and they evidenced a warm, caring, and supportive attitude toward clients.

Researchers, like therapists, experience countertransference toward their subjects.[51] The questions in the preceding paragraph were playing in my own head while at the same time I found myself initially neglecting to look at frequencies as well as means, instead writing warm, admiring paragraphs about the supportiveness and respectfulness of my respondents. But eventually, several factors began to give me those countertransferential rumbles in the stomach that suggest (just as in the course of a therapy) that "all is not well in Paradise." A contrary voice began to rise in my mind, one that was more in the tradition of Freud's hermeneutic of suspicion: Was I being lulled by the pleasantness and concern expressed by the survey participants in their essay responses? Was there, possibly, as human nature and Freudian hermeneutics would suggest, some erotic or aggressive, oedipal or pre-oedipal component lurking beneath the placid explanations of my subjects?

A number of factors beyond pure intuition reinforced the validity of my increasingly suspicious subjectivity: First, the prevalence of sexual boundary violations estimated by the respondents (12.0 to 14.5 percent) was somewhat higher than even the estimates of prevalence in the clinical literature. At the same time, one-third of my sample reported being told by other colleagues of sexual misconduct. Yet the means of reported levels of unethical enactments by my subjects were very low, with the most obvious sexual and aggressive violations rated unanimously as zero. Was there a parallel with the infamous 1990 CBS/*New York Times* racism poll, in which only 19 percent of New York City residents admitted to using racial slurs, but 50 percent said they knew others who did?[52] My respondents similarly seemed to be locating the problem entirely outside themselves. Where were those boundary-crossing practitioners, if they were not represented in my own sample?

Second, when it came to unethical enactments that my respondents did *not* unanimously report as zero, were the slightly elevated means really only reflecting the aberrant behavior of a few "outliers," as I was assuming? In going back to check the frequencies, the data showed that more—sometimes many more—than just a few lone individuals were reporting these enactments (see Table 1).

Third, a review of the most recent literature shows that the problem of professional boundary violations is not going away, in spite of greater general awareness and attention to training. In spite of recent prevalence studies based on self-reports of social workers, showing percentages of sexual boundary crossings with former or current clients in the range of only 0 to 4 percent, new studies compiled from adjudicated complaints and malpractice claims have shown sexual misconduct accounting for 29 percent of the seventy-two substantiated claims against social workers.[53] Sexual misconduct was the second-most common malpractice claim (18.5 percent). This perhaps suggests that, given the increased public awareness of sexual misconduct by therapists, respondents even on anonymous surveys have become more wary about disclosing unethical behavior. Although this type of study has not yet been conducted for pastoral psychotherapists per se, such new studies of evidence not relying on therapists' self-reports show that the problem of sexual misconduct continues.

Berkman and colleagues studied a form of denial or minimization by therapists based on a rationale of "mitigating circumstances" for continuing boundary violations.[54] Their study of social-work students showed that there continues to be a relatively high level of approval by social-work students of sexual contact between social workers and clients in certain "mitigating circumstances," especially sexual contact following termination. But nearly 10 percent of students in their study approved regardless of termination and even when the social worker's role was to provide intensive psychotherapy.[55] The authors called for greater attention to education and training, including emphasis on the founding ethics and values of the social-work profession, and better understanding of the potential damage to clients.[56] What was normative was not necessarily good or appropriate. In fact, in spite of the warm and caring tone of the qualitative data in this study, the enactment subscales indicate that a number of the respondents have treated at least one patient (and multiplied by the number of respondents, many more than one) unethically.

Even more disturbing, based on the therapists' frequent agreement that enactments occur more at a time of crisis, these situations likely occurred at a point when the patient was extremely fragile or vulnerable. Participants' responses to whether and how they explored the impact of enactments further suggest that these episodes may or may not have been processed or analyzed with the patient. And based on the qualitative reports of how these therapists reflected upon the impact on themselves, there may have been little or no self-scrutiny on the part of the therapists.

Real Relationship: Rationale or Rationalization?

In the play *Mrs. Klein,* the character of Melanie Klein confronts her daughter Melitta with the accusation, "You're a bad clinician!" Melitta spits back, "Why?!" Her mother replies, ". . . You *reassure* your patients . . . *You're bloody destructive!*"[57]

Appeals to the "real relationship" can be dangerous if they are used to justify therapists' inadequately processed enactments or grandiose caregiving fantasies. Glen O. Gabbard has described the thicket of self-deceptions with which therapists continue to deny, minimize, and justify sexual misconduct.[58] The "real relationship" can become an elaborate defense against the anxieties that can arise when one chooses to set a limit or hold the line, rather than do what is gratifying for either the patient or the therapist in the moment. Gabbard writes, "Analysts who have engaged in serious boundary violations with their patients often lose sight of the phenomenon of transference. They begin to emphasize the 'real' relationship and feel that their uniqueness as a human being is the therapeutic factor in the treatment, rather than their knowledge or technique."[59]

Sullivan's famous phrase that "we are all more human than otherwise"[60] championed early on a recognition that both patient and therapist are wounded and strong, fallible and knowing. The sense of mutuality between patient and therapist is, perhaps, a more readily acceptable and congenial idea to pastoral counseling and clinical social work as professions than to any other therapeutic discipline, because both these professions have always attended the wider social context of their patients. Although professional pastoral counselors and clinical social workers may never leave the hermetic *vas*[61] of the consulting room, both professions have their origins in, and carry a "species memory" of, direct care out in the communities in which they serve. For example, parish pastors and social-work case-workers both "hit the pavement" to do home and hospital visits and crisis interventions. They may have found it natural, then, to be called into more direct involvement at times in the lives of patients and their families. And neither discipline (certain individual practitioners excepted) has ever wholeheartedly embraced a therapeutic idea of total abstinence and neutrality. Therapeutic models, whether psychoanalytic, Rogerian, humanist-existential, or "eclectic," that emphasize personal warmth, concern, and a "real relationship" component have always had a strong appeal in both professions.

But this recognition of common grounding in the human condition can too easily slide into a facile acceptance of therapists' loosening of boundaries in the name of mutuality, and an abdication—or unconscious denial—of responsibility for the patient's well-being. As pastoral theologian Judith Orr wrote shortly before her death,

> Some kinds of boundaries (the structure and rules for interaction and fulfillment of roles) characterize all relationships, and some relationships reflect temporarily unequal power without being dominating and abusive, e.g., parent-child and teacher-parent relationships at their best. Differences in power do mean some different responsibilities: the parent/teacher/therapist has the special responsibility to take the lead in structuring a safe context for the nurture and learning of the child/student/client. Assuming we will not abandon these roles immediately, the adequacy of mutuality for the improvement of ethical therapy (and of teaching and parenting also) begs for clarification.[62]

The Specter of Narcissism

So we return to the question "So what?" What is being missed, primarily, in all such appeals to mutuality and the "real relationship" is an element of unconscious grandiosity in the countertransference. Disguised as altruism, the unconscious desire not just to be caring but to be a *special* carer can easily infect any caregiving relationship, especially in the absence of consistent, thoughtful self-analysis. In overt sexual misconduct, many typologies of offenders have been proposed, including the two-type "wanderer-predator" model,[63] an eight-fold and a fourfold typology developed from treatment of offenders,[64] and most recently a Jungian archetypology of the "naive prince," the "wounded warrior," the "dark king," etc.[65] Regardless of typology, however, there appears to be a through-line of narcissism in all cases of boundary violations.[66] Whether or not narcissism is entrenched as a predominant characterological feature (as in the pastoral care case of Terence in the previous chapter), an element of grandiosity and omnipotence can be detected in nearly all unexamined enactments, including those that do not constitute overt sexual misconduct but do represent departures from accepted ethical standards.

Many of the other enactments reported by practitioners might be seen in and of themselves as fairly benign. Some amount of enactment is probably inevitable.[67] Enactments can be signs that the therapeutic work has deepened to a place where unconscious dynamics at work in both patient and therapist are emerging at a level that cannot yet be symbolized or verbalized. Relational therapist Jodie Messler Davies has suggested that enactments may even be more likely to occur precisely at those moments in the therapy when "a vision of experience . . . has not found its way into the consciously articulated and ostensibly agreed-on rendition of events. Thus, the unconscious but coercive projective-introjective attempt to invade and shape the experience of the other ensues in bidirectional patterns that can become mystifying to patient and analyst alike."[68]

None of us is immune. The problem with many of the enactments reported in this study was not so much that they happened, but the prevailing pattern of lack of self-examination by these therapists of their own affects, dynamics, and motives and relative lack of sustained attention to processing enactments with clients. Without adequate exploration of what such enactments really mean, both to the therapist and to the patient, both partners can lapse into a collusive dynamic in which each is gratified—sometimes enormously—but their (often traumatic) origins remain unconscious and therefore potentially unaddressed, unchanged, and unhealed.

Barbara Pizer[69] and Jody Messler Davies[70] point to the perpetual seductiveness of a grandiose fantasy of oneself as omnipotent healer and needed rescuer, for whom enactments are no longer unethical but signs of one's greater caring for the patient's needs. Even nonpredatory therapists are easily lulled down the "slippery slope"[71] by unconsciously gratifying motives of caring for the patient in special and uniquely necessary ways. Being the "one and only" for a patient, Gabbard[72] points out, also may invoke an unconscious oedipal fantasy of aloneness in which only patient and therapist/patient and mother exist, a dangerous unconscious collusion that might be signaled subtly by a dimly recognized sense of secrecy, or "feeling cozy."[73]

At what point does a conscious intent to be warm, caring, and supportive, as in the case of Sara in this chapter, slip into a cozy, self-aggrandizing feeling of being uniquely special to the patient? At what point, then, does such a pattern become so entrenched that (unlike Miranda's case) the patient's anger, fear, rage, rebellion, or other negative feelings toward the therapist become impossible to express or even consciously acknowledge? How often does such a pattern reenact a destructive childhood dependency, in which ulterior sexual motives or narcissistic needs were fused with a parent's overtly caring and protective role?

To play on Sullivan's statement, quoted earlier, "We are all more narcissistic (or narcissistically wounded) than otherwise." Enactments are inevitable, and the desire to be a special helper is common. Not only is none of us immune to the occurrence of unanticipated enactment moments in deep therapeutic work, but I would venture that none of us is immune to at least occasional seductive desires to be the omnipotent healer. While this probably does not constitute an entrenched, predatory characterological pattern in most practitioners, the very dynamics that often draw individuals to pursue caregiving professions virtually guarantee an intensification of unconscious impulses along a healer-healed axis.

Grandiosity may not only appear in the guise of being the special healer of our patients. It may also appear in the form of overestimating our capacity to contain and analyze all the possible meanings that can arise when enactments do occur. As Arnold Goldberg has stated, many enactments may not in and of themselves constitute anything overtly unethical in the moral sense.[73] However, we must acknowledge our limitations in being able adequately to process these enactments and to contain the energies they generate.

Finally, even seemingly ethical enactments may not be so harmless after all. Although no overt sexual boundary violations were endorsed on the Therapist Enactment Subscale in my research, the correlation of so many enactments, both ethical and otherwise, with therapists' experiencing and communicating to patients both sexual and aggressive affects—especially erotic feelings—suggests that more may be going on beneath the conscious level of the "real relationship." Especially with regard to erotic feelings in the therapist, as Kenneth Pope, Janet Sonne, and Jean Holroyd have pointed out, "Therapists experiencing sexual attraction, arousal, or stimulation with a patient may become exceptionally confused about actions: the patient's or their own."[75] Thus, enactments that on the surface may appear within normal ethical boundaries may not be experienced that way by either therapist or patient in the presence of an erotic dynamic (whether conscious or unconscious for either or both). Further, the presence of erotic feelings may impair therapists' judgment about what constitutes a genuinely therapeutic enactment.

Recommendations for the Use of the Self in Pastoral Psychotherapy

Based on this discussion of the results of this research study, three recommendations are offered for clinical practice and for education, training, and ongoing development of pastoral counselors and psychotherapists:

1. The results of this study call for a renewed clinical focus on exploration of both transference and countertransference dynamics in the context of an intersubjective relationship that operates at multiple levels, both conscious and unconscious.

2. This renewal of attention to exploration and interpretation, in turn, calls for greater use by therapists of in-depth clinical consultation/supervision, with particular focus on the therapist's countertransference in the intersubjective relationship, and on the unconscious projective processes that may be at work in "pulls" and affective intensities as they manifest in the therapy. This may be augmented by a return to personal psychotherapy or analysis, especially when one's work begins to tap areas of deep pain or unresolved conflict.

3. This study calls for a deromanticization of the meaning of the term *empathy* and a recognition, or recuperation, of its diagnostic usefulness, in the Kohutian sense, in guiding the therapist to understand enactments as they occur.

Claiming or Reclaiming a More Exploratory Stance

Freud's original dictum concerning abstinence and neutrality, which he reputedly kept as a reminder to himself on a small placard on his desk, was "When in doubt, don't." Based on the results of this study, this dictum still seems like good advice. While new developments in psychoanalysis have clearly moved both analysis and psychotherapy beyond the illusion that a therapist can maintain perfect neutrality, new conceptualizations of transference and countertransference as part of a multilayered continuum of conscious and unconscious intersubjective experience do not necessarily justify a loosening of basic ethical boundaries. Increasing recognition of the power and importance of enactments to convey unconscious communications and diagnostic information about a patient's dynamics, if anything, requires therapists to use greater circumspection about intentionally allowing or initiating enactments, since there will inevitably be unanticipated and unpreventable enactment moments, and these will provide as much material as can be processed adequately in the therapy—sometimes more.

The key here is not attempting to eliminate all enactments, which is in any case probably impossible, but to maintain a consistently exploratory stance that continually keeps moving the therapeutic process from the realm of action back into symbolization, verbalization, and ultimately, comprehension. This mirrors the process that therapy should be engendering in patients' own lives over time—to learn to refrain from impulsive action and increase the capacity for reflection and understanding of the unconscious currents that animate relationships, choices, and everyday life.

If a therapist finds him- or herself justifying an action on the grounds of the "real relationship," this should be a red flag. Some unconscious process may be at work—including the very real possibility of some narcissistic gratification that, if attended early enough, may yield important information about the patient's unspoken needs and the righting of the therapeutic process.

Gabbard and Eva Lester have outlined the following four guidelines for determining when an enactment may be becoming potentially harmful to the patient or the therapeutic process:[76] First,

> "catching oneself" as the enactment is *in statu nascendi* may serve to prevent a near-crossing from becoming a violation. Second, the capacity of both analyst and patient to discuss and analyze the incident may determine whether a behavior is productive or destructive. Conversely, if an enactment is not discussable for one reason or another, it may bode poorly for the process. A third principle concerns whether the enactment is repetitive and unresponsive to the analyst's own self-analytic efforts. Finally, a determination of harm to the patient or the process may assist in judging the enactment's exploitiveness.

Although these authors are referring specifically to psychoanalysis, these principles of self-observation and interpretive exploration of the meaning of events with patients serve an important protective function in any psychotherapy, since it is precisely the enactments that spring, unconsidered, from the unconscious that have the most potential for harm.

The issue of repetitive or even quasi-ritualized enactments[77] that are accompanied by a feeling of resistance to exploration or interpretation, either within the therapist or in the larger atmosphere created by the intersubjective dyad, especially raises the need for the second recommendation of this study, namely, supervision and personal therapy.

Supervision and Personal Therapy

The late Rev. Bonnie Niswander, former director of training at the Lutheran General Pastoral Counseling Center, was fond of saying about the need for supervision, "No one can see the back of her own head!" Supervision and consultation need to be sought more routinely. Therapists in this study overwhelmingly endorsed both supervision and personal psychotherapy as the most important ways to get back on track when feeling overwhelmed by a patient's dynamics. Not just any consultation or supervision will be helpful, however. Supervision and consultation need to be conducted in such a way that the supervision itself does not become a parallel exercise in gratification or unconscious collusion with the dynamic already set up between patient and therapist.

Just as therapists can fall into the too-comfortable state of comforting and gratifying clients, supervisors, too, can fail to probe areas of unpleasant affect or anxious defense with their supervisees, in order to promote a surface atmosphere of supportiveness and encouragement in supervision. At its worst, consultation can be used by certain therapists as a hedge against legal liability, without any true intent to engage in genuine self-examination.[78]

Genuine supervision/consultation needs to gain access to multiple layers and dimensions of the therapist's conscious and unconscious motivations, pulls, affects, thoughts, dreams, and fantasies that may pertain to the case. Just as a therapist needs to move beyond exploration of the conscious, interpersonal relationship between therapist and patient, so, too, does the supervisor need to probe the unconscious as well as conscious dynamics of the case under supervision. This does not mean doing therapy or analysis with one's supervisees— on the contrary, the discovery of areas of previously untreated conflict, anxiety, or unhealed trauma should signal the supervisor or consultant to refer the therapist for further personal therapy or analysis. At the same time, supervision cannot simply be an examination solely based on the conscious interactions between therapist and patient or techniques for interpersonal management of the case.

Barbara Pizer, in her call for routine consultations as part of the ethical expectations of all psychotherapists, has identified a number of affects and typical defensive processes that, when present, should signal a need for consultation:[79]

- "Cognitive flummoxing," in which therapists are temporarily thrown into unfruitful cognitive focus on some specific, minute aspect of an event because the event itself has been experienced as affectively overwhelming and "indigestible"

- Secrecy

- Internal pressure to talk with others about the treatment, to "brag or bemoan"

- A rescue fantasy that "only I can help this patient through her difficult time"

- "Prolonged affects of excitement, boredom, anxiety, dread, withdrawal, anger, and, last but not least, feeling cozy"

Pizer distinguishes between "signal affect" (in which the therapist is able to use a strong affective reaction to inform clinical judgment, a regular part of any therapist's training and experience) and "affect as a signal of the need for consultation." The latter is characterized by the therapist's finding him- or herself unable to use strong reactions therapeutically, but instead, the affects remain "static, entrenched, intense, persistent, disconnected—as in an affective state, with affect now linked with a recognizable dissociative defense."[80]

Supervision and consultation need to address the level of enactment in the therapy and to explore its potential meanings directly and empathically. Especially in cases where there are repetitive, ritualized, or escalating enactments, some of the following questions might be fruitfully kept in mind throughout the consultation, as I have written previously:[81]

- What happened in the session at the level of action as well as words? Have certain enactments ever happened before? Are any of them repetitive actions in which the repetition or escalation of the level of enactment might carry conscious and potentially unconscious meaning?

- What might be some possible meanings of these enactments and rituals for the patient, based on what we know about his or her history, current behavior outside of therapy, and feelings evoked in the room?

- What about enactments and rituals on the part of the therapist? What meanings might they have for him or her? In what way does the interplay of these meanings with those of the patient provide new information that could be available for use in the interpretive task of therapy?

Based on the results of my study, I would further advocate that consultants and supervisors help therapists to be especially alert for signs of inflation and grandiosity in their choices of interventions. Narcissistic wounding in particular is shame laden and covered over with defensive attempts at disavowal of grandiosity. Supervision therefore needs to be accomplished in ways that are not accusing or shame provoking, but rather collaborative and empathic with the therapist's own internal worldview, desires, needs, wounds, and aspirations. When narcissistic currents are at play in a therapist's countertransference, gently uncovering them is an important task of supervision. Supervision, therefore, is as delicate an art as psychotherapy itself. It provides a container or holding environment for both the therapist and his or her case, not unlike Winnicott's question "Who holds the mother holding the baby?"[82]

A careful consideration of the questions suggested here can deepen and enrich the content of supervisory or consulting sessions and deepen the therapist–consultant relationship as well. This type of supervision or consultation models a stance of empathic curiosity about the meaning of everything that happens, based on a foundational assumption that every act has meaning. In this way, supervision or consultation creates a process parallel to the therapy itself and opens a "potential space"[83] for introspection and playful contemplation of multiple meanings and associations. By opening up this potential space with the therapist, to explore the inner dynamics of countertransference and the transference-countertransference relationship between therapist and patient, the supervisor can help the therapist maintain awareness of projective dynamics and use these to the ongoing benefit of the patient. To this end, empathy is a necessity, both in therapy and in supervision.

Empathy

Empathy is often misunderstood, even among therapists who claim a self psychological perspective, as caring, warmth, and being nice. Empathy, however, as the founder of self psychology, Heinz Kohut, repeatedly attempted to clarify,[84] is not caring but careful perspective taking, attempting to understand the world through the inner experience and perspective of the other, as a means of gathering information about the other's needs, affects, motives, and behaviors. It is an information-gathering "empirical" activity that does establish a powerful emotional bond between people, and as such is a *precondition* for both supportive, effective mothering and therapy but is not in and of itself warmth or kindness. Kohut defined empathy as a "mode of observation attuned to the inner life,"[85] or "vicarious introspection."[86] In this sense, empathy is often experienced as profoundly beneficial to patients—not because they feel warmly loved and reparented, but because they feel recognized and understood. In Kohut's understanding, the diagnostic information gained through empathy must be interpreted to the patient. Impulses and desires must be explored together for what they might mean, rather than being merely enacted.

Even in the Rogerian sense, empathy and genuine caring do not equate with gratification of a patient's most consciously expressed needs or with a therapist's own desire to please, heal, or rescue another. Empathy is not mere sympathy or concern. Empathy, even when meant in the sense of care for the other, requires an effort to stand in the other person's shoes and go beyond the interpersonal pressures of the moment—even when this is anxiety provoking—to consider what all the possible effects of an enactment on a patient might be, both positive and negative. A rush to momentary gratification, especially when coupled with a denial of potentially negative impact and failure to examine the act later, does not constitute either genuine caring or empathy, but rather gives the appearance of caring while sealing over more damaging negative effects.

Because of therapists' pervasive desire to be (or to experience themselves as) kind and caring, it is easy for therapists' understanding and use of the term *empathy* to drift away from its sharper usage in self psychology. This empathy-drift can easily carry therapists from the rockier shores of genuine analytic work, in which empathy is seen as an important diagnostic tool, to the warmer but less transmutative waters of cozy caretaking.

Narcissistic elements in the therapist, described in this chapter, are also a serious impediment to genuine empathy. Empathy, by definition, requires a turning toward the other in an effort to take the other's inner perspective. This process is effectively blocked by the narcissistic movement inward. Good supervision and personal therapy or analysis are therefore crucial to the capacity for empathy, because they make it possible to recognize, destigmatize, and, over time, heal the narcissistic turning away, in Neville Symington's language,[87] from the Lifegiver and from others in the external world.

Further, empathy is not to be confused with a blurry form of mutuality in which roles and boundaries are merged. Empathy is not only compatible with good boundary keeping, it is essential to it. One cannot maintain a safe and well-boundaried frame without an understanding of the potentially harmful impact of poor boundaries on the other.

Finally, empathy means more than sympathy or even empathic understanding of the patient in the present moment or as presenting in the present affect state. Recent movements in psychoanalytic theory have challenged a unitary notion of the self with views of subjectivity (including both conscious and unconscious dimensions) that are far more fluid, dynamic, and multiple than even Freud himself provided with his decentering of the conscious self in favor of a topographical, and later structural, model of consciousness and unconsciousness in a dynamic interplay. By giving in to the conscious pressures of the moment, a therapist is in danger from this new intersubjective or relational perspective to miss *other* aspects of the patient's self, other competing subjectivities that may desire or require something very different than the enactment that is overtly being demanded in the moment. Empathy requires perspective taking that considers the whole other, inasmuch as that can ever be approximately known, including possible effects that have not yet manifested in the conscious relationship and can only be guessed at through empathic glimpses of alternative affect states and alternative realities in the patient's mind. For this reason, classical ideas about abstinence and refraining make sense, not only because one's own neurotic conflicts may be intruding upon the therapy, but because all enactments will have resonance in multiple corridors of the patient's psyche, as well as deeply unpredictable effects in the intersubjective "between" of patient and therapist. Given this multiplicity, to deal with all the unavoidable enactments will more than fill the capacity of the therapist and the therapeutic relationship to contain and understand them, without inviting further unmanageable complexity by giving in to the avoidable ones.

CHAPTER SEVEN
Toward a Relational Theology
God-in-Relation

AS WE HAVE SEEN in the opening chapters of this book, Sigmund Freud's topographical model privileged a single "depth" model of the unconscious, and the early generations of psychoanalysts and their enthusiasts—including the Emmanuel movement and early pastoral psychologists (as described in chapter 2)—understood themselves in some sense as heroes. They often felt misunderstood and even persecuted by the uncomprehending masses, but they saw themselves as pioneers into uncharted territories where *deeper* truths would be unearthed to cathartic effect. The topographical model gave at least the illusion of a certain element of control over the unknown. The inner landscape could seem threatening and dangerous, but it constituted an increasingly recognizable region with categorizeable contents based on the cartography of Freud and his followers. This may feel more comfortable to us than the idea of our minds as "undefined spatiality, like the contours of a perfume."[1] Yet postmodernism and the relational paradigm have challenged us to entertain the possibility that our minds, and indeed our selves, are more like highly complex, networked systems, not discrete entities, more like the clouds of chaos theory than the clocks of Newtonian physics.[2] What might this do to our theology, our theological anthropology, and our work as pastoral theologians and caregivers?

It seems to me that as we embrace a model of greater complexity and multiplicity of the human mind, this will lead us not only to a more complex and nuanced appreciation for the diversity and mutability of human persons, but also, finally, to a more variegated, nonlimited, and nonlimiting imago Dei. Contemporary trinitarian process, liberation, and feminist theologies already contain elements to support such a theology of complexity, diversity, and mutability. Elizabeth Johnson, in the book *She Who Is*, describes how the very image of the

Figure 7. Rublev icon of the Trinity

Trinity is one that challenges unitary, totalizing images of God.[3] As in the Rublev icon [Figure 7] shown above, Johnson presents a trinitarian image of God as fluid, multiple, and profoundly relational:

> At its most basic the symbol of the Trinity evokes a livingness in God, a dynamic coming and going with the world that points to an inner divine circling

around in unimaginable relation. God's relatedness to the world in creating, redeeming, and renewing activity suggests to the Christian mind that God's own being is somehow similarly differentiated. Not an isolated, static, ruling monarch but a relational, dynamic, tripersonal mystery of love—who would not opt for the latter?[4]

In her vast mining of the Catholic theological tradition, Johnson finds support for this idea in numerous sources, including Aquinas: "Relation really existing in God is really the same as His essence, and only differs in intelligibility. In God relation and essence do not differ from each other but are one in the same."[5] She quotes the contemporary feminist theologian Catherine LaCugna, "To be God is to-be-relationally."[6] Similar themes are found in the work of liberation theologian Leonardo Boff, who writes, "We believe that God is communion rather than solitude,"[7] and, "In the beginning is communion."[8] Johnson continues with the Johannine statement:

Being related is at the very heart of divine being. God's being is not an enclosed, egocentric self-regard but is identical with an act of free communion, always going forth and receiving in. At the deepest core of reality is a mystery of personal connectedness that constitutes the very livingness of God. The category of relation thus serves as a heuristic tool for bringing to light not just the mutuality of trinitarian persons but the very nature of the holy mystery of God herself. Divine unity exists as an intrinsic *koinonia* of love, love freely blazing forth, love not just as a divine attitude, affect, or property but as God's very nature: "God is Love" (1 Jn 4:16).[9]

In another trinitarian approach, John Milbank argues for a "postmodern Christianity" that values diversity as a central organizing principle. For Milbank, the Trinity is a sign of God as community, "even a 'community in process,'[10] infinitely realized, beyond any conceivable opposition between 'perfect act' and 'perfect potential.'"[11] He writes:

Christianity can become "internally" postmodern . . . I mean by this that it is possible to construe Christianity as suspicious of notions of fixed "essences" in its approach to human beings, to nature, to community and to God, even if it has never fully escaped the grasp of a "totalizing" metaphysics. Through its belief in creation from nothing it admits temporality, the priority of becoming and unexpected emergence. A reality suspended between nothing and infinity is a reality of flux, a reality without substance, composed only of relational differences and ceaseless alterations (Augustine, *De Musica*). Like nihilism, Christianity can, should, embrace the differential flux.[12]

Milbank finds the expression of this Christianity not in creedal statements about God but in Christian practices of community. Christian community embodies a commitment to difference but, unlike nihilism, envisions the possibility of difference with harmony—borrowing from Augustine, a *concentus musicus*.[13]

All the detailed arguments of Milbank's postmodern Augustinian theology (including some internal contradictions, imported from postmodernist philosophy)[14] cannot be adequately explored here. It is interesting, though, in light of the focus of this book on intersubjectivity, both conscious and unconscious, the "known" and the "unknown" *(das Unbewüsst)*, that another of Milbank's propositions is that the mediator of reality is *desire* (which, for Milbank, is the expression of the third person of the Trinity), not "Greek knowledge" (cognitive or intellectual knowing, distinct from the knowledge of emotion and the body).[15] Desire for the other reaches across the gaps, the "transitional space," to generate an intersubjective arena of creation. If we accept the concept of the relational dimension of consciousness and its construction, our theology can be similarly understood as a mutual, coconstructive, cogenerative yearning between humans and the divine.[16]

Luce Irigaray's postmodern creation statement is "On the first day, the first days, the gods, God, make a world by separating the elements."[17] Irigaray emphasizes the act of creation as doubling and difference, rather than unity, which can all too easily translate into totalitarian oppression, the subsuming of all otherness into the One. What binds and heals in a relational model is not a vision of ultimate oneness, as in homogenization, but mutual desire and love that bridges toward the other, embracing difference.

Christianity is at heart a praxis of diversity in love, not what Milbank calls a "gnosis, in the sense of a formulaic wisdom that we must just recite or magically invoke."[18] A relational theology both models and makes room for difference, for a multiplicity of ways of knowing, and a flux among sensation, hunger, emotion, and rational thought. It is a theology that is not set abstractly apart from bodies but locates itself in and between them.

Such a view also works well with the idea from process theology that God is not monolithic or static, but fluid, changing, and in process. "God is a verb," to quote feminist theologians Mary Daly and Virginia Ramey Mollenkott.[19] Process theology offers us a vision of a God who does not interfere with the gift of human free will but is always present to transform suffering once again into healing, and each twist and turn of life into a new possibility, a new beginning.[20] Bernard Loomer speaks of the "size of God," large enough to contain everything in the universe, large enough to contain even our suffering.[21] This view respects and honors the depth of suffering, without trivializing or sugarcoating it, but also offers hope for transformation as always and eternally available, small resurrections possible every day.

A final caution regarding theology: a theology of multiplicity, like any theology, could under certain circumstances waft again into the realm of abstraction and disconnection from the body. In some postmodern constructions, cyberspace has been posited not only as a metaphor for the human mind, but for the divine. Graham Ward writes these words concerning cyberspace:

> In this land of fantasy and ceaseless journeying, this experience of tasting, sampling and passing, truth, knowledge, and facts are all only dots of light on a screen, evanescent, consumable. This is the ultimate in the secularization of the divine, for here is a God who sees and knows all things, existing in pure activity and realized presence, in perpetuity. Divinization as the dissolution of subjectivity within the immanent, amniotic satisfaction, is the final goal and object of postmodernity. Cyberspace is the realization of a metaphor used repeatedly by Derrida, Irigaray, and Kristeva—the Khora, the plenitudinous womb, dark, motile, and unformed, from which all things issue.[22]

What is problematic in this view, and why for me the analogy between cyberspace and the womb is incorrect, is precisely that cyberspace is so disembodied. The *Khora* signifies a profound origination in relation that cyberspace, for all its rapid-fire electronic connectivity, lacks. Surfing the Web can be as much an experience of profound isolation and alienation as one of connection. In the anonymous discourse of cyberspace, identity is not only fluid but also disconnected from bodies and from any ongoing commitment or responsibility either for oneself or for others. As Ward himself notes, it is also a realm that purports to offer universal access but in fact is heavily tied to capitalist venture and therefore available only to those with the financial resources to pay for the privilege of "surfing."

The image of the *Khora* does speak to something beyond sheer complexity and motility. God is in the body, not disembodied. Numerous feminist theologians have challenged Greek, New Testament, and Cartesian forms of mind-body dualism as perpetuating the subjugation of women's experience and glorifying disconnected rationality at the expense of the lived experiences of childbirth, sexuality, dying, suffering, and surviving.[23] Womanist, mujerista, and global feminist theologies in particular celebrate the power of sheer survival as a source of power and knowledge to inform and sustain faith.[24] God is experienced both in the community of solidarity and within the self, as in Ntozake Shange's often-quoted line of poetry: "I found God in myself and I loved her/I loved her fiercely."[25] God is understood in the Black Church tradition as immanent, a source of strength in the face of concrete racial and economic oppression, the

God "who makes a way out of no way."[26] In the words of Asian theologian Elizabeth Tapia, "Theology is not only a theoretical exercise. It is a commitment and participation in people's struggle for full humanity, and discernment of God's redemptive action in history. It is 'theology-in-action,' embodied, and integrated holistically with critical reflection."[27] This is a profoundly incarnational theology, in which God/Jesus/Spirit is recognized and celebrated as present and in motion in the world, in the dailiness of life, and in the body.

The imago Dei we embrace inevitably influences our theological anthropology. Faith in an incarnational God conceived as fluid, multiple, in motion, and in perpetual relation both with us and within us emancipates us from constraining, static, monolithic notions of both God and human beings. A multiple, relational theology, it seems to me, is hospitable to an embodied conception of mind and self that gives room enough for the human person to encompass a wide capacity for relationality, both with other people and with and among the *inner* selves that inhabit the time and spatial dimensions of one's own lived life. Freud's rigid hierarchy of "higher powers" and "infernal regions" collapses, as we recognize that all of us contain spheres of both rationality and irrationality, knowability and unknowability, of abstract thought, emotion, and animal sense, both within ourselves and in our relations with one another. Furthermore, these are not fixed positions but are in continual flux as we move in and out of different internal and external states of pressure, desire, conflict, and union.

Theological Implications for Pastoral Praxis

In conclusion, what are the implications for a pastoral praxis that is both healing and liberative? Especially for those of us who are practitioners of pastoral care and psychotherapy, the archetype of the heroic explorer of "dark continents," while seductive, is ultimately narcissistic and needs to be modified. This is not to say that as helping professionals we can jettison all authority or erase the boundaries that create a safe holding environment for those who come to us for help. Drawing again from the relational school of psychoanalysis, it is possible, however, to move from a more hierarchical model of the therapist as knowing explorer (active) and the patient as continent (acted upon). We can move toward a model that acknowledges an asymmetry of roles and responsibilities but at the same time honors that wisdom is shared as meanings are continually being coconstructed and reconstructed in the intersubjective space of the therapeutic relationship.

This emerging paradigm requires new capacities of us: complexity, a revaluing of subjectivity, empathy and mutuality, patience, emancipatory listening, and silence.

Complexity

Simplistic answers and once-for-all interpretations will not satisfy. They will tend again toward fixity, absolutism, and totalitarian force—even if only ideological. This will change the quality of our listening. Rather than listening only or primarily for unifying themes and overarching patterns, we will listen with greater attention for complexity and multiplicity.

Relational theorist Philip Bromberg has suggested a shift in the focus of our attention, involving a "dialogue between discontinuous domains of self-meaning held by a multiplicity of states of consciousness, some of which can be told and some only enacted . . . ['G]etting into a mood' represents a shift to a state of consciousness with its own internal integrity, its own reality, and sometimes its own 'truth.'"[28] He writes:

> A case could be made, for example, that the reason a state such as depression is difficult to alleviate even with medication is that it is not simply an "affective disorder" but an internally coherent aspect of the self . . . with its own narrative, its own memory configuration, its own perceptual reality, and its own style of relatedness to others . . . So the "curing" of depression must be a process that does not become an effort to cure the patient of "who he is" . . . [but] a dialectic with a multiplicity of different self-narratives, perceptual realities, and adaptational meanings to the patient, each of which speaks with its own voice.[29]

This also suggests a shift in listening from content to process, especially shifts in states of self and the quality of relatedness between subjects, between the multiple "I's" and the "Thou's" that may be present at any given moment. This calls for a second capacity, a revaluing of subjectivity.

Revaluation of Subjectivity

We are challenged to recognize more varied kinds of knowledge than just the positivist and argumentative versions of "truth" we were taught to render from our modernist grammar-school curricula onward. In the words of Mary Belenky and her colleagues, we are called to "passionate knowing."[30] In their book *Women's Ways of Knowing,* these researchers describe "passionate knowers" as those who "seek to stretch the outer boundaries of their consciousness—by making the unconscious conscious, by consulting and listening to the self, by voicing the unsaid, by listening to others and staying alert to all the currents and undercurrents of life about them, by imagining themselves inside the new poem or person or idea that they want to come to know and understand . . . knowers who enter into a union with that which is to be known." Like their example, geneticist Barbara McClintock, we are challenged not to look at the subjects of our investigation from the outside, but to get inside them as much as is humanly possible, to know one another and perhaps even God through experience and empathy, not just objective observation. The word *I* thus comes back into serious, even scholarly, discourse.

This subjectivity, this passionate knowing, will lead us naturally, I believe, to a third necessary quality or pairing of qualities: empathy and mutuality.

Empathy and Mutuality

A relational image of God works together with a relational humanity. Such a theology holds empathy and mutuality at the heart of an ethical stance toward one another. If reality is no longer seen as imposed, but coconstructed in relationship, then relations among people require a higher level of intentional listening and intentional speaking. The "ideal speech situation," to use the language of Jürgen Habermas,[31] will be one of *inter*-subjectivity. I find resonance for this idea in the Judaeo-Christian tenet of reciprocity of love of self and neighbor, the New Testament language of *agape* love, and the Catholic tradition's *caritas*.

We can perhaps find an intersubjective interpretation in the narratives of Jesus' life. For example, Jesus allowed himself to be changed by his encounters, as in the story of the Canaanite woman who dared to enter into a midrash-like debate with him on behalf of her sick daughter and won his admiration: "Great is your faith! Let it be done for you as you wish" (Matthew 15:21-28; Mark 7:24-30). Peter is able to walk on the water toward Jesus, upheld by his faith while held in a mutual gaze, but when he is distracted by his fear of the wind, the intersubjective moment is eclipsed, and Peter begins to sink. He is saved from drowning by Jesus' reaching out and restoring their relational connection (Matthew 14:22-32). A commitment to mutual engagement and intersubjectivity further leads to a fourth capacity, patience.

Patience

A recognition that the sacred and all life is a *process,* and a faith that God is in process with humanity, not just acting *upon* human beings from above, demands the capacity to allow time for changes to unfold. Nor can human beings simply act upon others. In this sense, even the most activist behaviors may participate in wrong if the activists seek to undo what they perceive as the wrongs of others with totalitarian moves themselves. Balance is required, and patience comes into play as time is taken for discernment and for process. When balance fails, patience will help in those times as well, to be of good courage, to seek one another's forgiveness, to begin again, and to take the long view.

Emancipatory Listening

The last capacity inspired by a relational paradigm is commitment to emancipatory listening, a justice making based on respect for difference. Jane Flax's formulations of a nonunitary self in the context of an emancipatory intersubjectivity lead to ethics, understood as the deconstruction of dominant discourses—even within the self, but certainly between and among selves, none of whom are conceived as static or monolithic. These selves are gendered, embodied, and embedded in contexts of culture, race, and class. Difference will emerge from the gaps and the margins. If God's own being is to be understood as multiple, fluid, relational, and in process, encompassing difference, then we will be attentive to finding God's own self/selves also in the gaps and on the margins.

Silence

This will involve silence as well as speech. Psychoanalyst Sheldon Roth writes, "We want to behave as if excessive movement puts all of nature into hiding, as it does at a woodland pond."[32] We will need—often—to still our own voices (including the internalized voices of our own socialization and enculturation) in order to seek and discern beyond the tacitly accepted "knowns" and "truths" of any particular time and place, to what voices and realities may be excluded or not yet recognized. Our practice of silence will not be one of "neutrality" but of profound respect for the complexity that might emerge from the not-yet-known-or-knowable. Far from a cold and aloof "blank screen," silence is the ground out of which much healing work is allowed to grow. This is the pastoral caregiver's discipline: to refrain from adding anything extraneous, anything unconsidered, anything born of his or her own need. There is a stillness in relational practice which is akin to the discipline of Zen sitting. We wait, with complete attention. And we wait with humility. The helpee is not an "It" to be acted upon, but a "Thou," a precious subject.

This is the heart of the theological task: to be with the other as a respectful companion and sometime guide on the journey. At the place of primordial silence, the pastor or pastoral counselor and the helpee share a common humanity filled with both joy and suffering. By casting together into the waters of meaning that lie within and between them both, respecting the spaces that silence opens, both can be transformed.

Shared Wisdom: Listening for God Within

Finally, all pastoral praxis, as distinct from other forms of care, is grounded in the "wideness in God's mercy"[33] and in the practice of listening for God in prayer and contemplation. The contemplative Christian tradition has long recognized the power of being still and quietly attending to the presence of God, both surrounding us in all of God's vastness and compassion, and welling up as the beloved Other within. We find, or at least catch glimpses, of the divine presence, both an Other as vast and incomprehensible and transcendent as the canopy of space beyond the stars themselves, and at the same time "more inward than my most inward part,"[34] "closer than breathing and nearer than hands and feet."[35] The Russian mystic Theophan the Recluse wrote, "To pray is to stand before the face of the Lord, ever-present, all-seeing, within you."[36] Prayer, meditation, and "practicing the presence of God" ground us in the loving embrace of God. Prayer envelops us in the "holding environment"[37] of God's compassion.

Relationality not only describes the intersubjective nature of human relations; it also, finally, describes the nature of the relationship between human persons and the divine. If God is not an "isolated, static, ruling monarch,"[38] but rather a dynamic, multiple, fluid creator/lover whose very nature is relation, then prayer itself is the practice that opens one up more and more to relationship with the divine desire and compassion. One enters through prayer into a state in which the exigencies of hourly living are reframed in the light of loving and being loved by God. One enters into God's passionate desire for one's own self, uniquely created and bestowed with the capacity for this very relation, however obscured it may be by the brokenness of creation and the obscuring preoccupations of daily human existence. In the words of Augustine:

> There is a light I love, and a food, and a kind of embrace when I love my God—a light, voice, odour, food, embrace of my inner [person], where my soul is floodlit by light which space cannot contain, where there is sound that time cannot seize, where there is a perfume which no breeze disperses, where there is a taste for food no amount of eating can lessen, and where there is bond of union that no satiety can part. That is what I love when I love my God.[39]

Such prayer is not a separating of spirit and mind from the body, but rather an experience of bringing all the multiple and diverse aspects of ourselves and our experience into communion with the multiple, diverse, relational One who made us and holds us. In the words of Julian of Norwich, "God is in our sensuality."[40] Echoing Augustine, she wrote, "God is closer to us than our own soul, for he is the foundation on which our soul stands, and he is the mean which keeps the substance and the sensuality together, so that they will never separate."[41]

In addition to quiet, contemplative prayer, we also are strengthened and sustained by forms of prayer in which we bring the cares of our heart to God. A relational understanding of God is as hospitable to intercessory prayer as to quiet, wordless meditation. Intercession takes on a different meaning and purpose, however. If God is no longer understood as remote, unchanging monarch, but rather as "verb," the active power of love in the world for healing, renewal, and resurrection, then our prayers of intercession are not petitions to a distant king, but rather, they are a focusing of the desire and compassion we find in relation with God toward the healing and wholeness of ourselves and others.

Even as God passionately desires and loves each of us, God desires and loves every other person and creature. The infinite embrace of God's love connects with the whole created chain of being. We, in turn, are all connected through this vast matrix of God's love for every part of creation. When we pray for another, our compassion resonates with the divine compassion in every part of this matrix, and we may even feel a subjective sense of connection, however far away we are geographically, with the one for whom we pray. There are times when, in prayer, I have even been given a sense of the state of the other person, a sense of healing, struggle, rest, and even the moment of their death. I do not ascribe to this experience any sort of extrasensory perception but, rather, the ineffable sense of the other that may come intersubjectively through immersion in this matrix of divine interconnection. We meet these others within, through the divine connectedness we all share, even as we meet the divine Other within.

When we pray for our family, friends, and ourselves, and for those who come to us for pastoral care or counseling, we find ourselves more able to relinquish the heroic need to rescue. We are restored to the recognition that healing and wholeness come from God, not our own interventions, and that God's love is vast enough to contain all the suffering that is beyond human efforts to save. Healing does happen, not always in the sense of immediate physical or emotional "cure," but in the restoration of self and others to harmony with divine wholeness, that "peace which passeth all understanding," God's eternal love and desire.

Finally, such practices of prayer are not only solitary, nor are they quietistic. The "peace that passeth all understanding" is not to be confused with acquiescence to the world's exercises of dominance through violence and power-over. Immersion in the interconnectedness of all life by meeting the other/others/Other within propels us out again, into communal worship, shared wisdom, and emancipatory practices that promote peace through justice. The labyrinth (Figure 7) is a powerful image for the journey into the heart.

One follows the winding path to the center, to rest awhile in the heart of God, but we cannot remain there, at least in this mortal life. One follows the interior path into communion with the divine Other, but then, having reached the innermost place, the rose at the center, one can rest there only so long. Eventually, one winds one's way back out again, renewed and sometimes even transformed,

Figure 8. Labyrinth and font at Grace Cathedral (Episcopal), San Francisco, California

to make one's way in the outward paths of the world, bringing whatever vision, strength, and compassion one has received back into interaction with the world's travail.

The flow is from solitary prayer to communal prayer and action and back again, seeking sustenance from our experience of God-with-us even as we seek encouragement, challenge, and the bracing winds of difference through community with others. In spite of being immersed in an obscurantist materialist culture, we help each other in community to hold fast to the belief that we are called by God: not to *leave* the world, but to enter ever more deeply *into* life in the world, trying faithfully to live the Good News of love.

A theology of God's intrinsic relationality and passionate love for creation leads, then, quoting LaCugna, from right belief to right action, from orthodoxy to ortho-*praxis* "to exist as persons in communion in a common household, living as persons from and for others, not persons in isolation or withdrawal or self-centeredness . . . Christian orthopraxis must correspond to what we believe is true about God: that God is personal, that God is ecstatic and fecund love, that God's very nature is to exist toward and for another."[42]

In conclusion, an intersubjective understanding of our relationships with both God and other human beings draws us more and more into the affairs of the world, and draws us especially toward those places where exclusion, oppression, and human suffering convict us and pierce our hearts with the cry for solidarity and agapic love.[43] The love and Good News we bring into the care we practice in the parish, in chaplaincy settings, and in the psychotherapy consulting room, from a relational perspective finally must spill over into action to address the wider causes of human suffering due to injustice, unequal distribution of wealth, and heedless degradation of the environment. As Christians who are also citizens, we are called to scrutinize and deconstruct the actions and words of our political leaders in the light of the Gospel message that God shows no partiality but loves all created beings alike.

Through prayer, worship, and a commitment to emancipatory practice, both alone and together with others, our hearts *will* be changed by the living God who calls us into relation with the divine and with one another. In this holy dance of shared wisdom, we join in mutual love and desire with the God who gives life for all, abundant, and eternal. Thus, from a relational perspective, this fluid, multiple, dynamic God of love and compassion is to be found in the interstices, in all the "potential spaces"[44] of our domestic, pastoral, therapeutic, social, political, and institutional life—and finally, in the least-expected places, even within the continents and internal spaces of our own selves.

Notes

Preface

1. This well-known term is borrowed from D. W. Winnicott, "Playing: A Theoretical Statement," in *Playing and Reality* (New York: Basic Books, 1971), 41.

2. For more information on pastoral case study method and process, see, e.g., H. S. Wilson, Takatso Mofokeng, Judo Poerwowidagdo, Robert A. Evans, and Alice Frazer Evans, *Pastoral Theology from a Global Perspective: A Case Study Approach* (Louisville: Westminster John Knox, 1996); Jeffrey Mahan, Barbara Troxell, and Carol Allen, *Shared Wisdom: A Guide to Case Study Reflection in Ministry* (Nashville, Tenn.: Abingdon, 1993); and Donald Capps and Gene Fowler, *The Pastoral Care Case: Learning about Care in Congregations* (St. Louis: Chalice Press, 2001).

Introduction

1. These cases are fictional composites, drawn only in broad outline from numerous real-life situations. Resemblance to any specific individual, living or dead, is coincidental.

2. The counseling profession has debated whether to use the term *patient* or *client,* and *patient* has been largely rejected. In my own clinical work, I have tended to use the term *patient,* following Virginia Beane Rutter in *Woman Changing Woman: Feminine Psychology Re-conceived through Myth and Experience* (San Francisco: HarperCollins, 1993, xiii), because *pathos,* the root of the word *patient* (like "passion"), refers to suffering, while the term *client* connotes a business transaction. While both elements are present in psychotherapy, I prefer to use the term that emphasizes the dimension of empathy with suffering rather than the contractual, consumer aspects of the relationship. Both words, however, convey certain partial truths about the experience of seeking healing and change in the context of a professional therapeutic relationship.

3. Sigmund Freud, "The Future Prospects of Psycho-analytic Therapy" (1910), in *The Standard Edition of the Complete Psychological Works of Sigmund Freud,* ed. and trans. J. Strachey (hereafter cited as *SE*), 11:141–51; and Freud, "Observations on Transference-Love" (1915), *SE* 12:157–71.

4. This view actually goes back at least as far as the 1950s, primarily based on Paula Heimann, "On Counter-transference," *International Journal of Psycho-analysis* 31 (1950): 81–84; and Heimann, "Counter-transference," *British Journal of Medical Psychology* 33 (1960): 9–15. See also D. W. Winnicott, "Hate in the Countertransference," *International Journal of Psycho-analysis* 30 (1949): 69–75. Even earlier traces of this view can be found in the work of one of Freud's first disciples, Sandor Ferenczi, in *Further Contributions to the Theory and Technique of Psycho-analysis* (London: Hogarth, 1926) and "The Confusion of Tongues between Adults and the Child: The Language of Tenderness and Passion" (1933), in *Final Contributions to the Problems and Methods of Psycho-analysis,* ed. M. Balint, trans. E. Mosbacher (London: Hogarth, 1955), 156–67.

5. Otto Kernberg, "Notes on Countertransference," *Journal of the American Psychoanalytic Association* 13 (1965): 38–56.

6. The terms *helper* and *helpee* are used here to refer in general to the two sides of any pastoral helping relationship, most broadly defined. The term *helpee* is meant to include anyone who is the recipient of pastoral care or counseling, including a parishioner or congregation member, a hospital patient receiving a chaplain's visit, a member of the armed forces seeking the counsel of a chaplain, and any counselee, client, or psychotherapy patient. *Helper* refers to any trained pastoral caregiver, including both the lay and the ordained pastor, priest, or rabbi, pastoral visitor, eucharistic minister, Stephen minister, chaplain, and pastoral counselor or psychotherapist. Some chapters will use more specific terms in reference to more specific helping roles.

7. E.g., Robert D. Stolorow and George E. Atwood, eds., *Faces in a Cloud: Intersubjectivity in Personality Theory*, rev. ed. (Northvale, N.J.: Jason Aronson, 1994); Robert D. Stolorow, George E. Atwood, and Bernard Brandchaft, eds., *The Intersubjective Perspective* (Northvale, N.J.: Jason Aronson, 1995); Donna M. Orange, George E. Atwood, and Robert D. Stolorow, *Working Intersubjectively: Contextualism in Psychoanalytic Practice* (Hillsdale, N.J.: Analytic Press, 2001).

8. This process is similar to one presented in Jody Messler Davies and Mary Gail Frawley, *Treating Adult Survivors of Childhood Sexual Abuse: A Psychoanalytic Perspective* (New York: Basic Books, 1994).

9. Pamela Cooper-White, "Soul-Stealing: Power Relations in Pastoral Sexual Abuse," *Christian Century*, February 20, 1991, 196–99; and idem, *The Cry of Tamar: Violence against Women and the Church's Response* (Minneapolis: Fortress Press, 1995).

10. E.g., Cooper-White, *The Cry of Tamar;* Carrie Doehring, *Taking Care: Monitoring Power Dynamics and Relational Boundaries in Pastoral Care and Counseling* (Nashville, Tenn.: Abingdon, 1995); Marie Fortune, *Is Nothing Sacred? When Sex Invades the Pastor-Parishioner Relationship* (San Francisco: Harper & Row, 1989); idem, *Clergy Misconduct: Sexual Abuse in the Ministerial Relationship Workshop Manual* (Seattle: Center for the Prevention of Sexual and Domestic Violence, 1992); Glen O. Gabbard, ed., *Sexual Exploitation in Professional Relationships* (Washington, D.C.: American Psychological Association, 1989); Nancy Hopkins and Mark Laaser, eds., *Restoring the Soul of a Church: Healing Congregations Wounded by Clergy Sexual Misconduct* (Collegeville, Minn.: Interfaith Sexual Trauma Institute/Alban Institute, 1995); Kenneth S. Pope, Janet L. Sonne, and Joan Holroyd, eds., *Sexual Feelings in Psychotherapy: Explorations for Therapists and Therapists-in-Training* (Washington, D.C.: American Psychological Association, 1993); Peter Rutter, *Sex in the Forbidden Zone* (Los Angeles: Jeremy Tarcher, 1989); Gary Schoener et al., *Psychotherapists' Sexual Involvement with Clients: Intervention and Prevention* (Minneapolis: Walk-In Counseling Center, 1989); among many others.

11. Pamela Cooper-White, "The Use of the Self in Psychotherapy: A Comparative Study of Pastoral Counselors and Clinical Social Workers," *American Journal of Pastoral Counseling* 4, no. 4 (2001): 5–35.

12. Doehring, *Taking Care*. See also, from a self psychological view, Arnold Goldberg's explication of the concept of sexualization of a usually nonsexual activity, "the intrusion of the sexual drive into an arena where it does not belong," as evidence of structural weakness or deficiency in the structure of the self, in *The Problem of Perversion: The View from Self Psychology* (New Haven: Yale University Press, 1995), 29. Robert Stoller, in *Perversion: The Erotic Form of Hatred* (New York: Jason Aronson, 1975) and *Observing the Erotic Imagination* (New Haven: Yale University Press, 1985), and Joyce McDougall, in *Plea for a Measure of Abnormality* (New York: Brunner/Mazel, 1992), further investigate the role of aggression in "normal" and "abnormal" expressions of sexuality.

1. Countertransference: A History of the Concept

1. Sigmund Freud, "The Future Prospects of Psychoanalytic Therapy" (1910), in *The Standard Edition of the Complete Psychological Works of Sigmund Freud*, ed. and trans. J. Strachey (New York: W. W. Norton, 2000) (hereafter cited as *SE*), 11:141–51; and Freud, "Observations of

Transference-Love" (1915), in *SE* 12:157–71. In spite of its seeming relevance, countertransference is not mentioned at all in Freud's comprehensive and important paper "The Dynamics of the Transference" (1912), in *SE* 12:99ff., nor does it appear in any of the later writings on clinical practice.

2. Freud, "The Future Prospects of Psychoanalytic Therapy," 144–45.

3. Freud, "Observations on Transference-Love," 164.

4. Sigmund Freud, "Recommendations to Physicians Pracccticing Psycho-analysis" (1912), in *SE* 12:115.

5. Sigmund Freud, "Fragment of an Analysis of a Case of Hysteria" (1905), in *SE* 7:7–122.

6. For a detailed history of this relationship, see A. Carotenuto, *A Secret Symmetry: Sabina Spielrein between Jung and Freud,* trans. A. Pomerans, J. Shepley, and K. Winston (New York: Pantheon, 1982); and Jean Kerr, *A Most Dangerous Method: The Story of Jung, Freud, and Sabina Spielrein* (New York: Vintage, 1993). Spielrein's complete diary from the years 1909–1912 and the correspondence among Spielrein, Jung, and Freud are reproduced in Carotenuto, *A Secret Symmetry,* 3–127.

7. Cited in Michael J. Tansey, "Sexual Attraction and Phobic Dread in the Countertransference," *Psychoanalytic Dialogues* 4, no. 2 (1994): 143.

8. Cited in Tansey, "Sexual Attraction and Phobic Dread," 144.

9. Freud, "Observations on Transference-Love," 169–70.

10. Freud, "Fragment of an Analysis of a Case of Hysteria."

11. Sigmund Freud, "Notes upon a Case of Obsessional Neurosis" (1909), in *SE* 10:155–318.

12. Sigmund Freud, "The Dynamics of the Transference" (1912), in *SE* 12:99ff.

13. Freud, "Dynamics of the Transference," 108.

14. Ibid.

15. Carotenuto, *A Secret Symmetry;* and Kerr, *A Most Dangerous Method.* Freud had become involved with Spielrein as a consultant to repair the damage caused by what Jung himself later called his "piece of knavery."

16. Cited in Tansey, "Sexual Attraction and Phobic Dread," 144.

17. Spielrein published a total of thirty-one papers in journals including the *Jahrbuch für Psychoanalytische und Psychopathologische Forschungen, Imago,* and the *Internationale Zeitschrift für Ärtzlihe Psychoanalyse.* Twelve of these appeared during the critical years of her relationship with Jung and Freud, 1911–1915.

18. Tansey, "Sexual Attraction and Phobic Dread."

19. Sandor Ferenczi and Otto Rank, *The Development of Psychoanalysis* (New York: Dover, 1956; orig. publ. 1923).

20. Sandor Ferenczi, "Child-Analysis in the Analysis of Adults" (1931), in *Final Contributions to the Problems and Methods of Psycho-analysis* (London: Hogarth, 1955), 133; and Ferenczi, "The Confusion of Tongues between Adults and the Child" (1933), in *Final Contributions,* 159.

21. These discussions of transference and countertransference were an outgrowth of Freud's fairly early "topographical model," first articulated in "The Interpretation of Dreams" (1900), in *SE,* vol. 5. At the same time Ferenczi was advancing his "active technique," Freud's work had taken a very different turn, building upon his earlier discovery of the Oedipus complex (also first named in "The Interpretation of Dreams") but taking new form with the advancement of the theory of the "drives" or "instincts" in "Beyond the Pleasure Principle" (1920), in *SE* 18:3–69. With "The Ego and the Id" (1923), in *SE* 19:3–66, Freud consolidated his new "structural theory" of ego, id, and superego. Those who were most vocally opposed to Ferenczi in the next generation, including Anna Freud—e.g., *The Ego and the Mechanisms of Defense* (New York: International Universities Press, 1966; orig. publ. 1936)—were conceptualizing countertransference in terms of ego defenses, that is, the displacement onto the analyst of sexual and aggressive wishes from the oedipal period. This view made transference interpretations become central to the therapeutic process but assigned no particular interest to countertransference. This model viewed the

analyst as a neutral, objective observer making insight-provoking interpretations at considerable remove from any emotional turmoil, which was seen as belonging entirely to the patient.

22. Alice Balint and Michael Balint, "On Transference and Countertransference," *International Journal of Psycho-analysis* 20 (1939): 223–30.

23. Michael Balint, *The Basic Fault* (London: Tavistock, 1968).

24. Balint and Balint, "On Transference and Countertransference," 228.

25. The only other significant reference to countertransference during this period was a brief mention of the concept by Helene Deutsch in "Occult Processes Occurring during Psychoanalysis" (1926), in *Psychoanalysis and the Occult,* ed. G. Devereux (New York: International Universities Press, 1953), 133–46. Although her viewpoint was mainly classical, Deutsch did suggest that there might be occasions where the analyst would identify with a patient from his or her own developmental experiences, and that this could be the basis for "intuitive empathy." Although Theodor Reik never used the term *countertransference,* he also advocated for the therapist to attend to his or her own affective responses to the patient in *Surprise and the Psychoanalyst* (New York: E. P. Dutton, 1937), 193.

26. Melanie Klein, "Notes on Some Schizoid Mechanisms," *International Journal of Psycho-analysis* 27 (1946): 99–110.

27. Paula Heimann, "On Countertransference," *International Journal of Psycho-analysis* 31 (1950): 81–84. See also Heiman, "Counter-transference," *British Journal of Medical Psychology* 33 (1960): 9–15. These papers alternated in print with two vigorous classical rebuttals by Annie Reich, "On Counter-transference," *International Journal of Psycho-analysis* 32 (1951): 25–31; and "Further Remarks on Countertransference," *International Journal of Psycho-analysis* 41 (1960): 389–95. Reich insisted, especially in her second paper, on the analytic posture of emotional neutrality out of respect for the patient's emotional autonomy. She argued against losing oneself in one's own affective reactions, thereby running the risk of "substituting a retranslation of her own feelings into those of the patient" ("Further Remarks," 392). In spite of her polemical tone and (in my view) incorrect prediction that the expansion of the concept of the countertransference would lead down a blind alley, Reich made a point that has continuing value today: there does need to be a balance between attention to the inner and outer life of the patient, both past and present, and between affective/intuitive and rational processes in the therapist.

28. D. W. Winnicott, "Hate in the Countertransference" (1949), in D. W. Winnicott, *Collected Papers: Through Paediatrics to Psycho-analysis* (New York: Brunner/Mazel, 1992), 194–203.

29. Opposition in addition to Annie Reich's came mainly from other classical theorists, both British (e.g., Edward Glover, Ella Sharpe) and American (e.g., Rene Spitz), who took up much the same position as Reich during the 1940s and 1950s. Robert Fliess (not to be confused with Freud's contemporary Wilhelm Fliess), in "Countertransference and Counteridentification," *Journal of the American Psychoanalytic Association* 1 (1953), forged a compromise position that was widely accepted. He differentiated between "trial identifications" and countertransference. The former were transient and only in the service of understanding the patient more fully. Fliess saw countertransference, however, as stimulating identifications from the therapist's own past that might have little to do with the patient at all. This, warned Fliess, was "a danger situation" (quoting Freud, "Analysis Terminable and Interminable" (1937), *SE* 23:211–53) that, using Freud's surgical metaphor, had the potential to contaminate the "sterile surgical field" of psychoanalysis. In France, Lacan (review of Margaret Little, "Countertransference" in *The Seminars of Jacques Lacan: Book I—Freud's Papers on Technique 1953–1954* [Cambridge, England: Cambridge University Press, 1988], 30–33; "Michael Balint's Blind Alleys: The Object Relation and the Intersubjective Relation," in *The Seminars of Jacques Lacan: Book I,* 209–19) scathingly rejected "Michael Balint's blind alleys," based on his general repudiation of any real knowability between two subjects. He considered Balint and Little to be mistaking as mutual recognition a mutual gaze across a vast gap between the two subjects of analyst and patient, only partially bridged by language. What the Balints and Little took for the analyst's attunement and the patient's ac-

knowledgment was, rather, simply a manifestation of the human desire for symmetry, as in a mirror, and not a real connection, which in Lacan's view was impossible. Lacan's view of the new theories of countertransference were not widely influential, however, outside of his own French circle. The openness to a broader definition of countertransference and its usefulness eventually began to be assimilated into classical analysts' thinking.

30. Nicholas Wright, *Mrs. Klein* (London: Nick Hern Books, 1998).

31. For a more detailed history of this relationship, see Janet Sayers, *Mothers of Psychoanalysis* (New York: W. W. Norton, 1991), 232.

32. Heimann, "On Countertransference," 81.

33. Ibid.

34. Ibid.

35. Ibid.

36. Ibid., 82.

37. Ibid.

38. Ibid.

39. Ibid., 83.

40. Ibid.

41. Ibid.

42. Winnicott, "Hate in the Countertransference."

43. D. W. Winnicott, "Counter-Transference" (1960), in *Maturational Processes and the Facilitating Environment* (London: Hogarth, 1965), 158–65.

44. Winnicott, "Hate in the Countertransference," 199.

45. Ibid., 195. Winnicott never abandoned the more classical view of the countertransference. In "Metapsychological and Clinical Aspects of Regression within the Psycho-analytical Set-up" (1954), in *Through Paediatrics to Psycho-analysis,* 289–94, he described countertransference as a type of reaction formation and "a limitation." In "Counter-Transference," Winnicott also disagreed with Jungian analyst Michael Fordham and with Jung's ("The Psychology of the Transference" [1946] in R. F. C. Hall, trans., *The Complete Works of C. G. Jung,* Bollingen Series 20, Vol. 16 [Princeton, N.J.: Princeton University Press, 1966], 163–326) concept of the transference/countertransference relationship as an alchemical *coniunctio* or symbolic marriage between analyst and patient. Winnicott refuted Fordham's idea that transference is a universal phenomenon in all relationships. He went on to say that countertransference contains "neurotic features *which spoil the professional attitude* and disturb the course of the analytic process as determined by the patient" ("Counter-Transference," 162; emphasis original).

46. For more detail on this concept in Winnicott's theory, see Winnicott, "The Antisocial Tendency" (1956), in *Through Paediatrics to Psycho-analysis,* 305–15.

47. For more on Winnicott's concepts of "True Self" and "False Self," see Winnicott, "Ego Distortions in Terms of True and False Self" (1960), in *Maturational Processes and the Facilitating Environment,* 140–52.

48. Winnicott, "Metapsychological and Clinical Aspects of Regression."

49. Winnicott, "Playing: a Theoretical Statement," in *Playing and Reality* (New York: Basic Books, 1979), 41.

50. D. W. Winnicott, "The Use of an Object and Relating through Identifications" (1969), in *Playing and Reality,* 86–94.

51. Margaret Little, "Winnicott Working in Areas Where Psychotic Anxieties Predominate: A Personal Record," *Free Associations* 3 (1985): 9–42.

52. Margaret Little, *Transference Neurosis and Transference Psychosis: Toward Basic Unity* (New York: Jason Aronson, 1986; a compilation of papers orig. publ. 1951–1965).

53. Racker's work constitutes the most systematic and highly technical codification of the British school's formulations on countertransference; see also Heinrich Racker, *Transference and*

Counter-transference (London: Hogarth; New York: International Universities Press, 1968). Racker further distinguished between "direct countertransference" in relation to the patient and "indirect countertransference" in relation to others such as the patient's family members, a referral source, or the therapist's own supervisor. Racker further differentiated between two types of identification with the patient in the countertransference: "Concordant identifications" are identifications by which the therapist feels empathically attuned with the patient. "Complementary identifications," a product of the patient's projective identification, are identifications with split-off unconscious parts of the patient's psyche, often archaic internal objects, and can result in a negative, judgmental stance or even retaliation toward the patient if not recognized.

54. Wilfred Bion, "Language and the Schizophrenic," in *New Directions in Psycho-analysis,* ed. M. Klein, P. Heimann, and R. E. Money-Kyrle (London: Hogarth, 1955), 220–39.

55. Ibid., 224.

56. Wilfred Bion, *Experiences in Groups and Other Papers* (London: Tavistock, 1961; repr. New York: Ballantine, 1974).

57. Harry Stack Sullivan, *The Interpersonal Theory of Psychiatry* (New York: W. W. Norton, 1953).

58. Frieda Fromm-Reichmann, *Principles of Intensive Psychotherapy* (Chicago: University of Chicago Press, 1950). See also Fromm-Reichmann, "Clinical Significance of Intuitive Processes of the Psychoanalyst," *Journal of the American Psychoanalytic Association* 3 (1955): 82–88.

59. Erich Fromm, *Escape from Freedom* (New York: Avon, 1941); and Fromm, *Man for Himself* (Greenwich, Conn.: Fawcett, 1947).

60. For a more detailed discussion of the contributions of the interpersonal school to the theory of countertransference, see Lawrence Epstein and Arthur H. Feiner, *Countertransference* (New York: Jason Aronson, 1979).

61. Fromm-Reichmann, *Principles of Intensive Psychotherapy,* 107–118.

62. *Funny Face,* directed by Stanley Donen (Paramount Pictures, 1957). Thanks to Deborah Hellerstein for making this connection.

63. E.g., Epstein and Feiner, *Countertransference,* 29.

64. During the same period, others were also writing influential papers on the topic of empathy from a more classical ego psychological perspective. Examples include Roy Schafer, *Aspects of Internalization* (New York: International Universities Press, 1981; orig. publ. 1959); and Ralph R. Greenson, "The Struggle against Identification," *Journal of the American Psychoanalytic Association* 2 (1954): 200–217. Schafer suggested that the therapist's ego function could provide sufficient mastery to allow for a "controlled regression," which in turn would lead to "generative empathy." More controversially, he proposed that there could be a "conflict free interplay of projective and introjective mechanisms" (p. 346). Greenson similarly suggested that the therapist would develop a "working model" of the patient, internalized over time, which made empathic identification possible. In the 1970s David Beres, Jacob Arlow, and David A. Shapiro were continuing investigations of empathy from an ego psychological viewpoint. See David Beres and Jacob Arlow, "Fantasy and Identification in Empathy," *Psychoanalytic Quarterly* 43 (1974): 26–50; and David A. Shapiro, "Empathy, Warmth and Genuineness in Psychotherapy," *British Journal of Social and Clinical Psychology* 8 (1969): 350–61. Beres and Arlow related empathy, intuition, and fantasy and identified the role of "signal affect" as a way the therapist could be triggered to shift away from useful identificatory thinking and feeling with the patient to thinking therapeutically about the patient. In the same year, Shapiro endeavored to delineate various categories of identification and link these with accurate versus distorted empathic understandings of the patient. There was also a parallel effort in clinical psychology to classify empathy in a scientific, empirical way: Charles B. Truax, "A Scale for the Measurement of Accurate Empathy," *Psychiatric Institute Bulletin* 1 (1961): 1–21; Barton A. Singer and Lester Luborsky, "Countertransference: The Status of Clinical vs. Quantitative Research," in *Effective Psychotherapy: Handbook of Research,* ed. A. Gurman

and A. Razin (New York: Pergamon Press, 1977), 433–51; David Liberman, "Affective Response of the Analyst to the Patient's Communications," *International Journal of Psycho-analysis* 59 (1978): 335–40; and Daniel Buie, "Empathy: Its Nature and Limitations," *Journal of the American Psychoanalytic Association* 29 (1981): 281–307. It remains to be seen—and is debatable on philosophical grounds—whether empathy will (or even should) lend itself to quantifiable scientific scrutiny.

65. E.g., Robert Fliess, "Metapsychology of the Analyst," *Psychoanalytic Quarterly* 11 (1942): 211–27; and Annie Reich herself in "On Counter-transference."

66. Heinz Kohut, "Introspection, Empathy and Psychoanalysis: An Examination of the Relationship between Mode of Observation and Theory," *Journal of the American Psychoanalytic Association* 7 (1959): 459–83.

67. Ibid.; and Kohut, "Introspection, Empathy, and the Semi-circle of Mental Health," *International Journal of Psycho-analysis* 63 (1982): 395–407.

68. Kohut, "Introspection, Empathy and Psychoanalysis"; and Kohut, *The Analysis of the Self* (New York: International Universities Press, 1971).

69. E.g., Heinz Kohut, "The Two Analyses of Mr. Z," *International Journal of Psycho-analysis* 60 (1979): 3–27.

70. Kohut, *The Analysis of the Self.* Kohut also developed the understanding of how empathy works in the therapeutic relationship in "The Psychoanalytic Treatment of Narcissistic Personality Disorders," *Psychoanalytic Study of the Child* 23 (1968): 86–113.

71. Kohut, *The Analysis of the Self*; and A. Goldberg, ed., with P. E. Stepansky, *How Does Analysis Cure?* (Chicago: University of Chicago Press, 1984).

72. For more detailed reviews of the psychoanalytic literature in the 1970s and 1980s and technical debates about the mechanisms of projection and introjection, see Michael Gorkin, *The Uses of Countertransference* (Northvale, N.J.: Jason Aronson, 1987); Lawrence Epstein and Arthur H. Feiner, *Countertransference* (New York: Jason Aronson, 1979); idem, *Countertransference: The Therapist's Contribution to the Therapeutic Situation* (Northvale, N.J.: Jason Aronson, 1995); and Michael J. Tansey and Walter F. Burke, *Understanding Countertransference: From Projective Identification to Empathy* (Hillsdale, N.J.: Analytic Press, 1989).

73. E.g., Carl Rogers, *Counseling and Psychotherapy* (Boston: Houghton Mifflin, 1942); Carl Rogers, *On Becoming a Person* (Boston: Houghton Mifflin, 1961); Virginia Satir, *Conjoint Family Therapy*, rev. ed. (Palo Alto: Science and Behavior Books, 1967); Murray Bowen, *Family Therapy in Clinical Practice* (New York: Jason Aronson, 1978); and Salvador Minuchin, *Family Kaleidoscope* (Cambridge: Harvard University Press, 1984).

74. Daniel Stern, *The Interpersonal World of the Infant* (New York: Basic Books, 1994).

75. E.g., Jacques Lacan, *Écrits: A Selection*, trans. B. Fink (New York: W. W. Norton, 2002).

76. E.g., Julia Kristeva, *The Kristeva Reader*, ed. Toril Moi (New York: Columbia University Press, 1986); Hélène Cixous, *The Hélène Cixous Reader* (New York: Routledge, 1994); Hélène Cixous, *Stigmata: Escaping Texts* (New York: Routledge, 1998); Luce Irigaray, *Speculum of the Other Woman*, trans. G. Gill (Ithaca, N.Y.: Cornell University Press, 1985).

77. E.g., Stephen A. Mitchell, *Relationality: From Attachment to Intersubjectivity* (Hillsdale, N.J.: Analytic Press, 2000); Stephen A. Mitchell and Lewis Aron, eds., *Relational Psychoanalysis: The Emergence of a Tradition* (Hillsdale, N.J.: Analytic Press, 1999); Lewis Aron, *A Meeting of Minds: Mutuality in Psychoanalysis* (Hillsdale, N.J.: Analytic Press, 1996); Jessica Benjamin, *The Bonds of Love: Psychoanalysis, Feminism and the Problem of Domination* (New York: Pantheon, 1988); idem, *Like Subjects, Love Objects: Essays on Recognition and Sexual Difference* (New Haven: Yale University Press, 1995); Phillip Bromberg, *Standing in the Spaces: Clinical Process, Trauma, and Dissociation* (Hillsdale, N.J.: Analytic Press, 1998); Jodie Messler Davies, "Love in the Afternoon: A Relational Reconsideration of Desire and Dread in the Countertransference," *Psychoanalytic Dialogues* 4, no. 2 (1994): 153–70; idem, "Dissociation, Repression, and Reality Testing in the Countertransference," *Psychoanalytic Dialogues* 6, no. 2 (1996): 189–219; idem, "Descending the

Slippery Slopes: Slippery, Slipperier, Slipperiest," *Psychoanalytic Dialogues* 10, no. 2 (2000): 219–30; Davies with Mary Frawley, *Treating Adult Survivors of Childhood Sexual Abuse: A Psychoanalytic Perspective* (New York: Basic Books, 1994); Irwin Hoffman, "Some Practical Implications of a Social-Constructivist View of the Psychoanalytic Situation," *Psychoanalytic Dialogues* 2, no. 3 (1992): 287–304; Theodore J. Jacobs, "Posture, Gesture and Movement in the Analyst: Cues to Interpretation and Countertransference," *Journal of the American Psychoanalytic Association* 21 (1973): 77–92; idem, "On Countertransference Enactments," *Journal of the American Psychoanalytic Association* 34, no. 2 (1986): 289–307; idem, *The Use of the Self Countertransference and Communication in the Analytic Situation* (Hillsdale, N.J.: Analytic Press, 1989); Stephen Mitchell, *Relational Concepts in Psychoanalysis* (Cambridge: Harvard University Press, 1988); Thomas Ogden, *Subjects of Analysis* (Northvale, N.J.: Jason Aronson, 1994); Ogden, *Reverie and Interpretation: Sensing Something Human* (Northvale, N.J.: Jason Aronson, 1997); and Otto Renik, "Analytic Interaction: Conceptualizing Technique in Light of the Analyst's Irreducible Subjectivity," *Psychoanalytic Quarterly* 62 (1993): 553–71.

2. The History of Countertransference in Pastoral Care and Counseling

1. Information on CPE training and certification is available from the Association for Clinical Pastoral Education, Decatur, Ga. (http://www.acpe.edu).

2. A more detailed history of pastoral care and counseling up to about 1980 is offered in E. Brooks Holifield, *A History of Pastoral Care in America: From Salvation to Self-Realization* (Nashville, Tenn.: Abingdon, 1983).

3. Ibid.

4. Ibid.; see also Orlo Strunk, "Emmanuel Movement," in *Dictionary of Pastoral Care and Counseling*, ed. R. J. Hunter (Nashville, Tenn.: Abingdon, 1990), 350–51.

5. William James, *The Varieties of Religious Experience* (New York: Longmans, 1902).

6. Holifield, *History of Pastoral Care in America*.

7. Charles A. Van Wagner II, *AAPC in Historical Perspective 1963–1991* (Fairfax, Va.: American Association of Pastoral Counselors, 1992), 1–14.

8. Anton Boisen, *The Exploration of the Inner World: A Study of Mental Disorders and Religious Experience* (Philadelphia: University of Pennsylvania Press, 1971; orig. publ. 1936).

9. Ibid.; see also Charles Gerkin, *The Living Human Document: Revisioning Pastoral Counseling in a Hermeneutical Mode* (Nashville, Tenn.: Abingdon, 1973).

10. Wayne Oates, *Protestant Pastoral Counseling* (Philadelphia: Westminster, 1962).

11. Seward Hiltner, *Pastoral Counseling* (New York: Abingdon, 1949).

12. E.g., Paul E. Johnson, *Psychology of Pastoral Care* (Nashville, Tenn.: Abingdon-Cokesbury, 1953).

13. Carl Rogers, *Counseling and Psychotherapy* (Boston: Houghton Mifflin, 1942); and idem, *On Becoming a Person* (Boston: Houghton Mifflin, 1961).

14. E.g., Thomas Oden, *Kerygma and Counseling* (Philadelphia: Westminster, 1966); idem, *Contemporary Theology and Psychotherapy* (Philadelphia: Westminster, 1967); Carroll Wise, *The Meaning of Pastoral Care* (New York: Harper & Row, 1966).

15. E.g., Russell Leslie Dicks, *Principles and Practices of Pastoral Care* (Philadelphia: Fortress Press, 1966).

16. Van Wagner, *AAPC in Historical Perspective*, 1–14.

17. Howard Clinebell, *Basic Types of Pastoral Care and Counseling: Resources for the Ministry of Healing and Growth* (Nashville, Tenn.: Abingdon, 1966; rev. ed. 1984).

18. In fact, before the publication of Clinebell's book, Rogers's own *Counseling and Psychotherapy* (New York: Houghton Mifflin, 1942) was a standard textbook for seminary courses in pastoral care. See Bonnie Miller-McLemore, "The Living Human Web: Pastoral Theology at

the Turn of the Century," in *Through the Eyes of Women: Insights for Pastoral Care,* ed. Jeanne Stevenson Moessner (Minneapolis: Fortress Press, 1996), 13.

19. William A. Clebsch and Charles R. Jaekle, *Pastoral Care in Historical Perspective* (Englewood Cliffs, N.J.: Prentice Hall, 1964).

20. Clinebell made a single reference to "transference," in the context of a brief mention of "psychoanalytic pastoral psychotherapy." He stated that this form of therapy was engaged with the analysis of dreams, fantasies, and transference feelings and followed this with a strong caveat that it should not be undertaken by any pastor without specialized training and supervision. Clinebell, *Basic Types of Pastoral Care and Counseling,* 275.

21. Karl Menninger, *Theory of Psychoanalytic Technique* (Northvale, N.J.: Jason Aronson, 1995; orig. publ. 1958).

22. Kenneth R. Mitchell, "Menninger, Karl (1893–)," in *Dictionary of Pastoral Care and Counseling,* ed. Rodney J. Hunter (Nashville, Tenn.: Abingdon, 1990), 707–8.

23. Karl Menninger, *Whatever Became of Sin?* (New York: Hawthorne, 1973).

24. Karl Menninger, *Love against Hate* (New York: Harcourt, Brace, 1989).

25. Karl Menninger, *Man against Himself* (New York: Harcourt, Brace, 1989).

26. Seward Hiltner and Karl Menninger, *Constructive Aspects of Anxiety* (Nashville, Tenn.: Abingdon, 1963).

27. Menninger, *Theory of Psychoanalytic Technique,* 77–98. Menninger's main citations included Sigmund Freud, Anna Freud, Edward Glover, Annie Reich, and others firmly rooted in the classical tradition, such as Otto Fenichel, Daniel Lagache, Ida Macalpine, and Robert Waelder.

28. Ibid., 88.

29. Here *interpersonal* refers to the psychoanalytic influence of Harry Stack Sullivan, described in chapter 1, e.g., Sullivan, *The Interpersonal Theory of Psychiatry* (New York: W. W. Norton, 1953).

30. Wayne Oates, ed., *Introduction to Pastoral Counseling* (Nashville, Tenn.: Broadman Press, 1959). In this volume, Samuel Southard cited Menninger in advocating for attention to the emotional health of the pastoral counselor (pp. 41–52). In the same anthology, Richard Young warned against problems of pastors attempting counseling beyond seven to ten sessions (p. 149), and James Lyn Elder emphasized the formation of pastoral counselors' attitudes as central to the pastoral task (pp. 53–65). Thomas Klink, who once worked at the Menninger Clinic, wrote about countertransference directly but only once in passing, defining it as the restimulation of infantile conflicts that may also have influenced clergy's vocational choice, in *Depth Perspectives in Pastoral Work* (Philadelphia: Fortress Press, 1965).

31. E. Mansell Pattison, "Transference and Countertransference in Pastoral Care," *Journal of Pastoral Care* 19 (1965): 193–202.

32. Sullivan, *Interpersonal Theory of Psychiatry.*

33. Menninger, *Theory of Psychoanalytic Technique.*

34. Maurice E. Wagner, "Role Conflict and Countertransference in the Pastor-Counselors," *Journal of Psychology and Theology* 1 (1973): 58–65. Wagner brought a focus on countertransference as classically defined into a discussion of other potential conflicts between "pastor-counselors'" roles as both clergyperson and counselor.

35. Paul E. Johnson, *Person and Counselor* (Nashville, Tenn.: Abingdon, 1967).

36. Charles A. Curran, *Religious Values in Counseling and Psychotherapy* (New York: Sheed and Ward, 1969).

37. Ana-Maria Rizzuto, *The Birth of the Living God: A Psychoanalytic Study* (Chicago: University of Chicago Press, 1979).

38. Paul Pruyser adopted the medical concept of diagnosis but did not turn specifically to

psychology or psychoanalysis and never used the terms *transference* or *countertransference* in *The Minister as Diagnostician: Personal Problems in Pastoral Perspective* (Philadelphia: Westminster, 1976).

39. Episcopal theologian Urban T. Holmes attempted a blend of Anglican tradition and Jungian images to articulate the role of the priest/minister in *Ministry and Imagination* (New York: Seabury, 1976) and *The Priest in Community: Exploring the Roots of Ministry* (New York: Seabury, 1978).

40. Don Browning, *The Moral Context of Pastoral Care* (Philadelphia: Westminster, 1976).

41. E.g., Paul Tillich, *The Courage to Be* (New Haven: Yale University Press, 1952).

42. E.g., Rollo May, *The Meaning of Anxiety* (New York: Ronald Press, 1950); and idem, *Love and Will* (New York: W. W. Norton, 1969).

43. Charles Gerkin, *The Living Human Document: Revisioning Pastoral Counseling in a Hermeneutical Mode* (Nashville, Tenn.: Abingdon, 1973), 11.

44. David Tracy, *Blessed Rage for Order: The New Pluralism in Theology* (New York: Seabury, 1975).

45. Seward Hiltner, *Theological Dynamics* (Nashville, Tenn.: Abingdon, 1972).

46. Carroll Wise, *Pastoral Psychotherapy: Theory and Practice* (Northvale, N.J.: Jason Aronson, 1983), 209–16.

47. Ibid., 210.

48. E.g., Margaret Kornfeld, *Cultivating Wholeness: A Guide to Care and Counseling in Faith Communities* (New York: Continuum, 1998).

49. Miller-McLemore, "The Living Human Web," 14.

50. E.g., Larry Kent Graham, *Care of Persons, Care of Worlds: A Psychosystems Approach to Pastoral Care and Counseling* (Nashville, Tenn.: Abingdon, 1992); Pamela Couture and Rodney Hunter, eds., *Pastoral Care and Social Conflict* (Nashville, Tenn.: Abingdon, 1995); Howard Clinebell, *Ecotherapy: Healing Ourselves, Healing the Earth* (Binghamton, N.Y.: Haworth Press, 1996).

51. The first pioneers, Edward Wimberly and Archie Smith Jr., developed pastoral theologies from the Black Church experience. See Edward Wimberly, *Pastoral Care in the Black Church* (Nashville, Tenn.: Abingdon, 1979); idem, *Pastoral Counseling and Spiritual Values: A Black Point of View* (Nashville, Tenn.: Abingdon, 1982); idem, *African American Pastoral Care* (Nashville, Tenn.: Abingdon: 1991); idem, *Counseling African American Couples and Families* (Louisville, Ky.: Westminster John Knox, 1997); idem, "The Cross-Culturally Sensitive Person"; idem, "Methods of Cross-Cultural Pastoral Care: Hospitality and Incarnation," *Journal of the Inter-denominational Theological Center* 23, no. 3 (1998): 170–202; and Archie Smith Jr., *The Relational Self: Ethics and Therapy from a Black Church Perspective* (Nashville, Tenn.: Abingdon, 1982). These publications were followed in the 1990s by Womanist pastoral theologians Linda Hollies, Emilie Townes, Marsha Foster Boyd, and Carroll Watkins Ali, who sought to integrate insights from African American theology and feminism with the unique experience, history, and culture of Black women. Linda Hollies, *Womanist Care: How to Tend the Souls of Women* (Joliet, Ill.: Woman to Woman Ministries, 1992); Emilie M. Townes, *A Troubling in My Soul: Womanist Perspectives on Evil and Suffering* (Maryknoll, N.Y.: Orbis, 1993); Marsha Foster Boyd, "Womanist Care: Some Reflections on Pastoral Care and the Transformation of African American Women," in *Embracing the Spirit: Womanist Perspectives on Hope, Salvation and Transformation*, ed. Emilie M. Townes (Maryknoll, N.Y.: Orbis, 1997), 197–202; and Carroll Watkins Ali, *Survival and Liberation: Pastoral Theology in African American Context* (St. Louis: Chalice Press, 1999). For a sample of essays on this subject, see also an anthology, Bonnie J. Miller-McLemore and Brita Gill-Austern, eds., *Feminist and Womanist Pastoral Theology* (Nashville, Tenn.: Abingdon, 1999).

52. Asian, Hispanic, and Native American perspectives are just beginning to be published in the pastoral literature in North America. This is partly because traditionally the whole notion of

pastoral care and counseling has been seen as embedded in an individualistic white, middle-class perspective that does not speak to other cultures' ways of providing spiritual care and emotional healing. As early as 1975, Virgilio Elizondo offered a description of the psychology and religious practices of Mexican-Americans in *Christianity and Culture: An Introduction to Pastoral Theology and Ministry for the Bicultural Community* (Huntington, Ind.: Our Sunday Visitor, 1975). This text provided helpful descriptions of Mexican-American cultural experience; it did not directly address approaches to pastoral care/*consejo pastoral*. Cross-cultural or multicultural approaches to pastoral counseling were mostly first published in the late 1980s by white, male authors and editors who respectfully acknowledged the limitations of their views. E.g., John E. Hinkle, "The Living Human Experience across Culture," in *At the Point of Need: Living Human Experience; Essays in Honor of Carroll A. Wise*, ed. James B. Ashbrook and John E. Hinkle (Landham, Md.: University Press of America, 1988), 185–94; David Augsburger, *Pastoral Counseling across Cultures* (Philadelphia: Westminster, 1986); and idem, *Conflict Mediation across Cultures: Pathways and Patterns* (Louisville, Ky.: Westminster John Knox, 1992). However, more recently, the North American pastoral literature has been enriched by more diverse authors, including Carole Bohn, Benoni Silva-Netto, Samuel Lee, and others. E.g., Carole R. Bohn, ed., *Therapeutic Practice in a Cross-Cultural World: Theological, Psychological, and Ethical Issues*, JPCP Monograph no. 7 (Decatur, Ga.: Journal of Pastoral Care Publications, 1995); Cullene Bryant, "Pastoral Care and Counseling in a Cross-Cultural Context: The Issue of Authority (Philippines)," *Journal of Pastoral Care* 49 (1995): 329–33; Benoni Silva-Netto, "Cultural Symbols and Images in the Counseling Process," *Pastoral Psychology* 42 (1994): 277–84; idem, "Toward a Multicultural Theology of Ministry," *Journal of Asian and Asian American Theology* 1, no. 1 (1996): 21–26; idem, "Pastoral Counseling in a Multicultural Context," *Journal of Pastoral Care* 46 (1992): 131–39; Christie Cozad Neuger, ed., *The Arts of Ministry: Feminist-Womanist Approaches* (Louisville, Ky.: Westminster John Knox, 1996); Kenneth G. Davis and Yolanda Tarango, eds., *Bridging Boundaries: The Pastoral Care of U.S. Latinos* (Scranton, Pa.: University of Scranton Press, 1999); Marsha Foster Boyd and Carolyn Stahl Bohler, "Womanist-Feminist Alliances: Meeting on the Bridge," in *Feminist and Womanist Pastoral Theology*, ed. Bonnie J. Miller-McLemore and Brita L. Gill-Austern (Nashville, Tenn.: Abingdon, 1999); Sharon Thornton, "Honoring Rising Voices: Pastoral Theology as Emancipatory Practice," *Pastoral Theology* 10 (2000): 64–80; and Samuel Lee, "Becoming Multi-cultural Dancers: The Pastoral Practitioner in a Multi-Cultural Society," *Journal of Pastoral Care* 55, no. 4 (2001): 389–95. In addition, pastoral theological works from a global perspective by Jorge Maldonado (Ecuador), Emmanuel Lartey (Ghana), Masamba MaMpolo (Congo), and others have been more widely available and increasingly influential in the North American context. See Jorge Maldonado, "My Basic Assumptions in Pastoral Counseling of Hispanic Families," *Covenant Quarterly* 42 (1994): 19–28; Emmanuel Lartey, *In Living Colour: An Intercultural Approach to Pastoral Care and Counseling* (London and Herndon, Va.: Cassell, 1997). See also Masamba MaMpolo, "Cultural Collisions: A Perspective from Africa," in *Handbook for Basic Types of Pastoral Care and Counseling (in Honor of Howard Clinebell)*, ed. Howard Stone and William Clements (Nashville, Tenn.: Abingdon, 1991), 103–20; Wilhelmina J. Kalu, "Gospel and Pastoral Counselling in Africa," in *Pastoral Care and Context*, ed. O. Stange (Nashville, Tenn.: Abingdon, 1992); Robert J. Wicks and Barry K. Estadt, eds., *Pastoral Counseling in a Global Church: Voices from the Field* (Maryknoll, N.Y.: Orbis, 1993); Emmanuel Lartey, Daisy Nwachuku, and Kasonga wa Kasonga, eds., *The Church and Healing: Echoes from Africa* (Frankfurt am Main: Peter Lang, 1994); Masamba MaMpolo, "Spirituality and Counselling for Healing and Liberation: The Context and Praxis of African Pastoral Activity and Psychotherapy," in Lartey et al., *The Church and Healing*, 11–34; Ernest Talibuddin, "Reflections on a Pastoral Ministry in a Pluralistic Society," *Bulletin of the Henry Martyn Institute of Islamic Studies* 15 (1996): 96–102; Philip Culbertson (New Zealand), "Pastoral Theology and Multiculturalism," *Anglican Theological Review* 79 (1997): 163–91; Christoph Schneider-Harpprecht (Brazil), "Aconselhamento Pastoral e

Diversidade," *Estudos Téologicos* 37, no. 1 (1997): 73–91; and Daniel Schipani (Brazil), "Psicología y Consejo Pastoral: Perspectivas Hispanas," *Apuntes* 18 (1998): 28.

53. E.g., Maxine Glaz, "Reconstructing the Pastoral Care of Women," *Second Opinion* 17, no. 2 (1991); Carrie Doehring, "Developing Models of Feminist Pastoral Counseling," *Journal of Pastoral Care* 46, no. 1 (1992): 23–31; Valerie DeMarinis, *Critical Caring: A Feminist Model for Pastoral Psychology* (Louisville, Ky.: Westminster John Knox, 1993); Christie Cozad Neuger, "Pastoral Theology and Pastoral Counseling: A Work in Progress," *Journal of Pastoral Theology* 2 (1992): 35–57; and idem, *Counseling Women: A Narrative, Pastoral Approach* (Minneapolis: Fortress Press, 2001).

54. E.g., Pamela Couture, *Blessed Are the Poor? Women's Poverty, Family Policy, and Practical Theology* (Nashville, Tenn.: Abingdon, 1991); Carroll Saussy, *God Images and Self Esteem: Empowering Women in a Patriarchal Society* (Louisville, Ky.: Westminster John Knox, 1991); Bonnie Miller-McLemore, *Also a Mother: Work and Family as Theological Dilemma* (Nashville, Tenn.: Abingdon, 1994); and Pamela Cooper-White, *The Cry of Tamar: Violence against Women and the Church's Response* (Minneapolis: Fortress Press, 1995). Three comprehensive anthologies containing essays on feminist perspectives in pastoral care and counseling also appeared in the 1990s and 2000, filling a gap in the pastoral literature with authoritative handbooks for pastoral caregivers working with women: Maxine Glaz and Jeanne Stevenson Moessner, eds, *Women in Travail and Transition: A New Pastoral Care* (Minneapolis: Fortress Press, 1991); Jeanne Stevenson Moessner, ed., *Through the Eyes of Women: Insights for Pastoral Care* (Minneapolis: Fortress Press, 1996); and Moessner, ed., *In Her Own Time: Women and Developmental Issues in Pastoral Care* (Minneapolis: Fortress Press, 2000).

55. E.g., Katherine Ragsdale, ed., *Boundary Wars: Intimacy and Distance in Healing Relationships* (Cleveland: Pilgrim Press, 1996).

56. Bert Cunin, Beth Cunin, and Sharona Benoff, "The Fifth Commandment and Orthodox Jews in Psychotherapy: Interventions, Transference and Countertransference," *Journal of Psychology and Judaism* 19 (1995): 241–49; Robert J. Wicks, "Countertransference and Burnout in Pastoral Counseling," in *Clinical Handbook of Pastoral Counseling* 1, ed. Robert Wicks et al. (New York: Integration Books/Paulist Press, 1985), 76–96; J. Stephen Muse, "Some Countertransference Distortions of Relationship between Male Pastors and Their Female Parishioners," *Journal of Pastoral Care* 46 (1992): 299–308; Bonnie Genevay and Renée S. Katz, "Countertransference and Older Clients," *Journal of Psychology and Christianity* 12 (1990): 181–92; idem, *Countertransference and Older Clients* (Newbury Park, Calif.: Sage, 1990); Pierre Emmanuel Lacocque and Anthony J. Loeb, "Death Anxiety: A Hidden Factor in Countertransference Hate," *Journal of Religion and Health* 27 (1988): 95–108; Suzanne Murphy Coyle, "A Covenanting Process in Pastoral Home Visits," *Journal of Pastoral Care* 39 (1985): 96–109. Additionally, David M. Moss and Carl W. Christensen investigated therapists' personal poetry as a possible means for recognizing countertransference in the classical sense, in "The Therapist's Poetry as a Therapeutic Incident," *Pastoral Psychology* 33 (1985): 273–87. Arthur Reisel considered countertransference from a Jungian point of view, in "The Trickster Made Me Laugh! A Study in Unexpected Laughter and Countertransference," *Journal of Pastoral Counseling* 24 (1989): 86–94.

57. John McDargh, "Crucial Observations Which Need to Be Extended: Commentary on 'Psychopathology, Sin and the DSM,'" *Journal of Psychology and Theology* 22 (1994): 277–85; Peter Cohen, "An Interesting Contradiction: A Study of Religiously Committed, Psychoanalytically Oriented Clinicians," *Journal of Psychology and Theology* 22 (1994): 304–18; Robert Carbo and John Gartner, "Can Religious Communities Become Dysfunctional Families? Sources of Countertransference for the Religiously Committed Psychotherapist," *Journal of Psychology and Theology* 22 (1994): 264–71; Bruce Narramore, "Are Religious Therapists More Susceptible to Countertransference? Commentary on 'Can Religious Communities Become Dysfunctional Families?' (Reply to Robert Carbo and John Gartner)," *Journal of Psychology and Theology* 22 (1994): 264–74; Timothy Kochems, "Countertransference and Transference Aspects of Religious Material in

Psychotherapy: The Isolation of Integration of Religious Material," in *Exploring Sacred Landscapes: Religious and Spiritual Experiences in Psychotherapy,* ed. Mary Lou Randour (New York: Columbia University Press, 1993); Nancy Kehoe and Thomas Gutheil, "Ministry or Therapy: The Role of Transference and Countertransference in a Religious Therapist," in Randour, *Exploring Sacred Landscapes;* and Donald Cole, "Haloing: An Investigation of the Implications of Shared Religious Identity in the Pastoral Counseling Relationship" (PhD diss., Garrett-Evangelical Theological Seminary, 1993). See also Timothy Kochems, "The Relationship of Background Variables to the Experiences and Values of Psychotherapists in Managing Religious Material" (PhD diss., George Washington University, 1983).

58. A combined search for the terms *countertransference* and *pastoral* in three databases—Dissertations Abstracts, PsycINFO, and the American Theological Library Association (ATLA) database—uncovered only seven dissertations since 1983, and none at all before 1969. The earliest dissertation dealing with countertransference and pastoral counseling was John Biersdorf's "Appraising the Presuppositions of the Pastoral Counselor: Some Applications of Michael Polanyi's Understanding of Personal Knowledge and Psychoanalytic Investigations of Countertransference to Issues in Pastoral Counseling" (PhD diss., Union Theological Seminary, New York, 1969). While very interesting, this dissertation introduced a line of philosophical investigation that has not been developed further by others.

59. Howard E. Friend, "A Training Text and Workshop to Identify and Work Creatively with Dynamics of Transference and Countertransference in the Pastoral Helping Relationship" (DMin project, Eastern Baptist Theological Seminary, 1977).

60. Gregory Scott Elkins, "The Development and Implementation of a Divorced Persons' Support Group" (DMin project, Drew University, 1985); Wayne Kendall, "Pastors' Countertransference in Relation to a Difficult Church" (PhD diss., Boston University, 1992).

61. William J. Collins, "The Pastoral Counselor's Countertransference as a Therapeutic Tool," *Journal of Pastoral Care* 36 (1982): 125–35.

62. Otto F. Kernberg, "Notes on Countertransference," *Journal of the American Psychoanalytic Association* 13 (1965): 38–56.

63. Joseph Sandler, "Countertransference and Role-Responsiveness," *International Review of Psycho-analysis* 3 (1976): 43–47.

64. Gary Ahlskog, "The Paradox of Pastoral Psychotherapy," *Journal of Pastoral Care* 41 (1987): 311–18. In a more recent anthology, *The Guide to Pastoral Counseling and Care,* ed. Gary Ahlskog and Harry Sands (Madison, Conn.: Psychosocial Press, 2000), Ahlskog and coauthor Alida Margolin refer to new uses of countertransference but define countertransference idiosyncratically in terms of actual enactments, not the therapist's feelings. The authors warn against overreliance on a totalist understanding of countertransference as an avoidance of the therapist's own unconscious contribution to the therapeutic situation.

65. Chris Schlauch, "Defining Pastoral Psychotherapy," *Journal of Pastoral Care* 41 (1987): 319–27. This emphasis was not carried into Schlauch's more recent overview of pastoral counseling, *Faithful Companioning: How Pastoral Counseling Heals* (Minneapolis: Fortress Press, 1995).

66. Richard Schwartz, "A Psychiatrist's View of Transference and Countertransference in the Pastoral Relationship," *Journal of Pastoral Care* 43 (1989): 42–46.

67. *Contra* Ahlskog, "Paradox of Pastoral Psychotherapy"; and Schlauch, "Defining Pastoral Psychotherapy."

68. Richard G. Bruehl, in Hunter, *Dictionary of Pastoral Care and Counseling,* 239–41.

69. Three very brief British dictionary entries also reflect awareness of the totalist view: D. D. Howell, "Transference," in *A Dictionary of Pastoral Care,* ed. Alastair Campbell (London: SPCK; New York: Crossroad, 1987), 284–85; J. R. Guy, "Transference," in *New Dictionary of Christian Ethics and Pastoral Theology,* ed. David Atkinson (Downers Grove, Ill., and Leicester, England: InterVarsity Press, 1995), 861; and "Countertransference" in Wesley Carr, ed., *The New Dictionary*

of Pastoral Studies (London: SPCK; Grand Rapids, Mich.: Eerdmans, 2002), 77. British pastoral counselor Barrie Hinksman, while using a largely classical definition of countertransference, also distinguishes between "proactive" (neurotic) and "reactive" (induced) countertransference and acknowledges the complexity of the transference-countertransference dynamic. Hinksman, "Transference and Countertransference," in *Clinical Counselling in Pastoral Settings*, ed. Gordon Lynch (London: Routledge, 1999), 94–106, terminology based on Petrushka Clarkson, *The Therapeutic Relationship in Psychoanalysis, Counselling Psychology and Psychotherapy* (London: Whurr, 1995).

70. Hans-Friedrich Stängle, "Countertransference in Ministry: 'The Best of Servants, but the Worst of Masters'" (PhD diss., Iliff School of Theology and University of Denver, 1996).

71. In a similar vein, Mary Lautzenhiser Fraser wrote a four-case study, "The Use of Transitional Space in Pastoral Counseling: Psychological and Theological Meaning Making" (unpublished PhD dissertation, Claremont School of Theology, 1996), in which she explored the utility of Winnicottian concepts of transitional space and transitional objects to effect healing in the pastoral sense of awareness of life as holy. Both Stängle and Fraser advocate the integration of psychoanalytic constructs—particularly drawing on object relations—into pastoral care and counseling.

72. Randour, *Exploring Sacred Landscapes.*

73. Rizzuto, *The Birth of the Living God.*

74. John McDargh, *Psychoanalytic Object Relations Theory and the Study of Religion* (Lanham, Md.: University Press of America, 1983); see also McDargh, "Concluding Clinical Postscript: On Developing a Psychotheological Perspective," in Randour, *Exploring Sacred Landscapes*, 172–93.

75. A number of other books and articles have been written recently by scholars of psychology and religion grappling with the integration of religion and psychoanalytic thought. For an overview of this literature, see Diane Jonte-Pace and William Parsons, eds., *Religion and Psychology: Mapping the Terrain* (New York: Routledge, 2000). See also James Jones, *Religion and Psychology in Transition: Psychoanalysis, Feminism, and Theology* (New Haven: Yale University Press, 1991); idem, *Contemporary Psychoanalysis and Religion: Transference and Transcendence* (New Haven: Yale University Press, 1993); Diane Jonte-Pace, *Speaking the Unspeakable: Religion, Misogyny, and the Uncanny Mother in Freud's Cultural Texts* (Berkeley: University of California Press, 2000); idem, "Object Relations Theory, Mothering, and Religion: Toward a Feminist Psychology of Religion," *Horizons* 14, no. 2 (1987): 310–27; idem, "Situating Kristeva Differently: Psychoanalytic Readings of Woman and Religion," in *Body/Text in Julia Kristeva: Religion, Women and Psychoanalysis*, ed. David Crownfield (Albany, N.Y.: SUNY Press, 1992), 1–22; idem, "At Home in the Uncanny: Freudian Representations of Death, Mothers, and the Afterlife," *Journal of the American Academy of Religion* 64 (1996): 61–88; Kirk Bingaman, *Freud and Faith: Living in the Tension* (Albany, N.Y.: SUNY Press, 2003). While these publications have important implications for clinical practice, they do not appear to have been widely disseminated beyond the academic community.

3. The Relational Paradigm: Postmodern Concepts of Countertransference and Intersubjectivity

1. For a discussion of "power-over" and "power-with," see Pamela Cooper-White, *The Cry of Tamar: Violence against Women and the Church's Response* (Minneapolis: Fortress Press, 1995), 31–40; Martha Ellen Stortz, *Pastor Power* (Nashville, Tenn.: Abingdon, 1993). See also Michel Foucault, *Power/Knowledge: Selected Interviews and Other Writings, 1972–1977*, ed. and trans. Colin Gordon (New York: Pantheon, 1980); Roy Herndon SteinhoffSmith, *The Mutuality of Care* (St. Louis: Chalice Press, 1999); and Judith Orr, "Review of 'The Mutuality of Care,'" *Journal of Pastoral Theology* 10 (2000): 126–29.

2. The term *intersubjectivity* in psychotherapy is a development of self psychology, found in Robert D. Stolorow and George E. Atwood, eds., *Faces in a Cloud: Intersubjectivity in Personality*

Theory, rev. ed. (Northvale, N.J.: Jason Aronson, 1994); Robert D. Stolorow, George E. Atwood, and Bernard Brandchaft, eds., *The Intersubjective Perspective* (Northvale, N.J.: Jason Aronson, 1995); and Donna M. Orange, George E. Atwood, and Robert D. Stolorow, *Working Intersubjectively: Contextualism in Psychoanalytic Practice* (Hillsdale, N.J.: Analytic Press, 2001).

3. The term *relational* here refers to a parallel development in object relations theory, first articulated by Stephen Mitchell in *Relational Concepts in Psychoanalysis: An Integration* (Cambridge: Harvard University Press, 1988). The "relational" school of psychoanalysis now includes numerous authors, especially those represented in the journal *Psychoanalytic Dialogues.* The term *relational* is also used by feminist writers affiliated with the Jean Baker Miller Institute (formerly the Stone Center for Developmental Services and Studies), Wellesley College (http://www.wcwonline.org), e.g., Jean Baker Miller, *Toward a New Psychology of Women,* 2d ed. (Boston: Beacon Press, 1987); Alexandra G. Kaplan, Jean Baker Miller, Irene Pierce Stiver, Janet L. Surrey, and Judith V. Jordan, *Women's Growth in Connection* (New York: Guilford Press, 1991); Judith Jordan, ed., *Women's Growth in Diversity* (New York: Guilford Press, 1997); Jean Baker Miller and Irene Pierce Stiver, *The Healing Connection: How Women Form Relationships in Therapy and Life* (Boston: Beacon Press, 1997).These authors challenge the developmental ideal of an autonomous self, replacing it with the paradigm of "self-in-relation." Both schools of thought have roots in Sullivanian interpersonal theory, and both value reciprocity and mutuality in the therapeutic relationship. The psychoanalytic group tends to emphasize unconscious relationship more, while the Stone Center group takes a more explicitly feminist view of the social and political dimensions of persons and relationships, particularly gender oppression.

4. I am using the term *paradigm* in the scientific and not the general sense, as articulated by Thomas Kuhn in *The Structure of Scientific Revolutions,* 2d ed. (Chicago: University of Chicago Press, 1970). The intersubjective, or relational, paradigm presents a comprehensive enough worldview and epistemology, and transpired as a sufficiently abrupt and revolutionary break with the previous prevailing Cartesian model, to fit Kuhn's model of how scientific "paradigm shifts" take place in a mainly revolutionary rather than evolutionary manner.

5. E. M. Forster, *Howard's End* (New York: Knopf, 1921; orig. publ. 1910), ch. 22, p. 214.

6. William Safire, "On Language: Connect! The New Imperative to Establish Rapport," *New York Times Magazine,* July 29, 2001, 18–20.

7. There are various uses of the term *modernism,* including late-nineteenth- and early-twentieth-century revolutionary movements in art, politics, and theology. The term is used here in the sense of what preceded "postmodernism" and as a corollary to positivism.

8. Richard Bernstein, *Beyond Objectivism and Relativism: Science, Hermeneutics, and Praxis* (Philadelphia: University of Pennsylvania Press, 1983). See also Egon Guba, "The Alternative Paradigm Dialog," in *The Paradigm Dialog,* ed. E. Guba (Newbury Park, Calif.: Sage Publications, 1990), 19.

9. John Caputo, *Radical Hermeneutics: Repetition, Deconstruction, and the Hermeneutic Project* (Bloomington: Indiana University Press, 1987), 262. See also Patti Lather, "Reinscribing Otherwise: The Play of Values in the Practices of the Human Sciences," in Guba, *The Paradigm Dialog,* 315–32.

10. See especially Zygmunt Bauman, *Modernity and the Holocaust* (Ithaca, N.Y.: Cornell University Press, 1989). This disillusionment was foreshadowed by the decline of optimistic philosophy in the wake of the Lisbon earthquake of 1755. Leibniz's "best of all possible worlds" collapsed in the face of ten thousand deaths in one night. See Jürgen Moltmann, "The Question of Theodicy and the Pain of God," in *History and the Triune God: Contributions to Trinitarian Theology,* trans. John Bowden (New York: Crossroad, 1992), 28–29.

11. Ibid., cited in Thomas Docherty, "Postmodernism: An Introduction," in *Postmodernism: A Reader,* ed. Thomas Docherty (New York: Columbia University Press, 1993), 12.

12. For further discussion of this point, see Docherty, "Postmodernism: An Introduction," 12ff.

13. Many other writers could be named and discussed in this chapter. I have selected only a few. Fissures in the Western Modernist universalizing worldview can be traced as early as some eighteenth- and nineteenth-century philosophers, including Kant, Hegel, and especially Nietzsche (see Jürgen Habermas, "The Entry into Postmodernity: Nietzsche as a Turning Point," in Docherty, *Postmodernism: A Reader*, 51–61). However, the movement to challenge tacit Western assumptions of privilege and preeminence began in earnest in the mid-twentieth century around the onset of World War II with the writings of Theodor Adorno and the Frankfurt School. These challenges blossomed in the 1960s and 1970s with such French writers as Gilles Deleuze, *Difference and Repetition*, trans. Paul Patton (New York: Columbia University Press, 1995; orig. publ. 1968); Jean Baudrillard, *Simulacra and Simulation*, trans. Sheila Glaser (Ann Arbor: University of Michigan Press, 1995); Jean-François Lyotard, *The Postmodern Condition: A Report on Knowledge*, trans. Geoff Bennington and Brian Massumi (Minneapolis: University of Minnesota Press, 1984; orig. publ. 1979); and, in America, Richard Rorty, *Philosophy and the Mirror of Nature* (Princeton, N.J.: Princeton University Press, 1981). An important thinker who also challenged modern Western assumptions of power from an explicitly political analysis was Jürgen Habermas, whose writings at Frankfurt in the generation after Adorno might be seen as a bridge between Marxist social theory and postmodern philosophy. E.g., Habermas, *Legitimation Crisis*, trans. Thomas McCarthy (Boston: Beacon Press, 1975); Habermas, *The Theory of Communicative Action: Reason and the Rationalization of Society*, trans. Thomas McCarthy (Boston: Beacon Press, 1985); and idem, *The Inclusion of the Other: Studies in Political Theory*, ed. Pablo DeGreiff and Ciaran Cronin (Cambridge: MIT Press, 2000).

14. E.g., Foucault, *Power/Knowledge*.

15. Docherty, "Postmodernism: An Introduction," 13.

16. For more discussion on this point, particularly regarding the role of reason, see ibid., 14.

17. E.g., Jacques Derrida, *Writing and Difference*, trans. Alan Bass (Chicago: University of Chicago Press, 1978).

18. E.g., Elisabeth Schüssler Fiorenza, *In Memory of Her: A Feminist Theological Reconstruction of Christian Origins* (New York: Crossroad, 1994); idem, *Wisdom Ways: Introducing Feminist Biblical Interpretation* (Maryknoll, N.Y.: Orbis, 2001); Letty Russell, *Feminist Interpretation of the Bible* (Louisville, Ky.: Westminster John Knox, 1991).

19. E.g., Joseph Natoli, *Postmodern Journeys: Film and Culture 1996–1998* (Albany, N.Y.: SUNY Press, 2001), and other titles in the SUNY Series in Postmodern Culture.

20. Jacques Derrida, "White Mythology," in *Margins of Philosophy*, trans. Alan Bass (Chicago: University of Chicago Press, 1982), 213.

21. Simone de Beauvoir, *The Second Sex*, trans. H. M. Parshley (New York: Knopf, 1953), cited in Deborah Anna Luepnitz, "Bateson's Heritage: Bitter Fruit," *Family Therapy Networker* (September/October 1988): 49.

22. Julia Kristeva has written numerous volumes in both French and English, including *In the Beginning Was Love* (New York: Columbia University Press, 1987); *Strangers to Ourselves*, trans. Leon Roudiez (New York: Columbia University Press, 1994); and, with Catherine Clément, *The Feminine and the Sacred*, trans. Jane Marie Todd (New York: Columbia University Press, 2001). For an anthology of selected writings, see also Kristeva, *The Kristeva Reader*, ed. Toril Moi (New York: Columbia University Press, 1986).

23. Luce Irigaray, *The Sex Which Is Not One*, trans. Catherine Porter and Carolyn Burke (Ithaca, N.Y.: Cornell University Press, 1985); idem, *Speculum of the Other Woman*, trans. Gillian Gill (Ithaca, N.Y.: Cornell University Press, 1985); and idem, *An Ethics of Sexual Difference*, trans. Carolyn Burke and Gillian Gill (Ithaca, N.Y.: Cornell University Press, 1993). For an anthology of selected writings, see also Irigaray, *The Luce Irigaray Reader*, ed. Margaret Whitford, trans. David Macey (London: Blackwell, 1991). For a third important French feminist essayist, not discussed in detail in the present chapter, see also Hélène Cixous, *"Coming to Writing" and*

Other Essays, ed. Deborah Jenson (Cambridge: Harvard University Press, 1992); idem, *Stigmata* (London: Routledge, 1998); and idem, *The Hélène Cixous Reader,* ed. Susan Sellers (London: Routledge, 1994).

24. Many of Lacan's writings in French remain untranslated in English. A good beginning collection of translated essays is Jacques Lacan, *Écrits: A Selection,* trans. Alan Sheridan (New York: W. W. Norton, 1977). A number of books about Lacan are now appearing. Two good introductions are Bruce Fink, *A Clinical Introduction to Lacanian Psychoanalysis: Theory and Technique* (Cambridge: Harvard University Press, 1999), written for psychotherapists, and Joël Dor, *Introduction to the Reading of Lacan: The Unconscious Structured like a Language,* ed. Judith Feher Gurewich, trans. Susan Fairfield (New York: Other Press, 1998), emphasizing the linguistic dimension of Lacan's psychoanalytic theory and practice.

25. Guba, "The Alternative Paradigm Dialog," 19; see also Lather, "Reinscribing Otherwise."

26. Tom McDonough, "In Memory of Carl Sagan: Star-Stuff," *Skeptic* 4, no. 4 (1996): 10–17, reprinted at http://www.skeptic.com/0.4.sagan-tribute.html.

27. John Polkinghorne, *Quarks, Chaos, and Christianity* (New York: Crossroad, 1997), 55–56.

28. Phrase adopted from seminal text in the sociology of knowledge by Peter Berger and Thomas Luckman, *The Social Construction of Reality* (Garden City, N.Y.: Doubleday, 1966).

29. There are several competing alternatives to the positivist paradigm. Egon Guba, in *The Paradigm Dialog,* summarizes these as Postpositivism or Critical Realism (which in the humanities is also referred to as Nonfoundationalism), Critical Theory (which is also similar to Poststructuralism in literary criticism), and Constructivism (and Social Constructionism, e.g., Berger and Luckman, *The Paradigm Dialog*). These fall on a spectrum from the least radical departure from positivism to the most. Postpositivism (see Denis Phillips, "Postpositivistic Science: Myths and Realities," in Guba, *The Paradigm Dialog,* 31–45) retains the Enlightenment belief that there is a reality "out there" that obeys natural laws, but rejects the confidence of positivism that it is possible to know that reality in an objective, distanced way. Postpositivist epistemologies emphasize the impact of the observer on the observed and the impossibility of ridding oneself of bias or embeddedness in context. There are no a priori foundations or standards existing apart from nature by which knowledge or truth can be authoritatively asserted. Critical theory (see Thomas Popkewitz, "Whose Future? Whose Past?" in Guba, *The Paradigm Dialog,* 46–66) shares these assumptions of postpositivism but adds the emphasis, drawing from Marx, Weber, and Durkheim, on social and political context and the impossibility of value-free knowledge. Critical theory attempts to uncover hidden values and biases in stated truth claims, particularly those that contribute to social, political, and economic oppression. The Frankfurt School, French structuralism, literary poststructuralism, sociology of knowledge, cultural Marxism, and feminist theory all utilize this epistemology. Contructivism is the most radical alternative to positivism, as described in this chapter. (See Guba, *The Paradigm Dialog,* 25–27; Irwin Z. Hoffman, "Discussion: Toward a Social-Constructivist View of the Psychoanalytic Situation," *Psychoanalytic Dialogues* 1 (1991): 74–105; and idem, "Some Practical Implications of a Social-Constructivist View of the Analytic Situation," *Psychoanalytic Dialogues* 2 (1992): 287–304. See also idem, "The Patient as Interpreter of the Analyst's Experience," *Contemporary Psychoanalysis* 19 (1983): 389–422; and Hoffman, *Ritual and Spontaneity in the Psychoanalytic Process: A Dialectical-Constructivist View* (Hillsdale, N.J.: Analytic Press, 1998).

30. Immanuel Kant, *Critique of Pure Reason,* ed. and trans. Paul Guyer and Allen Wood (Cambridge, Mass.: Cambridge University Press, 1998; orig. publ. 1780).

31. Friedrich Nietzsche, "The Epistemological Starting Point," cited in Luepnitz, "Bateson's Heritage," 52.

32. Ibid.

33. See Denis Phillips, "Postpositivistic Science: Myths and Realities," in Guba, *The Paradigm Dialog,* 31–45.

34. Thomas Popkewitz, "Whose Future? Whose Past?" in Guba, *The Paradigm Dialog,* 46–66.

35. Berger and Luckman, *Social Construction of Reality.* For application to the field of psychology, see also Kenneth Gergen, "The Social Constructionist Movement in Modern Psychology," *American Psychologist* 40, no. 3 (1985): 266–75.

36. Thanks to Joseph Palombo, Institute for Clinical Social Work, Chicago, whose own schematics on the philosophical strands within psychoanalysis helped me formulate this graphic representation.

37. John Polkinghorne, 1991 Trinity Institute Lecture Series, Trinity Episcopal Church, New York; and idem, *Quarks, Chaos and Christianity* (New York: Crossroad, 1977), 58–59.

38. William Arndt and F. Wilbur Gingrich, *Greek-English Lexikon of the New Testament,* translation and adaptation of Lexikon by Walter Bauer (Chicago: University of Chicago Press, 1971), 23; and *Analytical Greek Lexikon* (Grand Rapids, Mich.: Zondervan, 1972), 91.

39. Arndt and Gingrich, *Greek-English Lexikon,* 506; and *Analytical Greek Lexikon,* 264.

40. Buber, *I and Thou.*

41. Kuhn, *Structure of Scientific Revolutions.*

42. Jessica Benjamin, *The Bonds of Love: Psychoanalysis, Feminism, and the Problems of Domination* (New York: Pantheon, 1998); idem, *Shadow of the Other: Intersubjectivity and Gender in Psychoanalysis* (New York and London: Routledge, 1998); and idem, *Like Subjects, Love Objects: Essays on Recognition and Sexual Difference* (New Haven: Yale University Press, 1998).

43. E.g., Roy Schafer, *Retelling a Life: Narration and Dialogue in Psychoanalysis* (New York: Basic Books, 1994); see also clinical social work theorist Carolyn Saari, *The Creation of Meaning in Clinical Social Work* (New York: Guilford Press, 1991); and idem, "The Created Relationship: Transference, Countertransference and the Therapeutic Culture," *Clinical Social Work Journal* 14, no. 1 (1987): 39–51.

44. The term *intersubjectivity* was first developed by theorists working from a self psychology framework and developing a very similar, parallel movement to "relational theory," with its origins in object relations and interpersonal psychoanalysis (Stolorow and Atwood, *Faces in a Cloud*). The term has slowly been adopted into relational theory and other contemporary psychoanalytic writings more generally.

45. In the most rigorous discussions within postmodern philosophy, the "subject" itself has become a matter of some crisis, due to the impossibility from a postmodern perspective for the subject to reflect with any sort of accuracy on itself. Alain Badiou, *Théorie du sujet* (Paris: Seuil, 1982). Docherty writes, "In the postmodern, it has become difficult to make the proposition 'I know the meaning of postmodernism'—not only because the postmodern is a fraught topic, but also because the 'I' who supposedly knows is itself the site of a postmodern problematic." Docherty "Postmodernism: An Introduction," 5.

46. Jodie Messler Davies, "Love in the Afternoon: A Relational Reconsideration of Desire and Dread in the Countertransference," *Psychoanalytic Dialogues* 4, no. 2 (1994): 153–70; idem, "Dissociation, Repression, and Reality Testing in the Countertransference: False Memory in the Psychoanalytic Treatment of Adult Survivors of Childhood Sexual Abuse," *Psychoanalytic Dialogues* 6, no. 2 (1996): 189–219; idem, "Descending the Slippery Slopes: Slippery, Slipperier, Slipperiest," *Psychoanalytic Dialogues* 10, no. 2 (2000): 219–30; and Jodie Messler Davies and Mary Frawley, *Treating Adult Survivors of Childhood Sexual Abuse: A Psychoanalytic Perspective* (New York: Basic Books, 1994).

47. Jody Messler Davies, "Multiple Perspectives on Multiplicity," *Psychoanalytic Dialogues* 8, no. 2 (1998): 195.

48. Davies, "Dissociation, Repression, and Reality Testing in the Countertransference," 197. See also Adrienne Harris, "This model of consciousness is less archaeologically organized and

more a set of surfaces or representations with boundaries of varying permeability," writing in "False Memory? False Memory Syndrome? The So-Called False Memory Syndrome?" *Psychoanalytic Dialogues* 6, no. 2 (1996): 159, n. 2.

49. Philip Bromberg, "'Speak! That I May See You': Some Reflections on Dissociation, Reality, and Psychoanalytic Listening," *Psychoanalytic Dialogues* 4, no. 4 (1994): 517–47.

50. Robert Emde, "The Affective Self: Continuities and Transformation from Infancy," in *Frontiers of Infant Psychiatry* 2, ed. J. D. Call et al. (New York: Basic Books, 1984), 38–54; idem, "The Prerepresentational Self and Its Affective Core," *Psychoanalytic Study of the Child* 38 (1983): 165–92.

51. Daniel Stern, *The Interpersonal World of the Infant* (New York: Basic Books, 1985).

52. Beatrice Beebe and Frank M. Lachmann, "The Contribution of Mother-Infant Mutual Influence to the Origins of Self- and Object Representations," in *Relational Perspectives in Psychoanalysis,* ed. N. J. Skolnick and S. C. Warshaw (Hillsdale, N.J.: Analytic Press, 1992), 83–117.

53. Stern's "representations of interactive experience as generalized" (RIGs), ibid.

54. Jean-Martin Charcot, *Clinical Lectures on Diseases of the Nervous System,* trans. T. Savill (London: New Sydenham Society, 1889).

55. Pierre Janet, *The Major Symptoms of Hysteria* (New York: Macmillan, 1907).

56. Sandor Ferenczi, "The Confusion of Tongues between Adults and Children: The Language of Tenderness and Passion," in *Final Contributions to the Problems and Methods of Psychoanalysis,* ed. M. Balint, trans. E. Mosbacher (London: Karnac Books, 1980; orig. publ. 1933), 156–67.

57. Bruce Perry, Richard Pollard, Toi L. Blakley, William L. Baker, and Domenico Vigilante, "Childhood Trauma, the Neurobiology of Adaptation, and Use-Dependent Development of the Brain: How States Become Traits," *Infant Mental Health Journal* 16, no. 4 (1995): 271–91; Bessel van der Kolk, "The Body Keeps the Score: Memory and the Evolving Psychobiology of Post Traumatic Stress," *Harvard Review of Psychiatry* 1, no. 5 (1994): 253–65; Allan N. Schore, "The Effects of Early Relational Trauma on Right Brain Development, Affect Regulation, and Infant Mental Health," *Infant Mental Health Journal* 22 (2001): 201–69.

58. Bessel van der Kolk and Rita Fisler, "Dissociation and the Fragmentary Nature of Traumatic Memories: Overview and Exploratory Study," *Journal of Traumatic Stress* 8 (1995): 505–26.

59. For example, Michael Moskowitz et al., *The Neurobiological and Developmental Basis for Psychotherapeutic Intervention* (Northvale, N.J.: Jason Aronson, 1997); Allan Schore, *Affect Regulation and the Origin of Self* (New York: Lawrence Erlbaum, 1994).

60. Van der Kolk and Fisler, "Dissociation and the Fragmentary Nature of Traumatic Memories," 508, citing the work of L. R. Squire and others.

61. Ibid., 511; Perry et al., "Childhood Trauma, the Neurobiology of Adaptation and Use-Dependent Development of the Brain: How States Become Traits" (available online at http://www.trauma-pages.com/perry96.htm).

62. Van der Kolk, "The Body Keeps the Score." Gender differences also have been seen. Adult males and older male children may be more likely to respond to threat with a fight-or-flight response associated with hormonal hyperarousal and sensitization of brain-stem and midbrain mediated catecholamine systems. Children and adult females are more likely to respond with a freeze-and-surrender reaction, involving CNS activation but also increased vagal tone, increased dopaminergic system activity, and in some cases the appearance of endogenous opioids, which reduce pain sensation and induce dissociative responses. Perry et al., "Childhood Trauma."

63. Van der Kolk and Fisler, "Dissociation and the Fragmentary Nature of Traumatic Memories." See also James Hopper and Bessel van der Kolk, "Retrieving, Assessing, and Classifying Traumatic Memories: A Preliminary Report on Three Case Studies of a New Standardized Method," *Journal of Aggression, Maltreatment, and Trauma* 4 (2001): 33–71.

64. In Elizabeth Loftus's often-cited study of implanting memories of being lost in a shopping mall, only 10 percent of research subjects actually came to accept the story as their own, and 90 percent resisted. Noted in "Miscoding Is Seen as the Root of False Memory," *New York Times*, May 31, 1994, C1, C8; cited in Davies, "Dissociation, Repression and Reality Testing," 193.

65. Cf. Harris, "False Memory?" 171.

66. Donnel Stern likens the constructivist view of memory to figures emerging from a dense fog: "They do have shapes, rough or 'fuzzy' shapes, and those shapes, while allowing a number of interpretations, forbid many others...We are not free to assign any interpretation we please to our experience, not without violating the semiotic regularities of our culture...Such violations are so meaningful that we notice them immediately, and the conclusions we draw from them are either dire or terribly interesting: that is, when the wrong use of signs does not indicate psychosis, it either indicates willful disregard (a lie) or playful disrespect (as in art) of the codes of communication in which we live." Stern, "Commentary on Papers by Davies and Harris," *Psychoanalytic Dialogues* 6, no. 2 (1996): 262–63.

67. The question thus shifts from the narrow forensic one of "Did 'it' happen?" to "What does 'its' presence—in my feelings, senses, thoughts, fantasies, memories, and behavior—mean?" Different meanings will then lead to different choices and actions at different times. There is no one right action (i.e., prescriptions for confrontation, litigation, or forgiveness), and "right" actions will also change over time as meanings continue to grow in subtlety and complexity.

68. Graham Ward, "Introduction, or, A Guide to Theological Thinking in Cyberspace," in *The Postmodern God: A Theological Reader* (Malden, Mass.: Blackwell, 1997), xv.

69. William Bechtel and Adele Abrahamsen, *Connectionism and the Mind: An Introduction to Parallel Processing in Networks* (Cambridge, Mass.: Blackwell, 1991).

70. Jane Flax, "Multiples: On the Contemporary Politics of Subjectivity," in *Disputed Subjects: Essays on Psychoanalysis, Politics and Philosophy* (New York: Routledge, 1993), 93.

71. Christopher Bollas, *The Shadow of the Object: Psychoanalysis of the Unthought Known* (New York: Columbia University Press, 1987).

72. Cf. Carolyn Saari, "Identity Complexity as an Indicator of Mental Health," *Clinical Social Work Journal* 21, no. 1 (1993): 11–23.

73. For further elaboration of the relationship between postmodernism and justice, including an appropriation of Winnicott's *Playing and Reality*, see Jane Flax, "The Play of Justice," in *Disputed Subjects*, 111–128.

74. Buber, *I and Thou*.

75. Even this might be challenged; the postmodern suspicion of rational cognition goes deep. For example, thinking politically about the other can become an exercise in abstraction that distances the other from oneself even while thinking about that other. Citing Adorno and Horkheimer, Docherty writes, "They were anxious that what should be a properly political engagement which involves the Subject in a process called intellection or thinking could be reduced to a ritual of thinking, to a merely formal appearance of thinking which would manifest itself as a legitimation not of a perception of the world but of the analytical modes of mathematical reason itself. The political disturbance of the Subject proposed by an engagement with a materially different Other would be reduced to a confirmation of the aesthetic beauty and validity of the process of mathematical reason itself, a reason whose object would thus be not the world in all its alterity but rather the process of reason which confirms the identity of the Subject, an identity untrammeled by the disturbance of politics. In short, the Subject would be reduced to an engagement with and a confirmation of its own rational processes rather than being committed to an engagement with the material alterity of the world...'Political engagement' would be characterized by the rupture of such ritual, the eruption of history into the consciousness in such a way that the aesthetic or formal structures of consciousness must be disturbed." Docherty, "Postmodernism: An Introduction," 8. Similar arguments have been made regarding literature—that

the meaning of a text is not what the reader abstractly thinks about it, but what the text does to the reader, or "performs" upon him or her, as in J. L. Austin's "performative linguistics" in *How to Do Things with Words* (Cambridge: Harvard University Press, 1975); Kenneth Burke, *Language as Symbolic Action* (Berkeley: University of California Press, 1972); and John R. Searle, *Expression and Meaning: Studies in the Theory of Speech Acts* (Cambridge, Mass.: Cambridge University Press, 1985).

76. Buber, *I and Thou*, 114.

77. Ibid., 123. (Kaufman's translation reads, "the eternal You.")

78. These four areas of subjectivity have also been identified in the traumatology literature as the domains into which traumatic memory may be stored, split off from one another by the protective mechanism of dissociation. See, for example, the BASK model of dissociation developed by Bennet G. Braun in "The BASK Model of Dissociatoin: Clinical Appliations," *Dissociation* 1 no. (1988): 116–23, and discussed in Cooper-White, *The Cry of Tamar*, 152, 158.

79. E.g., Lewis Aron, *A Meeting of Minds: Mutuality in Psychoanalysis* (Hillsdale, N.J.: Analytic Press, 1996); Theodore Jacobs, "Posture, Gesture and Movement in the Analyst: Cues to Interpretation and Countertransference," *Journal of the American Psychoanalytic Association* 21 (1973): 77–92; idem, "On Countertransference Enactments," *Journal of the American Psychoanalytic Association* 34, no. 2 (1986): 289–307; and idem, *The Use of the Self* (Hillsdale, N.J.: Analytic Press, 1989).

80. Ludwig Wittgenstein, *Philosophical Investigations* (Oxford: Blackwell, 1953), cited in Aron, *A Meeting of Minds*, 192. Parallel contemporary trends, not cited, which support this view include Kenneth Burke's *Language as Symbolic Action* and Searle's *Expression and Meaning*.

81. Aron, *A Meeting of Minds*, 192.

82. Jacobs, "Posture, Gesture and Movement in the Analyst"; idem, "On Countertransference Enactments"; and idem, *The Use of the Self.*

83. Carter Heyward, *When Boundaries Betray Us: Beyond Illusions of What Is Ethical in Therapy and Life* (San Francisco: HarperSanFrancisco, 1995); Katherine Ragsdale, ed., *Boundary Wars: Intimacy and Distance in Healing Relationships* (Cleveland: Pilgrim Press, 1996).

84. SteinhoffSmith, *The Mutuality of Care; contra* Orr, "Review of 'The Mutuality of Care.'"

85. For a fuller discussion of professional ethics from a constructivist perspective, see Hoffman, "Some Practical Implications," 287–304. See also Karen Maroda, "Countertransference Techniques: Constructing the Interpersonal Analysis," in *The Power of Countertransference: Innovations in Analytic Technique* (Northvale, N.J.: Jason Aronson, 1991), 110–56.

86. Hoffman, "Some Practical Implications," 303.

87. Joseph Sandler, "Countertransference and Role Responsiveness," *International Review of Psychoanalysis* 3 (1976): 43–47.

88. Hoffman, "Discussion: Toward a Social-Constructivist View," 92; Aron, *A Meeting of Minds*, 87, 96–100 et passim. From a Jungian point of view, see Andrew Samuels, *Jung and the Post-Jungians* (London: Routledge, 1985), 175.

89. Stortz, *Pastor Power;* Cooper-White, *The Cry of Tamar.*

90. Hoffman, "Some Practical Implications," 299.

4. The Relational Paradigm in Pastoral Assessment and Theological Reflection

1. African American spiritual, in *This Far by Faith: An African American Resource for Worship* (Minneapolis: Augsburg Fortress, 1999), hymn 66.

2. Redlining is a racist and economically discriminatory practice, now illegal, in which banks and retail stores draw a "red line" around neighborhoods, usually in the inner city, in which they refuse to locate branches or franchises, deny loans to residents, or provide lower quality services and goods. The term originated in the 1930s in mortgage banking, when, under the New Deal, the Home Owners Loan Corporation (HOLC) devised a four-color rating system to determine neighborhoods' level of eligibility for mortgage loans. "Part of the theory in the

'30s and '40s was that race and prosperity were interconnected. A green neighborhood meant low-risk, while blue and yellow neighborhoods were more risky. Red neighborhoods were considered the riskiest and were to be avoided. As a result of that coding, less than 20 percent of FHA and VHA loans were made to people of color in the 1930s and 1940s." Gary Warth, "Research Project Looking at Red-lining," *The Californian/North County Times,* May 5, 2002, citing researcher Richard Marciano at the University of San Diego. The trend spread to supermarket chains in the 1960s, along with the building of megastores in the suburbs, resulting in serious lack of availability of affordable, fresh food in the inner cities. "As supermarkets close, urban residents must travel further to purchase competitively priced, high quality groceries. Low-income families who tend not to own cars take public transportation or pay for cabs in order to reach larger, cheaper markets in the suburbs. Those lucky enough to have friends willing to carpool may find themselves paying child care costs while they gather their families' groceries. Many residents patronize smaller, independent inner city stores that often lack the wholesale purchasing power of big chains. Customers patronizing corner stores often find retail prices as much as 49% higher for a selection of food long on canned goods and short on fresh meat and produce." Judy Heany and Tamara Hayes, "Redlining Food: How to Ensure Community Food Security," Food First/Institute for Food and Development Policy, http://www.foodfirst.org/progs/humanrts/ redlining.html, also citing Bill Turque, Deborah Rosenberg, and Todd Barrett, "Where the Food Isn't," *Newsweek,* February 24, 1992.

3. Emilie Townes, *Breaking the Fine Rain of Death: African American Health Issues and a Womanist Ethic of Care* (New York: Continuum, 1998).

4. Larry Kent Graham, "From Relational Humanness to Relational Justice: Reconceiving Pastoral Care and Counseling," in *Pastoral Care and Social Conflict,* ed. P. Couture and R. Hunter (Nashville, Tenn.: Abingdon, 1995), 220–34.

5. Betty Carter and Monica McGoldrick, *The Expanded Family Life Cycle: Individual and Social Perspectives,* 3d ed. (Boston: Allyn & Bacon, 1999), 6.

6. I am grateful for consultations from the Rev. Carla Harris, Dr. Eloise Scott, and the Rev. Margaret Tyson, whose rich feedback has helped to bring Linda to voice in relation to the experience of African American women ministers. As a white author of cases with multiple cultural and class dimensions throughout this book, I am aware that I stand on "holy ground," and I approach the task of writing cases with a deep sense of humility and circumspection. I do so out of a commitment to including social and cultural context in our pastoral theological casework, a dimension that has been too long neglected. I have engaged in "vicarious introspection" to the extent that is possible, but true to my own constructivist position, I am aware that one can never fully represent the experiences of another, particularly one outside one's own social location. Each case study is finally meant to tell the story of an individual, with his or her own unique, particular intrapsychic dynamics and social location. Neither Linda, Gary, Terence, nor Sara is intended to be paradigmatic of an entire cultural, ethnic, or class group. I am deeply grateful for the honest, illuminating feedback of readers from diverse backgrounds. Any errors or infelicities of expression are mine alone.

7. Thandeka, in *Learning to Be White: Money, Race, and God in America* (New York: Continuum, 2000), 3, describes an exercise called the Race Game: "The Race Game, as my luncheon partner very quickly discovered, had only one rule. For the next seven days, she must use the ascriptive term white whenever she mentioned the name of one of her Euro-American cohorts. She must say, for instance, 'my white husband, Phil,' or 'my white friend Julie,' or 'my lovely white child Jackie.'... I guaranteed her that if she did this for a week and then met me for lunch, I could answer her question [what it felt like to be black] using terms she would understand. We never had lunch together again. Apparently my suggestion had made her uncomfortable. African Americans have learned to use a racial language to describe themselves and others. Euro-Americans also have learned a pervasive racial language. But in their racial lexicon, their

own racial group becomes the great unsaid [also citing labor historian David Roediger, *Towards the Abolition of Whiteness* (London: Verso, 1994), 12]. I wanted my luncheon partner to give voice to her whiteness as the racial unsaid in her life."

8. Cf. Jacques Derrida, *Positions,* trans. Alan Bass (Chicago: University of Chicago Press, 1985), 39. For Derrida, the "play of differences" and his term *différance* refer to the distance between signifiers and what they signify, in both time and space, erasing all essentialisms. I am using this term to mean *both* this slipperiness of verbal meaning and also the phenomenologically felt differences among various groups as they are socially and culturally constructed through gender, race, class, etc.

9. Emmanuel Lartey, *In Living Colour: An Intercultural Approach to Pastoral Care and Counselling* (London and Herndon, Va.: Cassell, 1997). This distinction was first made by anthropologist Florence Kluckhohn, "Dominant and Variant Value Orientations," in *Personality in Nature, Society, and Culture,* ed. Clyde Kluckholn, Henry Alexander Murray, and D. M. Schneider (New York: Knopf, 1953), 342–57. For more on Kluckhohn's value orientations approach to culture, see Florence Kluckhohn and Frederick L. Strodtbeck, *Variations in Value Orientations* (Evanston, Ill.: Row Peterson, 1961). See also Orlo Strunk Jr., "Multicultural Counseling and the Systemic Notion: Implication for Pastoral Psychotherapy," in *Therapeutic Practice in a Cross-Cultural World: Theological, Psychological, and Ethical Issues,* ed. Carole Bohn (Decatur, Ga.: Journal of Pastoral Care Publications, 1995), 1–16.

10. Marsha Foster Boyd stresses the key role of listening in pastoral care with African American women in terms of "the privilege one is afforded to listen as another tells her or his story. A theology of Womanist Care, then, seeks to ensure that African American women are 'listened into life.'" Boyd, "Womanist Care: Some Reflections on the Pastoral Care and the Transformation of African American Women," in *Embracing the Spirit: Womanist Perspectives on Hope, Salvation, and Transformation,* ed. Emilie M. Townes (Maryknoll, N.Y.: Orbis, 1997), 200.

11. Because this book focuses on countertransference and use of the self, the sample assessments given here will not be formal, extensive diagnostic reports. For more extensive discussion of classical pastoral assessment methods, see Nancy Ramsay, *Pastoral Diagnosis* (Minneapolis: Fortress Press, 1998). Paul Pruyser's *The Pastor as Diagnostician* (Philadelphia: Westminster, 1976) also is a valuable reference, from the perspective of a classical, more medically informed model. See also Pruyser, "Evaluation and Diagnosis, Religious," *Dictionary of Pastoral Care and Counseling,* ed. Rodney Hunter (Nashville, Tenn.: Abingdon, 1990), 371–73; Seward Hiltner, "Toward Autonomous Pastoral Diagnosis," *Bulletin of the Menninger Clinic* 40 (1975): 574–78; Ralph Underwood, "Personal and Professional Integrity in Relation to Pastoral Assessment," *Pastoral Psychology* 31 (1982): 109–17; and George Fitchett, *Spiritual Assessment in Pastoral Care: A Guide to Selected Resources* (Decatur, Ga.: Journal of Pastoral Care Publications, 1993). It may also be useful to consider human development including "faith development" in more extended assessments, while remaining circumspect about the hierarchical or "progress" model implied in some stage theories, e.g., James Fowler, *Stages of Faith: The Psychology of Human Development and the Quest for Meaning* (San Francisco: Harper & Row, 1981); Robert Kegan, *The Evolving Self* (Cambridge: Harvard University Press, 1982); Theodore Loder, *The Logic of the Spirit: Human Development in Theological Perspective* (San Francisco: Jossey-Bass, 1998); Evelyn Whitehead and James Whitehead, *Christian Life Patterns: The Psychological Challenges and Religious Invitations of Adult Life* (New York: Crossroad, 1995); Sharon Parks, *The Critical Years: The Young Adult Search for a Faith to Live By* (San Francisco: Harper & Row, 1986); Jeanne Stevenson Moessner, ed., *In Her Own Time: Women and Developmental Issues in Pastoral Care* (Minneapolis: Fortress Press, 2000); Felicity Kelcourse, ed., *Human Development and Faith: Life Cycle Change in Body, Mind and Spirit* (St. Louis: Chalice Press, forthcoming). For a summary of critiques of faith development theory, see Sharon Parks, "The North American Critique of James Fowler's Theory of Faith Development," in *Stages of Faith and Religious Development: Implications for Church, Education, and Society,*

ed. James Fowler, Karl Ernst Nipkow, and Friedrich Schweitzer (New York: Crossroad, 1991), 101–29.

12. Patrick Casement, *Listening to the Patient* (New York: Guilford Press, 1985), 38–41.

13. *Free association* was first used by Sigmund Freud as early as the 1890s; see Josef Breuer and Sigmund Freud, "Studies on Hysteria" (1893), in *The Standard Edition of the Complete Psychological Works of Sigmund Freud,* ed. and trans. J. Strachey (New York: W. W. Norton, 2000) (hereafter cited as *SE*), 2:303–5. The term was defined in the technique papers of 1912–1914; e.g., idem, "Dynamics of the Transference," *SE* 12:97–108; idem, "Recommendations to Physicians Practicing Psychoanalysis," *SE* 12:111–120; and idem, "On Beginning the Therapy," *SE* 12:121–44). Free association was the "fundamental rule" of psychoanalysis, in which the patient was exhorted to try to say everything that crossed his or her mind. I use the term more broadly, as it is commonly used in contemporary psychoanalysis, to mean noticing everything that comes to mind: thoughts, feelings, images, ideas, music, bodily sensations, fantasies, or anything else that floats into consciousness.

14. A number of methods and resources for theological reflection have been published, e.g., David Tracy, *The Analogical Imagination: Christian Theology and the Culture of Pluralism* (New York: Crossroad, 1981); Theodore W. Jennings Jr., "Pastoral Theological Methodology," in *Dictionary of Pastoral Care and Counseling,* ed. Rodney Hunter (Nashville, Tenn.: Abingdon, 1990), 862–64; Patricia Killen and John DeBeer, *The Art of Theological Reflection* (New York: Crossroad, 1994); James D. Whitehead and Evelyn Eaton Whitehead, *Method in Ministry: Theological Reflection and Christian Ministry* (Kansas City: Sheed & Ward, 1995); Howard Stone and James Duke, *How to Think Theologically* (Minneapolis: Fortress Press, 1996); Robert Kinast, *Let Ministry Teach: A Guide to Theological Reflection* (Collegeville, Minn.: Liturgical Press, 1996); *Making Faith-Sense: Theological Reflection in Everyday Life* (Collegeville, Minn.: Liturgical Press, 1999); Kinast, *What Are They Saying about Theological Reflection?* WATSA Series (New York: Paulist Press, 2000); and Donald Capps and Gene Fowler, *The Pastoral Care Case: Learning about Care in Congregations* (St. Louis: Chalice Press, 2001). For a specifically feminist methodology, see Carrie Doehring, "A Method of Feminist Pastoral Theology," in *Feminist and Womanist Pastoral Theology,* ed. Bonnie Miller-McLemore and Brita Gill-Austern (Nashville, Tenn.: Abingdon, 1999), 95–111. A method for group reflection may be found in Jeffrey Mahan, Barbara Troxell, and Carol Allen, *Shared Wisdom: A Guide to Case Study Reflection in Ministry* (Nashville, Tenn.: Abingdon, 1993).

15. Anton Boisen, *Exploration of the Inner World: A Study of Mental Disorder and Religious Experience* (Philadelphia: University of Philadelphia Press, 1971; orig. publ. 1936). This expression was later developed by Charles Gerkin, *The Living Human Document: Revisioning Pastoral Counseling in a Hermeneutical Mode* (Nashville, Tenn.: Abingdon, 1973).

16. Clifford Geertz, *Interpretation of Cultures: Selected Essays* (New York: Basic Books, 1973).

17. Loren Eiseley, *The Star Thrower* (New York: Harvest, 1979); Barbara Kingsolver, "Creation Stories" and "Making Peace," in *High Tide in Tucson: Essays from Now or Never* (New York: Harper Perennial, 1996), 17–34; Stephen Hawking, *A Brief History of Time* (New York: Bantam, 1988). See also Freeman Dyson, *Infinite in All Directions* (New York: Harper & Row, 1988); Jane Goodall, *Reason for Hope: A Spiritual Journey* (New York: Warner, 2000); John Polkinghorne, *Quarks, Chaos, and Christianity* (New York: Crossroad, 1997); Oliver Sacks, *The Man Who Mistook His Wife for a Hat and Other Clinical Tales* (New York: Summit, 1985); and Lewis Thomas, *Late Night Thoughts on Listening to Mahler's Ninth Symphony* (New York: Viking, 1983).

18. Jennings, "Pastoral Theological Methodology," 862ff.

19. Karen Baker Fletcher, "The Strength of My Life," in Townes, *Embracing the Spirit,* 122–39; and Cheryl A. Kirk-Duggan, "Justified, Sanctified, and Redeemed: Blessed Expectation in Black Women's Blues and Gospels," in Townes, *Embracing the Spirit,* 140–66.

20. Delores Williams, *Sisters in the Wilderness: The Challenge of Womanist God-Talk* (Maryknoll, N.Y.: Orbis, 1993).

21. Boyd describes this ministry of presence using the image of the "empowered cojourner" in "Womanist Care," 200, also citing Cecilia Williams Bryant, *Kujua: A Spirituality of the Hidden Way* (Baltimore, Md.: Akosua Visions, 1993), 35, 39.

22. Boyd states the importance of affirming African American women's life stories: "affirmation, validating and affirming the stories and the places of African American women" as well as confronting "structures and strictures," holding one another accountable, and healing through "lifting, straightening and strengthening" (Hebrews 12:12), "Womanist Care," 201.

5. The Relational Paradigm in Pastoral Care

1. Thanks to chaplains the Rev. Dr. Florence Gelo and the Rev. Dr. Charles Lindholm for their consultations about Gary's story.

2. Such interdisciplinary collaboration is not to be assumed in all hospital settings, of course. For a discussion of the role of chaplaincy in patient care and the need for increased awareness of chaplains' role among medical, nursing, and other hospital staff, see, e.g., Larry VandeCreek and Jerry Royer, "Education for Interdisciplinary Teamwork," *Journal of Pastoral Care* 29 (1975): 176–84; VandeCreek, *The Chaplain-Physician Relationship* (New York: Haworth, 1991); George Fitchett, Peter Meyer, and Laurel Burton, "Spiritual Care in the Hospital: Who Requests It? Who Needs It?" *Journal of Pastoral Care* 54, no. 2 (2000): 173–86; VandeCreek and Burton, "Professional Chaplaincy: Its Role and Importance in Health Care," *Journal of Pastoral Care* 55, no. 1 (2001): 81–97; and Charles Lindholm, "The Increased Utilization of Pastoral Care in an Active Medical Center" (DMin project, Lutheran Theological Seminary at Philadelphia, 2002).

3. My own social location is both like and unlike that of the composite cases in this book. As a woman born in 1955 and educated in the nontraditional professions of ministry and psychoanalytic therapy, I have experienced much of what has been written about gender discrimination and both the oppression and the empowerment of women through movements for social change in the radical decades of the 1960s and 1970s. My class background presents a mixed-class picture. The home in which I grew up was much like Tex Sample's "respectables" (right down to the chain-link fence!) in *Blue Collar Ministry: Facing Economic and Social Realities of Working People* (Valley Forge, Pa.: Judson Press, 1984), 74. My family was settled, "church-going, tee-totaling, politically and socially conservative" as described by Joseph T. Howell, *Hard Living on Clay Street* (New York: Doubleday/Anchor, 1973), 6, cited in Sample, *Blue Collar Ministry,* 73. The town in which I lived was a bedroom community both for the small industrial city of Lynn, Massachusetts, and for the more cosmopolitan but subjectively distant city of Boston. Lynn was dominated by two General Electric Company plants, where my great-great-uncle, great-uncle, and father all worked, moving up over the decades from bookkeeping and accounting to upper-middle management, while my grandfather worked a variety of blue-collar jobs, including Brinks truck driver, private security police, mechanic, and service station owner. Both my father and grandfather were veterans, the former during the Korean occupation, and the latter in the cavalry ride against Pancho Villa in 1917 and as a fighter pilot in World War I. My parents and grandparents were deeply involved in both the American Legion and the Masons, where my father continues to volunteer indefatigably in his retirement. The population of my hometown was all white, with strong religious and white-ethnic enclaves, most predominantly Italian Catholics, white Anglo-Saxon Protestants (our family's religious and ethnic identity), and a large population of Conservative and Reform Jews. There were many first- and second-generation Holocaust survivors. By virtue of my father's rising economic and social status and my own university and Ivy League graduate education and academic profession, I understand the experience of Gary's

trajectory into the "professional class." Like many academics and therapists, my present-day life best fits a blend of Paul Fussell's upper-middle and "X" classes, in *Class: A Guide through the American Status System* (New York: Summit, 1983), 146–74, 212–23, defined more by education and the conscious adoption of certain social values than by income. Like many of my white peers, I am simultaneously privileged, distressed by privilege, and anxious to work for social change and justice.

4. Fussell, *Class*, 230–33. See also Meck Groot, "On Being Working-Class Educated," in "Hearing the Voices of Poor and Working-Class Women," special issue, *Journal of Women and Religion* 12 (1993): 11–15.

5. Tex Sample describes the "blue-collar respectable" group, for whom dignity, discipline, hard work, and a home that symbolizes security and decency are prevailing values, in *Blue Collar Ministry*, 71–83. For further discussions of working-class life in America, see Karen Bloomquist, *The Dream Betrayed: Religious Challenges of the Working Class* (Minneapolis: Fortress Press, 1990); Herbert Gutman, *Power and Culture: Essays on the American Working Class*, ed. Ira Berlin (New York: Pantheon, 1987); John Raines and Donna Day-Lower, *Modern Work and Human Meaning* (Philadelphia: Westminster John Knox, 1986); Lillian Breslow Rubin, *Worlds of Pain: Life in the Working-Class Family* (New York: Basic Books, 1976), 128; Rubin, *Families on the Fault Line: America's Working Class Speaks about the Family, the Economy, Race and Ethnicity* (New York: HarperCollins, 1994); Richard Sennett and Jonathan Cobb, *The Hidden Injuries of Class* (New York: Knopf, 1972); Roy Theriault, *Unmasking the American Working Class* (New York: New Press, 2003); and Erik Olin Wright, "American Class Structure," *American Sociological Review* 47 (1982): 709–26.

6. Sample, *Blue Collar Ministry*, documents the aspirations of "respectable" parents for their children to go to college. For a more nuanced view of working-class parents' pride and ambivalence, see also Rubin, *Worlds of Pain*, 207–9.

7. Barbara Ehrenreich describes the "professional-managerial class" in *Fear of Falling: The Inner Life of the Middle Class* (New York: Pantheon, 1989).

8. First-person account by bel hooks, "Crossing Class Boundaries," in *Where We Stand: Class Matters* (New York: Routledge, 2000), 143.

9. For a number of first-person essays on this liminal state from similar perspectives of academics from the working class, see C. L. Barney Dews and Carolyn Leste Law, eds., *This Fine Place So Far from Home: Voices of Academics from the Working Class* (Philadelphia: Temple University Press, 1995). See also bel hooks, "Coming to Class Consciousness," in *Where We Stand*, 24–37; and "Hearing the Voices of Poor and Working-Class Women," special issue, *Journal of Women and Religion* 12 (1993): 1–73.

10. Barbara Ehrenreich documents how, in spite of minuscule increases in the minimum wage, the rising cost of housing in particular has exacerbated the divide between rich and poor, and created a growing but largely invisible subclass of working poor. Wage gains have not kept pace with inflation, and the poorest workers "have made the least progress back to their 1973 wage levels." *Nickel and Dimed: On (Not) Getting By in America* (New York: Metropolitan Books/Henry Holt, 2001), 203. Further, "the shift from a blue-collar industrial economy to a service and information/technology economy will eventually dislocate 15 to 45 million workers in urban America." Judith Orr, "Hard Work, Hard Lovin', Hard Times, Hardly Worth It," in *The Care of Men*, ed. Christie Cozad Neuger and James Newton Poling (Nashville, Tenn.: Abingdon, 1997), 77, citing Richard Gillett, "Church Role Vital for Justice in New Workplaces," *The Witness* 69, no. 2 (1986): 12–15.

11. Pertti Alasuutari explains drinking among working-class men as both an act of freedom from social constraints at work and at home, and a form of self-medication to "numb the pain of not feeling man enough," in "Alcoholism in Its Cultural Context: The Case of Blue Collar Men," *Contemporary Drug Problems* 12 (winter 1986): 641–86, cited in Orr, "Hard Work, Hard

Lovin'," 95–96. Alasuutari also notes that the pattern of binge drinking is more prevalent among blue-collar men, while white-collar drinking tends to be more continual (p. 674). On binge drinking, see also Sample, *Blue Collar Ministry*. Sample identifies binge drinking in particular with "blue collar hard living." Orr states, "Drinking is especially common among hard-living men, but is not uncommon among others as well," p. 80, citing Ben Hamper, *Rivethead: Tales from the Assembly Line* (New York: Warner, 1986), 55.

12. For pastoral perspectives on patterns of alcoholism, see Stephen P. Apthorp, *Alcohol and Substance Abuse: A Clergy Handbook* (Wilton, Conn.: Morehouse-Barlow, 1985); Howard Clinebell, *Understanding and Counseling Persons with Alcohol, Drug, and Behavioral Addictions*, rev. ed. (Nashville, Tenn.: Abingdon, 1998); Clinebell, "Alcohol Abuse, Addiction, and Therapy," in *Dictionary of Pastoral Care and Counseling*, ed. Rodney J. Hunter (Nashville, Tenn.: Abingdon, 1990), 18–21. See also Richard Wallace, ed., *Journal of Ministry in Addiction and Recovery* 1 (Binghamton, N.Y.: Haworth Press, 1994).

13. Orr, "Hard Work, Hard Lovin'," 74, documents how the simplistic stereotype of the working-class male as "drunken, overweight, hedonistic, licentious, violent, loud, boyish, inarticulate, boring, and stupid" persists and is reinforced by media portrayals such as sitcom characters Archie Bunker and Al Bundy—in spite of the diversity of working-class experiences, lifestyles, self-perceptions, and levels of employment and wage.

14. "The six-pack of beer is merely the working-class version of the idle-class multiple martini lunch." Orr, "Hard Work, Hard Lovin'," 80.

15. Pierre Bourdieu, *Language and Symbolic Power* (Cambridge: Harvard University Press, 1991), describes the domestication of language and body as one moves up the socioeconomic scale, the denial of social and sexual identity of working-class men, and the blunting of expression of appetites, feelings, and outspokenness. Cited in Orr, "Hard Work, Hard Lovin'," 240.

16. The most commonly used brief assessment tool, designed by doctors to determine whether a referral for further assessment and treatment is in order, is the CAGE acronym: (1) Have you ever tried to *cut back* or *control* your drinking? (2) Have you ever become *angry* or *annoyed* because someone asked you about your drinking? (3) Have you ever felt *guilty* about your drinking? (4) Have you ever needed an "*eye-opener*" (i.e., another drink) to get going the next morning after drinking? (Words in italics added by this author.) Affirmative responses to the first three questions suggest a problem with alcohol, ranging from abuse to addiction, depending on the number of yeses. The fourth question confirms physiological addiction due to the presence of withdrawal symptoms. For further discussion of the distinctions among substance use, abuse, and addiction, see the *Diagnostic and Statistical Manual of Mental Disorders*, 4th ed., text rev. (DSM-IV-TR) (Washington, D.C.: American Psychiatric Press, 2000), 212–23. For a comparative discussion of other brief assessment tools, see Hans-Jürgen Rumpf et al., "Development of a Screening Questionnaire for the General Hospital and General Practices," *Alcoholism: Clinical and Experimental Research* 21, no. 5 (1997): 894; and Cheryl Cherpitol, "Screening for Alcohol Problems in the U.S. General Population: Comparison of the CAGE, RAPS4, and RAPS4-QF by Gender, Ethnicity, and Service Utilization," *Alcoholism: Clinical and Experimental Research* 26, no. 11 (2002): 1,686–91.

17. Robert Wicks, "Burnout," in *Essentials for Chaplains*, ed. Sharon Cheston and Robert Wicks (New York: Paulist Press, 1993), 2–3. On reflective practices in working life, see also Parker Palmer, *The Active Life: A Spirituality of Work and Creativity* (San Francisco: Jossey-Bass, 1999); and *Let Your Life Speak: Listening for the Voice of Vocation* (San Francisco: Jossey-Bass, 1999).

18. Owen Renik, "Countertransference, Enactment and the Psychoanalytic Process," in *Structure and Psychic Change: Essays in Honor of Robert Wallerstein*, ed. Mardi Jon Horowitz, Otto Kernberg, and Edward Weinshel (Madison, Conn.: International Universities Press, 1993), 135–58.

19. On pastoral self-care, see, e.g., Donald R. Hands and Wayne L. Fehr, *Spiritual Wholeness for Clergy: A New Psychology of Intimacy with God, Self, and Others* (Washington, D.C.: Alban

Institute, 1993); Rochelle Melander and Harold Eppley, *The Spiritual Leader's Guide to Self-Care* (Bethesda, Md.: Alban Institute, 2002); Roy Oswald, *Clergy Self-Care: Finding a Balance for Effective Ministry* (Washington, D.C.: Alban Institute, 1991); Oswald, *How to Build a Support System for Your Ministry* (Washington, D.C.: Alban Institute, 1991); Robert Wicks, *Christian Introspection: Self-Ministry through Self-Understanding* (New York: Crossroad, 1983).

20. For detailed guidance in drawing a genogram, see Monica McGoldrick, Randy Gerson, and Sylvan Shellenberger, *Genograms: Assessment and Intervention*, 2d ed. (New York: W. W. Norton, 1999). Good instructions are also included in a number of pastoral resources, including Herbert Anderson and Robert Cotton Fite, *Becoming Married* (Louisville, Ky.: Westminster John Knox, 1993); and Edwin Friedman, *Generation to Generation: Family Process in Church and Synagogue* (New York: Guilford Press, 1985).

21. If Carol had direct evidence of alcohol impairing Gary's professional life or interfering with his relationships, a referral to a specialized alcohol treatment facility for assessment would be preferable to a general counseling referral.

22. Carroll A. Watkins Ali, *Survival and Liberation: Pastoral Theology in African American Context* (St. Louis: Chalice Press, 1999), 6.

23. Alice Miller, *The Drama of the Gifted Child: The Search for the True Self* (New York: Basic Books, 1981).

24. Ibid.

25. Gary Harbaugh and Evan Rogers, "Pastoral Burnout: A View from the Seminary," *Journal of Pastoral Care* 38 (1984): 99–106; William Hulme, "Coming to Terms with Clergy Burnout," *Christian Ministry* 15, no. 1 (1984): 5–7; Christina Maslach, *Burnout: The Cost of Caring* (Englewood Cliffs, N.J.: Prentice Hall, 1982); Christina Maslach and Michael Leiter, *The Truth about Burnout: How Organizations Cause Personal Stress and What to Do about It* (San Francisco: Jossey-Bass, 1997); John A. Sanford, *Ministry Burnout* (Lousville, Ky.: Westminster John Knox, 1982); Wicks, "Burnout," *Essentials for Chaplains*, 1–8.

26. *My Life as a Dog*, directed by Lasse Hallström, written by Reidar Jönsson and Lasse Hallström (Sweden, 1985).

27. Monologue from *My Life as a Dog*, trans. Eivor Martinus.

28. Bernard Loomer, *The Size of God: Theology of Bernard Loomer in Context*, ed. William Dean and Larry Axel (Macon, Ga.: Mercer University Press, 1987).

29. Augustine, *Confessions*, trans. Henry Chadwick (Oxford: Oxford World's Classics/Oxford University Press, 1998), 193.

30. Glen O. Gabbard and Eva P. Lester, *Boundaries and Boundary Violations in Psychoanalysis* (New York: Basic Books, 1995), 78, 88–89 et passim; Kenneth Pope, Janet Sonne, and Jean Holroyd, *Sexual Feelings in Psychotherapy* (Washington, D.C.: American Psychological Association, 1995), 180–82.

31. Men who cross sexual boundaries frequently minimize the impact of their behaviors. Often, in fact, men do not believe they have violated a boundary if they did not engage in sexual intercourse. The extended public discourse regarding President Bill Clinton's rhetoric about what constituted "having sex" has highlighted gender differences in the interpretation of sexual behavior, and the extent of rationalizing use of language itself, i.e., what *is* is. Feminist literature has explored the patriarchal equation of all sexuality with heterosexual intercourse, and the equation of intercourse itself with rape, e.g., Andrea Dworkin, *Intercourse* (New York: Free Press, 1987). For more detailed discussion of the aspect of minimization and denial of sexual and aggressive behaviors in male sex offenders, see Timothy Beneke, *Men on Rape* (New York: St. Martin's, 1986); Philip Culbertson, *Counseling Men*, Creative Pastoral Care and Counseling Series (Minneapolis: Fortress Press, 1994); Paul Kivel, *Men's Work: How to Stop the Violence That Tears Our Lives Apart* (New York: Ballantine, 1992); David Livingston, *Healing Violent Men: A Model for*

Christian Communities (Minneapolis: Fortress Press, 2002); James Newton Poling, *The Abuse of Power: A Theological Problem* (Nashville, Tenn.: Abingdon, 1991); Poling, "Masculinity, Competitive Violence and Christian Theology," in *The Spirituality of Men*, ed. Philip Culbertson (Minneapolis: Fortress Press, 2002), 113–31.

32. For a negative example of this myth, see Louis McBurney, "Seduced," *Leadership* (fall 1998): 101–6.

33. Ann Janine Morey, "Blaming the Woman for the Abusive Male Pastor," *Christian Century*, October 5, 1988, 866–69; Pamela Cooper-White, *The Cry of Tamar: Violence against Women and the Church's Response* (Minneapolis: Fortress Press, 1995), 138.

34. This fictional case is a composite based on extensive experience as therapist and consultant with many situations similar to Terence's and Elaine's. Terence is here depicted as a white, educated, middle-class clergyman, working in the context of a middle- or upper-middle-class congregation; however, similar scenarios of temptation and exploitation occur across all racial and class lines.

35. John Gottman, *Why Marriages Succeed or Fail* (New York: Fireside/Simon and Schuster, 1994), 68–102.

36. It was my thesis in *The Cry of Tamar*, reconfirmed in my most recent research, that narcissistic wounding is a factor in virtually all situations of clergy boundary violations. For more detailed discussions, see *The Cry of Tamar*, 137–38; Cooper-White, "The Therapist's Use of Self: Countertransference in Pastoral Counseling and Clinical Social Work" (PhD diss., Institute for Clinical Social Work, Chicago, 2000).

37. Cooper-White, *The Cry of Tamar*, 208–11, 220.

38. Peter Rutter describes how men gradually test the boundaries and sexualize the professional relationship in *Sex in the Forbidden Zone* (Los Angeles: Jeremy Tarcher, 1986), 137–58; see also Pope et al. on unacknowledged sexual feelings, *Sexual Feelings in Psychotherapy*, 103–18.

39. Neville Symington, *Narcissism: A New Theory* (London: Karnac Books, 1993).

40. These books represent a wide range of theoretical perspectives: Otto Kernberg, *Borderline Conditions and Pathological Narcissism* (Northvale, N.J.: Jason Aronson, 1985); Heinz Kohut, *The Analysis of the Self: A Systematic Approach to the Psychoanalytic Treatment of Narcissistic Personality Disorders* (New York: International Universities Press, 1971); idem, *The Restoration of the Self* (New York: International Universities Press, 1976), and idem (published posthumously), *How Does Analysis Cure?* ed. Arnold Goldberg and Paul Stepansky (Chicago: University of Chicago Press, 1984); Peter Giovacchini, *Impact of Narcissism: The Errant Therapist on a Chaotic Quest* (Northvale, N.J.: Jason Aronson, 2001); Alexander Lowen, *Narcissism: Denial of the True Self* (New York: Touchstone Books, 1997); Andrew P. Morrison, ed., *Essential Papers on Narcissism* (New York: New York University Press, 1986); Elsa Ronningstam, ed., *Disorders of Narcissism: Diagnostic, Clinical and Empirical Implications* (Northvale, N.J.: Jason Aronson, 2000); Nathan Schwarz-Salant, *Narcissism and Character Transformation: The Psychology of Narcissistic Character Disorders* (San Francisco: Inner City Books, 1986); Hyman Spotnitz, *Treatment of the Narcissistic Neuroses* (Northvale, N.J.: Jason Aronson, 1995); Symington, *Narcissism: A New Theory*. From a pastoral perspective, see also Conrad Weiser, *Healers: Harmed and Harmful* (Minneapolis: Fortress Press, 1994), 67–81.

41. Kohut, *Analysis of the Self*; idem, *The Restoration of the Self*; idem, *How Does Analysis Cure?*; and Miller, *The Drama of the Gifted Child*, drawing from D. W. Winnicott, "Ego Distortion in Terms of True and False Self," in *Maturational Processes and the Facilitating Environment* (London: Hogarth, 1965), 140–52.

42. Miller, *The Drama of the Gifted Child*.

43. Narcissism is a prevalent concern in the dominant culture of North America. A recent count revealed over 220 books in print on the subject. See also Christopher Lasch's still-relevant

social analysis, *The Culture of Narcissism: American Life in an Age of Diminishing Expectations,* rev. ed. (New York: W. W. Norton, 1991).

44. Cooper-White, *The Cry of Tamar,* 137–38.

45. Heinz Kohut, "The Two Analyses of Mr. Z," *International Journal of Psycho-analysis* 60 (1979): 3–27.

46. Arnold Goldberg, *Being of Two Minds: The Vertical Split in Psychoanalysis and Psychotherapy* (Hillsdale, N.J.: Analytic Press, 1999).

47. Ibid., 10. The original distinction between repression and disavowal goes back to Sigmund Freud. Freud coined the term *disavowal (Verleugnung),* in connection with sexual perversion, and the internal mechanism he called "splitting of the ego" *(Ichspaltung),* in "Fetishism" (1927), in *The Standard Edition of the Complete Psychological Works of Sigmund Freud* 21, ed. and trans. J. Strachey (New York: W. W. Norton, 2000), 149–59.

48. Kohut, "The Two Analyses of Mr. Z," 11.

49. Followers of Kohut, including Ernest Wolf, identified additional types of selfobjects, e.g., Ernest Wolf, *Treating the Self* (New York: Guilford Press, 1988). Kohut himself introduced a third selfobject, the alter-ego-twinship, in *The Restoration of the Self,* 44.

50. For a postmodern discussion of narcissism and its origins in lack (drawing on both Freud and Jacques Lacan), see Gilles Deleuze, *Difference and Repetition,* trans. Paul Patton (New York: Columbia University Press, 1994), esp. 110ff.

51. Augustine, *Confessions,* 10.33.50: 208.

52. Ibid., 193.

53. D. W. Winnicott, "The Antisocial Tendency" (1956), in *Through Paediatrics to Psychoanalysis: Collected Papers* (New York: Brunner/Mazel, 1992), 306–15.

54. Weiser, *Healers: Harmed and Harmful,* 75.

55. Pamela Cooper-White, "Dynamics of Sexual Exploitation and Responding to Victims," ELCA Leadership Training Event, Chicago, December 4–6, 1998, 17–18.

56. Kohut discussed the concept of "transmuting internalization" in all three of his major works. He first introduced it in *The Analysis of the Self* and elaborated in his subsequent works *The Restoration of the Self* and *How Does Analysis Cure?*

57. Michael J. Tansey, "Sexual Attraction and Phobic Dread in the Countertransference," *Psychoanalytic Dialogues* 4, no. 2 (1994): 139. Tansey describes how a woman's tears and depression signal vulnerability, heightening erotic countertransference.

58. Heinz Kohut, "On Courage," in *Self Psychology and the Humanities: Reflections on a New Psychoanalytic Approach,* ed. Charles Strozier (New York: W. W. Norton, 1985), 5–50; see also D. W. Winnicott on play and giving, "The Depressive Position in Normal Emotional Development" (1958), in *Through Paediatrics to Psycho-analysis,* 271.

59. For information on spiritual direction, including training and ethics, see the Web site of Spiritual Directors International, http://www.sdiworld.org.

60. C. S. Lewis, *The Problem of Pain* (New York: Macmillan, 1947), 135, 139. Similar imagery is found in Blaise Pascal, *Pensées,* 11.181, in *Pensées and Other Writings,* trans. Honor Levi (Oxford: Oxford University Press, 1995), 52.

61. Phillip Bennett, *Let Yourself Be Loved* (Mahwah, N.J.: Paulist Press, 1997), 20, 25.

62. E.g., Imago Relationship Therapy, Harville Hendrix, *Getting the Love You Want: A Guide for Couples* (New York: Harper & Row, 1990); object relation couples therapy, David E. Scharff and Jill Savege Scharff, *Object Relations and Couple Therapy* (Northvale, N.J.: Jason Aronson, 1991).

63. Winnicott, "Ego Distortion in Terms of True and False Self," 145.

64. Gabbard and Lester, *Boundaries and Boundary Violations*; Pope, Sonne and Holroyd, *Sexual Feelings in Psychotherapy.*

65. Susan Schechter, *Guide for Mental Health Professionals* (Washington, D.C.: National Coalition Against Domestic Violence, 1987). Specific to pastoral care, see also Cooper-White,

The Cry of Tamar, 123–24; and Carol Adams, *Woman-Battering,* Creative Pastoral Care and Counseling Series (Minneapolis: Fortress Press, 1994), 47–49.

66. E.g., Rita Nakashima Brock, *Journeys by Heart: A Christology of Erotic Power* (New York: Crossroad/Herder & Herder, 1989); and Carter Heyward, *Touching Our Strength: The Erotic as Power and the Love of God* (San Francisco: HarperSanFrancisco, 1989).

67. Nancy Eiesland, *The Disabled God: Toward a Liberatory Theology of Disability* (Nashville, Tenn.: Abingdon, 1994).

68. A version of the "miracle question" used in solution-focused brief therapy, described in Margaret Zipse Kornfeld, *Cultivating Wholeness: A Guide to Care and Counseling in Faith Communities* (New York: Continuum, 1998), 114–43. For a more in-depth discussion of the solution-focused method, see Peter DeJong and Insoo Kim Berg, *Interviewing for Solutions,* 2d ed. (Florence, Ky.: Wadsworth, 2001); for brief pastoral counseling approaches, see Howard Stone, *Strategies for Brief Pastoral Counseling* (Minneapolis: Fortress Press, 2001).

69. Pastors should be alert to signs of clinical depression and for suicidality. If any such symptoms are present or if there is any doubt about the possibility of suicidal ideation, the individual should be referred immediately to a psychotherapist, psychologist, or psychiatrist or mental health facility for a professional clinical evaluation. For more detailed information on suicide assessment and intervention, see Cooper-White, *The Cry of Tamar,* 231–36; Kornfeld, *Cultivating Wholeness,* 325–27; and Alan Berman, *Suicide Prevention* (New York: Springer, 1990).

70. Seward Hiltner, *Preface to Pastoral Theology* (New York: Abingdon, 1958).

71. Watkins Ali, *Survival and Liberation,* 5–6.

72. Larry Kent Graham, "From Relational Humanness to Relational Justice: Reconceiving Pastoral Care and Counseling," in *Pastoral Care and Social Conflict,* ed. P. Couture and R. Hunter (Nashville, Tenn.: Abingdon, 1995), 220–34.

73. Philip Krey, plenary address to "Common Mission in the City," conference at General Theological Seminary, New York, February 29, 2000.

74. Bonnie Miller-McLemore, "The Living Human Web: Pastoral Theology at the Turn of the Century," in *Through the Eyes of Women: Insights for Pastoral Care,* ed. Jeanne Stevenson Moessner (Minneapolis: Fortress Press, 1996), 9–26.

75. Kornfeld, *Cultivating Wholeness.*

76. Anton Boisen, *The Exploration of the Inner World* (New York: Harper & Brothers, 1952), cited in Charles Gerkin, *The Living Human Document: Revisioning Pastoral Counseling in a Hermeneutical Mode* (Nashville, Tenn.: Abingdon, 1973, 1984).

77. Miller-McLemore, "The Living Human Web," 16.

78. Jeanne Stevenson Moessner, "From Samaritan to Samaritan: Journey Mercies," in Moessner, *Through the Eyes of Women,* 322ff.

79. Ibid., 322.

80. Anne Katherine, *Boundaries: Where You End and I Begin* (New York: Fireside/Parkside, 1991).

81. Dorothy McRae-McMahon, *Being Clergy, Staying Human: Taking Our Stand in the River* (Washington, D.C.: Alban Institute, 1992).

82. Ibid., 46.

83. Ibid., 72.

6. The Relational Paradigm in Pastoral Psychotherapy

1. Pamela Cooper-White, "The Therapist's Use of the Self: Countertransference in Pastoral Counseling and Clinical Social Work" (PhD diss., Institute for Clinical Social Work, Chicago, 2000), research funded largely by the Episcopal Church Foundation; research findings summarized in Cooper-White, "The Use of the Self in Psychotherapy: A Comparative Study of Pastoral Counselors and Clinical Social Workers," *American Journal of Pastoral Counseling* 4, no. 4 (2001): 5–35.

2. In my study, only 5 percent of respondents, including both pastoral counselors and clinical social workers, self-identified as cognitive-behavioral, and less than 1 percent (one therapist) identified as humanistic-existentialist.

3. Adapted from Vincent D'Andrea and Peter Salovey, *Peer Counseling: Skills and Perspectives* (Palo Alto, Calif.: Science and Behavior Books, 1983), 63, citing Joseph Luft, *Group Processes: An Introduction to Group Dynamics,* 3d ed. (New York: McGraw-Hill, 1984).

4. On gentle confrontation as proclamation in pastoral care, see Charles Taylor, *The Skilled Pastor: Counseling as the Practice of Theology* (Minneapolis: Fortress Press, 1991).

5. I am indebted to several Puerto Rican professional church women, whose consultation helped me bring Linda authentically to voice: Sara Calderón, the Rev. Ivis LaRiviere-Mestre, and Melissa Ramirez, as well as consultation with the Rev. Nelson Rivera.

6. For a discussion of the internalization of culture in counselors' assumptions, see D. Y. F. Ho, "Internalized Culture, Culturocentrism, and Transcendence," *The Counseling Psychologist* 23 (1995): 4–24. See also John Hinkle and Gregory Hinkle, "Surrendering the Self: Pastoral Counseling at the Limits of Culture and Psychotherapy," in *Therapeutic Practice in a Cross-Cultural World: Theological, Psychological, and Ethical Issues,* JCPC Monograph no. 7, ed. Carole Bohn (Decatur, Ga.: Journal of Pastoral Care Publications, 1995), 77–98.

7. For a discussion of the history and challenges of Puerto Rican women and attendant pastoral issues, see Irma S. Corretjer-Nolla, "The Pastoral Care of the Puerto Rican Woman in the United States," in *Bridging Boundaries: The Pastoral Care of U.S. Hispanics,* ed. Kenneth Davis and Yolanda Tarango (Scranton, Pa.: University of Scranton Press, 2000), 65–80. See also Ivis LaRiviere-Mestre, "Working with Latinos: The Ministerial Implications of Reaching Out to Latino/Hispanic Families," in *Reaching the Latino Community: A Manual for Congregational Leaders,* ed. Hector Carrasquilo and Giacomo Cassese (Chicago: Evangelical Lutheran Church in America, 2002), 45–52.

8. Male pastoral counselors in the American Association of Pastoral Counselors outnumber women five to one at the two levels of certification for independent practice (Fellow and Diplomate). This is due in part to a continuing gender imbalance in the ordained clergy more generally (women still represent approximately 8 percent of all clergy in denominations ordaining women). Of all AAPC members, 87 percent are white (breakdown by Fellow and Diplomate not available), followed by 2 percent African Americans, 1.5 percent Asians, 0.4 percent Hispanics/Latinos, and less than 0.1 percent Native Americans, with a balance of approximately 9 percent "Other" or "Unlisted." Data provided by AAPC office, March 21, 2003. While there are still very few Hispanic/Latino pastoral psychotherapists, there are many more Puerto Rican women active in pastoral ministries more generally, and in church leadership in the United States, especially in the Roman Catholic Church. See Corretjer-Nolla, "The Pastoral Care of the Puerto Rican Woman," 72–73.

9. On issues of shame and dignity, see LaRiviere-Mestre, "Working with Latinos," 50.

10. Hispanic/Latino families have a 27 percent poverty rate (1993 U.S. Census figure), over twice the U.S. average. Over one-third of those poor Latino families are Puerto Rican. Corretjer-Nolla, "The Pastoral Care of the Puerto Rican Woman," 79.

11. For a description of the positive cultural-social messages, practices, and traditions in the Latino community, see LaRiviere-Mestre, "Working with Latinos," 48–50.

12. I am using the term *difference* in a somewhat different sense than that of Jacques Derrida in *Positions,* trans. Alan Bass (Chicago: University of Chicago Press, 1985), 39. For Derrida, the "play of differences" and his term *"différance"* refers to the distance between signifiers and what they signify, in both time and space, erasing all essentialisms. I am using this term to mean *both* this slipperiness of verbal meaning and *also* the phenomenologically felt differences among various groups as they are socially and culturally constructed through gender, race, class, etc.

13. Emmanuel Lartey, *In Living Colour: An Intercultural Approach to Pastoral Care and Counseling* (London and Herndon, Va.: Cassell, 1997); and idem, "Pastoral Counselling in Multi-

cultural Contexts," in *Counselling in Pastoral Settings*, ed. Gordon Lynch (London and New York: Routledge, 1999), 22–36. For a review of the literature on multicultural counseling theory and practice, see also Jairo Fuertes and Denise Gretchen, "Emerging Theories of Multicultural Counseling," in *Handbook of Multicultural Counseling*, 2d ed., ed. Joseph Ponterotto, J. Manual Casas, Lisa Suzuki, and Charlene Alexander (Thousand Oaks, Calif.: Sage, 2001).

14. Ellen Ruderman, "Creative and Reparative Uses of Countertransference by Women Psychotherapists Treating Women Patients: A Clinical Research Study," in *The Psychology of Today's Woman: New Psychoanalytic Visions*, ed. T. Bernay and D. Cantor (Cambridge: Harvard University Press, 1986), 339–63.

15. Heinz Kohut, *The Restoration of the Self* (New York: International Universities Press, 1977); and Ernest Wolf, *Treating the Self* (New York: Guilford Press, 1988).

16. Corretjer-Nolla notes that indigenous Taino culture was matrilineal, and women in Puerto Rico have not been entirely subjugated even to the present day. A heritage of women's strength thus lived on. However, systematic oppression of women, including sexual exploitation and constriction of roles and opportunities for women, was imposed on the culture by the Spanish conquistadors and missionaries. While Puerto Rican women in the United States are still disproportionately poor, divorced, and single mothers, increasing numbers of Puerto Rican women, especially in second and third generations in the States, are achieving "higher education and better professional job opportunities." Corretjer-Nolla, "The Pastoral Care of the Puerto Rican Woman," 74.

17. Ivis LaRiviere-Mestre points out the distinction between being "strong" and being "tough," in that survival is usually coupled with "the characteristic Puerto Rican gracious behavior of Puerto Rican women even when we encounter difficulties and undue pressures in our lives." Personal communication, February 2003.

18. Owen Renik, "Countertransference, Enactment and the Psychoanalytic Process," in *Structure and Psychic Change: Essays in Honor of Robert Wallerstein*, ed. Mardi Jon Horowitz, Otto Kernberg, and Edward Weinshel (Madison, Conn.: International Universities Press, 1993), 135–58.

19. Glen O. Gabbard and Eva P. Lester, *Boundaries and Boundary Violations* (New York: Basic Books, 1995), 78, 88–89 et passim; Kenneth Pope, Janet Sonne, and Jean Holroyd, *Sexual Feelings in Psychotherapy* (Washington, D.C.: American Psychological Association, 1995), 180–82.

20. On post-traumatic memory, see, e.g., Pamela Cooper-White, *The Cry of Tamar: Violence against Women and the Church's Response* (Minneapolis: Fortress Press, 1995), 145–52, 157–63; and Judith Herman, *Trauma and Recovery* (New York: Basic Books, 1992), 110–12.

21. David Finkelhor, *Child Sexual Abuse: New Theory and Research* (New York: Free Press, 1984), 28, 31.

22. Sor Juana Inés de la Cruz is a fitting saintly Latina woman with whom Sara might identify. Sor Juana was "a Latina nun with a thirst for knowledge and learning and concern for the poor. She was a well versed Mexican theologian who was told to stop her writing. She sold her private library and gave the money to the poor, since the church hierarchy had interpreted her intellectual abilities as a threat to the 'status quo.' If she refused, she would have faced the cruelty of the Inquisition." Ivis LaRiviere-Mestre, personal communication, February 2003.

23. Term first used by Eric Kris, "Ego Psychology and Interpretation in Psychoanalytic Therapy," *Psychoanalytic Quarterly* 20, no. 1 (1951): 15–30. See also Sydney Pulver, "The Psychoanalytic Process and Mechanisms of Therapeutic Change," in *Psychoanalysis: The Major Concepts*, ed. Burness Moore and Bernard Fine (New Haven: Yale University Press, 1995), 87.

24. This term is used frequently in the survivor literature. It was originally used by Ernest Hemingway in *A Farewell to Arms:* "The world breaks everyone, and afterward many are strong at the broken places. But those that will not break it kills" (New York: Scribner's Sons, 1995), 249.

25. Jody Messler Davies, "Love in the Afternoon: A Relational Consideration of Desire and Dread in the Countertransference," *Psychoanalytic Dialogues* 4, no. 2 (1994): 153–70.

26. Thanks to Sara Calderón for this suggestion.

27. Text and music by Cesareo Gabarain, 1979, *Ediciones Paulinas,* OCP Publications, 5536 NE Hassalo, Portland, OR 97213, 800-547-8992; trans. Madeleine Forell Marshall, Editorial Avance Luterano. Reprinted in *With One Voice: A Lutheran Resource for Worship* (Minneapolis: Augsburg Fortress, 1995), hymn 784.

28. Larry VandeCreek, Hilary Bender, and Merle R. Jordan, *Research in Pastoral Care and Counseling: Quantitative and Qualitative Approaches* (Decatur, Ga.: Journal of Pastoral Care Publications, 1994).

29. Cooper-White, "The Therapist's Use of the Self."

30. Although face-to-face interviewing would have been preferable for the ethnographic aspect of the research, I judged the subject matter to be too sensitive to elicit honest information in all cases through a face-to-face method. This is especially critical in a research survey of subject matter for which there has been little or no previous research, as was the case for pastoral counselors and clinical social workers. A future follow-up study using Grounded Theory (Juliet Corbin and Anselm Strauss, *Basics of Qualitative Research: Techniques and Procedures for Developing Grounded Theory,* 2d ed. [Newbury Park, Calif.: Sage, 1998]) or another similar purely qualitative method should generate interesting results for comparison. Psychoanalytic small-group research methods that in their design use the researcher's own countertransference and the group's unconscious process as a source of data would be another elegant method paralleling the subject matter of countertransference itself.

31. The members of the comparison group were zip-code matched to eliminate regional differences as an extraneous variable and then drawn from random samples wherever possible within each zip code. Pilot testing was conducted to check length, clarity of wording to accommodate the widest possible range of theoretical viewpoints of participants, and test for content validity (i.e., consistency of meaning across pilot test subjects). Standard ethical research guidelines were observed, to protect participants' anonymity due to the private or sensitive nature of some of the questions and to minimize any potential for harm. To preserve the anonymity of participants, the questionnaire was preceded by a paragraph indicating that completion and return of the questionnaire signified voluntary informed consent. Steps taken to minimize risk included anonymity and a disclosure statement that some of the material contained in this survey could be unsettling. Participants were informed that they were under no obligation to respond and might feel free to stop at any point. Participants were invited to call anonymously for debriefing if needed, and referrals were prepared in case of any distress; however, no participants called requesting debriefing. Risk was further minimized by framing questions in a nonconfrontational, respectful style, with no implied right, wrong, or obviously unethical answers.

32. Questionnaire developed by Ricardo Chouhy, "On Countertransference: An Exploratory Study of Analysts' Attitudes toward the Use of Self as a Therapeutic Tool in the Analytic Situation" (PhD diss., Derner Institute, Adelphi University, 1986), summarized in Robert Mendelsohn, Wilma Bucci, and Ricardo Chouhy, "Transference and Countertransference: A Survey of Attitudes," *Contemporary Psychoanalysis* 28, no. 2 (1992): 364–90.

33. There were two additional hypotheses, based on the literature. One tested for a significant difference among therapists of different theoretical orientations in both their conceptualization and utilization of countertransference (founded). The other hypothesis tested whether therapists who specialize in, or whose caseload includes a proportion greater than 25 percent of, patients whom they classify according to DSM-IV criteria as suicidal, borderline, psychotic, or post-traumatic would be more likely to give a totalist definition of countertransference in their own words on the TRQ and score significantly more "Totalist" on the ATC in attitudes, behavior, and total score (not founded). Details of these results appear in the complete study, Cooper-White, "The Therapist's Use of the Self," available through University Microfilms, Inc.

34. The complete questionnaire is available in the complete study, ibid.

35. Quantitative data were tested using the computer software Statistical Package for the Social Sciences (SPSS). Tests for difference, used to compare responses by discipline and by gender, included chi-square for nominal data and *t*-test for interval and ratio data. Tests for association were also run between subscales and with demographic data, including coefficient of contingency for nominal data and Pearson's *r* for correlations of ratio-level data. Multiple regression was run in cases where several correlations appeared to be interrelated. Qualitative data (responses to essay questions) was examined using content analysis by independent raters, plus narrative analysis of longer responses. Dictionaries were created to rate definitional responses; variables were created for specific enactments mentioned in respondents' narrative answers; and qualitative codes were developed for longer narrative discussions of experience and meaning, using the "nodes" method from the Sage NUD*ist software.

36. Ralph R. Greenson, "The 'Real' Relationship" (1971), in *Explorations in Psychoanalysis,* ed. Ralph R. Greenson (New York: International Universities Press, 1978), 425–40.

37. Stephen Pepper, *World Hypotheses* (Berkeley: University of California Press, 1982).

38. Irvin Yalom, *Existential Psychotherapy* (New York: Basic Books, 1980).

39. Some additional correlations included the following: Theoretical beliefs and attitudes about transference and countertransference as reported on the ATC mostly correlated negatively with enactments, particularly client enactments. Self-reports of clinical practices on the ATC generated mostly positive correlations with actual enactments, especially therapist enactments.

40. Heinz Kohut, "Introspection, Empathy, and the Semi-Circle of Mental Health," *International Journal of Psycho-analysis* 63 (1982): 397.

41. Carl Rogers, *Counseling and Psychotherapy* (Boston: Houghton Mifflin, 1942).

42. $p \leq .001$.

43. $t = 4.19, p \leq .0001$.

44. $t = 9.05, p \leq .0001$.

45. Male AAPC practitioners still outnumber women five to one at the Fellow and Diplomate levels. Initial sample selection had to be corrected for gender imbalance. This is due in part to a gender imbalance in the ordained clergy more generally (women still represent only approximately 8 percent of all clergy in denominations ordaining women). Nevertheless, a number of independent gender differences were found for which discipline did not factor in as a significant covariable.

46. Similar to findings by Ruderman, "Creative and Reparative Uses of Countertransference."

47. It should be noted that the qualitative questions on the TRQ were phrased in a carefully neutral way, so as not to elicit any particular type of response. In fact, the researcher's bias was a psychoanalytic one, predisposed to expecting many reflections about therapists' inner dynamics and unconscious material, so the absence of this came as a surprise.

48. Greenson, "The 'Real' Relationship." The very notion of a "real relationship," as Greenson first proposed it, depends upon a classical definition of transference and countertransference as distortions in perception of reality. Greenson's need to distinguish that in every transference reaction there is a germ of reality, and in all "real relationships" there is an element of transference, becomes less important from a totalist point of view, in which the "admixtures and blendings of real and transference components" (p. 429) are all subsumed under a totalist definition of transference and countertransference as the sum total of all feelings, thoughts, and reactions. Thus, when a therapist is working from a truly totalist understanding, the notion of a "real relationship" apart from the transference-countertransference relationship becomes irrelevant.

49. D. W. Winnicott, "Counter-Transference" (1960), in *Maturational Processes and the Facilitating Environment* (London: Hogarth, 1965), 164.

50. Franz Alexander, *Fundamentals of Psychoanalysis* (New York: W. W. Norton, 1948).

51. Université de Paris, "Rigorousness, Countertransference of the Researcher," Clinical Psychology 8th Colloquium of the Clinical Psychology Laboratory of the University of Paris, *Bulletin de Psychologie* 39, nos. 16–18 (1986): 739–838.

52. WCBS-TV News/*New York Times* Race Relations Poll, June 1990, cited in Maurice Berger, "A Pitiless Mirror Where Audiences See Themselves," *New York Times,* July 23, 1990, p. AR 5.

53. C. S. Berkman, S. G. Turner, M. Cooper, D. Polnerow, and M. Swartz, "Sexual Contact with Clients: Assessment of Social Workers' Attitudes and Educational Preparation," *Social Work* 45, no. 3 (2000): 223–35.

54. Ibid., also citing Glen O. Gabbard, "Sexual Excitement and Countertransference Love in the Analyst," *Journal of the American Psychoanalytic Association* 42, no. 4 (1994): 1,083–106; Peter Rutter, *Sex in the Forbidden Zone: When Men in Power Abuse Women's Trust* (Los Angeles: Jeremy Tarcher, 1989); and Herbert Strean, *Therapists Who Have Sex with Their Patients: Therapy and Recovery* (New York: Brunner/Mazel, 1994), among others.

55. Berkman et al., "Sexual Contact with Clients," 226.

56. Ibid., 229.

57. Nicholas Wright, *Mrs. Klein* (London: Nick Hern Books, 1988), 31.

58. Gabbard, "Consultation from the Consultant's Perspective," *Psychoanalytic Dialogues* 10, no. 2 (2000): 209–18; Gabbard and Lester, *Boundaries and Boundary Violations in Psychoanalysis,* 89–91.

59. Gabbard, "Consultation," 211–212.

60. Harry Stack Sullivan, *The Interpersonal Theory of Psychiatry* (New York: W. W. Norton, 1953).

61. C. G. Jung, "The Psychology of the Transference," in *The Complete Works of C. G. Jung* 16, Bollingen Series 20, trans. F. C. Hull (Princeton, N.J.: Princeton University Press, 1966), 163–326.

62. Judith Orr, review of *The Mutuality of Care* by Roy Herndon SteinhoffSmith, *Journal of Pastoral Theology* 10 (2000): 218.

63. Marie Fortune, *Is Nothing Sacred? When Sex Invades the Pastor-Parishioner Relationship* (San Francisco: Harper & Row, 1989).

64. Gary Schoener and John Gonsiorek, "Assessment and Development of Rehabilitation Plans for the Therapist," in *Psychotherapists' Sexual Involvement with Clients: Intervention and Prevention,* ed. G. Schoener et al. (Minneapolis: Walk-In Counseling Center, 1989), 401–4; and Gabbard and Lester, *Boundaries and Boundary Violations,* 92–117.

65. Richard Irons and Jennifer Schneider, *The Wounded Healer: Addiction-Sensitive Approach to the Sexually Exploitative Professional* (Northvale, N.J.: Jason Aronson, 1999).

66. Cooper-White, *The Cry of Tamar,* 137–38; Gabbard and Lester, *Boundaries and Boundary Violations,* 117.

67. Theodore Jacobs, *The Use of the Self: Countertransference and Communication in the Analytic Situation* (Hillsdale, N.J.: Analytic Press, 1989); Owen Renik, "Analytic Interaction: Conceptualizing Technique in Light of the Analyst's Irreducible Subjectivity," *Psychoanalytic Quarterly* 62 (1993): 553–71.

68. Jody Messler Davies, "Descending the Therapeutic Slopes—Slippery, Slipperier, Slipperiest: Commentary on Papers by Barbara Pizer and Glen O. Gabbard," *Psychoanalytic Dialogues* 10, no. 2 (2000): 220.

69. Barbara Pizer, "The Therapist's Routine Consultations: A Necessary Window in the Treatment Frame," *Psychoanalytic Dialogues* 10, no. 2 (2000): 197–208.

70. Davies, "Descending the Therapeutic Slopes."

71. Gabbard and Lester, *Boundaries and Boundary Violations,* 78.

72. Gabbard, "Consultation," 211.

73. Pizer, "The Therapist's Routine Consultations."

74. Arnold Goldberg, Panel on Ethics in Psychoanalysis, Institute for Psycho-analysis, Chicago, May 1999.

75. Pope, Sonne, and Holroyd, *Sexual Feelings in Psychotherapy,* 96.

76. Gabbard and Lester, *Boundaries and Boundary Violations*, 127.

77. Cooper-White, "The Ritual Reason Why: Explorations of the Unconscious through Enactment and Ritual in Pastoral Psychotherapy," *Journal of Supervision and Training in Ministry* 19 (1999): 68–75.

78. Gabbard, "Consultation," 67.

79. Pizer, "The Therapist's Routine Consultations."

80. Ibid., 205.

81. Cooper-White, "The Ritual Reason Why," 73.

82. E.g., D. W. Winnicott, "The Theory of the Parent-Infant Relationship," in *The Maturational Processes and the Facilitating Environment* (London: Hogarth, 1965), 37–55; *Babies and Their Mothers* (Reading, Mass.: Addison-Wesley, 1987), 17, 71.

83. D. W. Winnicott, "Playing: A Theoretical Statement," in Winnicott, *Playing and Reality* (New York: Basic Books, 1971), 41.

84. In a late paper, presented posthumously in Chicago in 1981 by his son, Kohut revisited his landmark 1959 paper on empathy, stating that both critics and supporters of self psychology had failed to grasp his concept of empathy. He reiterated that empathy is not some sort of telepathic activity or intuition, nor is it associated with any particular emotion such as compassion or affection. Heinz Kohut, "Introspection, Empathy and Psychoanalysis: An Examination of the Relationship Between Mode of Observation and Theory," *Journal of the American Psychoanalytic Association* 7 (1959): 459–83; and Kohut, "Introspection, Empathy, and the Semi-Circle of Mental Health," 395–407.

85. Kohut, "Introspection, Empathy, and the Semi-Circle of Mental Health," 397.

86. Kohut, "Introspection, Empathy, and Psychoanalysis," 459 et passim; Patrick Casement uses a similar term, *trial identification*, in *Learning from the Patient* (New York: Guilford Press, 1985), originally from Robert Fleiss, "The Metapsychology of the Analyst," *Psychoanalytic Quarterly* 11 (1942): 211–27.

87. Neville Symington, *Narcissism: A New Theory* (London: Karnac Books, 1993), 40, 42, et passim.

7. Toward a Relational Theology: God-in-Relation

1. Graham Ward, "Introduction, or, A Guide to Theological Thinking in Cyberspace," in *The Postmodern God: A Theological Reader* (Malden, Mass.: Blackwell, 1997), xv.

2. John Polkinghorne, Trinity Institute Lectures, Trinity Episcopal Church, New York, 1997; see also idem, *Quarks, Chaos and Christianity: Questions to Science and Religion* (New York: Crossroad, 1997).

3. As Johnson herself exhaustively catalogs (p. 210), there are numerous twentieth-century articulations of trinitarian theology, many of which could be considered relational. E.g., Jürgen Moltmann's influential idea of the Trinity as "divine society," *The Trinity and the Kingdom*, trans. M. Kohl (San Francisco: Harper & Row, 1981); John Macquarrie's rendering of the Trinity as primordial source, expressive dynamism, and unitive Being in Love, *Principles of Christian Theology*, 2d ed. (New York: Scribner's Sons, 1977), 190–210; Sallie McFague's feminist trinity of mother-lover-friend, *Models of God* (Philadelphia: Fortress Press, 1987), 35 et passim.

4. Elizabeth Johnson, *She Who Is* (New York: Crossroad, 1994), 192.

5. Ibid., 227–28.

6. Ibid., 228, citing Catherine LaCugna, *God for Us: The Trinity and Christian Life* (San Francisco: HarperSanFrancisco, 1991).

7. Leonardo Boff, *Holy Trinity, Perfect Community*, trans. Phillip Berryman (Maryknoll, N.Y.: Orbis, 2000), xvi.

8. Ibid., 1, 3.

9. Johnson, *She Who Is*, 228.

10. Milbank's trinitarian formulations may be understood within a larger trend in contemporary Anglican theology of understanding the Trinity as community, e.g., S. H. Ford, "Perichoresis and Interpretation: Samuel Taylor Coleridge's Trinitarian Concept of Unity," *Theology* 89, no. 727 (1986): 20–23; British Council of Churches, *The Forgotten Trinity: The Report of the BCC Study Commission on Trinitarian Doctrine Today* (London: BCC, 1989); J. O'Donnell, "The Trinity as Divine Community," *Gregorianum* 69, no. 1 (1988): 5–74; and Catherine Mowry LaCugna and J. O'Donnell, "Returning from 'the Far Country': Theses for a Contemporary Trinitarian Theology," *Scottish Journal of Theology* 41 (1988): 191–215, reviewed in Jürgen Moltmann, *The Trinity and the Kingdom*, xii.

11. John Milbank, "Postmodern Critical Augustinianism: A Short *Summa* in Forty-two Responses to Unasked Questions," in *The Postmodern God*, ed. Graham Ward (Oxford: Blackwell, 1997), 274.

12. Ibid., 267.

13. Ibid., 268–69. This idea echoes earlier formulations of the social trinity; cf. Moltmann, *The Trinity and the Kingdom*; and Boff, *Holy Trinity, Perfect Community*, esp. 118–19. In Milbank's attempt to work within a postmodern framework, a subtle shift has occurred in which the implicit ethic is not justice based on equality (cf. Luce Irigaray's critique, "Equal to Whom?" in *Differences: A Journal of Feminist Cultural Studies* 1, no. 2 [1989]: 59–76, reprinted in Ward, *The Postmodern God*, 198–214) as much as a nonviolence based on valuing differences. For a further discussion of Irigaray's critique of equality, see also Susan Jones, "This God Who Is Not One: Irigaray and Barth on the Divine," in *Transfigurations: Theology and the French Feminists*, ed. C. Kim, S. St. Ville, and S. Simonaitis (Minneapolis: Fortress Press, 1993), 109–41; and Grace Jantzen, "Luce Irigaray: Introduction," in Ward, *The Postmodern God*, 191–97.

14. Milbank's theology imports one of the central problems of postmodernist philosophy—that of ethical criteria. In his own words, "Postmodernism claims to refuse dialectic, but this is the instance of its failure to do so; it is right to make the effort" ("Postmodern Critical Augustinianism," 270). Like many postmodern writers, Milbank links violence with exclusion of the other, but he does not resolve the real social and political problems resulting from the inclusion even of oppressors (e.g., p. 273).

15. Milbank, "Postmodern Critical Augustinianism," 275. This line of thought draws in part on Gilles Deleuze, e.g., *The Logic of Sense*, trans. Mark Lester and Charles Stivale (New York: Columbia University Press, 1990); *Difference and Repetition*, trans. Paul Patton (New York: Columbia University Press, 1994); and Deleuze and Félix Guattari, *A Thousand Plateaus*, trans. Brian Massumi (London: Athlone Press, 1988).

16. Cf. ibid., 274–75.

17. Luce Irigaray, *An Ethics of Sexual Difference*, trans. Carolyhn Burke and Gillian Gill (London: Athlone Press, 1993), 7. Also cited in Ward, "Introduction," *The Postmodern God*, xxvi.

18. Milbank, "Postmodern Critical Augustinianism," 274.

19. First proposed by Mary Daly in *Beyond God the Father: Toward a Philosophy of Women's Liberation* (Boston: Beacon Press, 1985), 34–35; also in Virginia Ramey Mollenkott, *Godding: Human Responsibility and the Bible* (New York: Crossroad, 1987).

20. See, for example, Marjorie Suchocki, *God Christ Church: A Practical Guide to Process Theology* (New York: Crossroad, 1982); and John Cobb, *Christ in a Pluralistic Age* (Philadelphia: Westminster, 1975). I am using process theology selectively. Certain themes in process theology, especially a tendency toward binary formulations, are not so useful in constructing a theological model of multiplicity—e.g., Alfred North Whitehead's polarities of conceptual and physical, and God's "primordial nature" and "consequent nature," part V in *Process and Reality: An Essay in Cosmology* (New York: Free Press, 1978; orig. publ. 1929), diagrammed by Suchocki as a *yin-yang* in *God Christ Church*, 113. See also John Cobb's discussion of "binity" in "Relativization of

the Trinity," in *Trinity in Process: A Relational Theology of God,* ed. Joseph Bracken and Majorie Suchocki (New York: Continuum, 1997), 1–22. Such language in process theology as God's "feeling of the world" (ibid.) also—perhaps—ascribes an unnecessarily monistic and conscious subjectivity to God. Whitehead's category of subjective unity of "actual entities," including God (part III), does not encourage a normative model of multiplicity.

21. Bernard Loomer, "Two Conceptions of Power," *Process Studies* 6 (1976): 5–32; William Dean and Larry Axel, eds., *The Size of God: The Theology of Bernard Loomer in Context* (Macon, Ga.: Mercer University Press, 1987).

22. Ward, "Introduction," in *The Postmodern God,* xvi.

23. See, e.g., Elisabeth Moltmann-Wendel, *I Am My Body: A Theology of Embodiment* (New York: Continuum, 1995).

24. See, e.g., Delores Williams, *Sisters in the Wilderness: The Challenge of Womanist God-Talk* (Maryknoll, N.Y.: Orbis, 1993); Emilie Townes, ed., *Embracing the Spirit: Womanist Perspectives on Hope, Salvation and Transformation* (Maryknoll, N.Y.: Orbis, 1997); Chung Hyun Kyung, *Struggle to Be the Sun Again: Introducing Asian Women's Theology* (Maryknoll, N.Y.: Orbis, 1990); Ada-María Isasi-Díaz, *Mujerista Theology* (Maryknoll, N.Y.: Orbis, 1996); Mercy Amba Oduyoye, *Introducing African Women's Theology* (Cleveland: Pilgrim Press, 2001); and Virginia Fabella and Oduyoye, eds., *With Passion and Compassion: Third World Women Doing Theology,* trans. Phillip Berryman (Maryknoll, N.Y.: Orbis, 1988).

25. Ntozake Shange, *for colored girls who have considered suicide/when the rainbow is enuf: a choreopoem* (New York: Macmillan, 1977), 63.

26. Williams, *Sisters in the Wilderness,* 6; and Karen Baker-Fletcher, "The Strength of My Life" in Townes, *Embracing the Spirit,* 125.

27. Elizabeth Tapia, "The Contribution of Philippine Women to Asian Women's Theology" (PhD diss., Claremont Graduate School, 1989), cited in Chung Hyung Kyung, *Struggle to Be the Sun Again,* 100–101.

28. Philip Bromberg, "'Speak! That I May See You': Some Reflections on Dissociation, Reality, and Psychoanalytic Listening," *Psychoanalytic Dialogues* 4, no. 4 (1994): 533. On the intrinsic relationship between reflection and liberative praxis, see also Isasi-Díaz, *Mujerista Theology,* 116.

29. Bromberg, 522–23.

30. Mary Belenky et al., *Women's Ways of Knowing* (New York: Basic Books, 1986), 141ff.

31. Jürgen Habermas, *Legitimation Crisis,* trans. Thomas McCarthy (Boston: Beacon Press, 1975). Also cited in Belenky et al., *Women's Ways of Knowing,* 145.

32. Sheldon Roth, *Psychotherapy: The Art of Wooing Nature* (Northvale, N.J.: Jason Aronson, 1987), 441.

33. Frederick William Faber, "There's a Wideness in God's Mercy," *The Hymnal* 1982 (New York: Church Publishing Corp., 1982), hymns 469, 470.

34. Augustine, *Confessions,* trans. Henry Chadwick (Oxford: Oxford University Press, 1991), 3.7, p. 43.

35. Alfred Lord Tennyson, "The Higher Pantheism," in *The Holy Grail and Other Poems* (London: Strahan, 1870), 10.

36. Theophan the Recluse, in *The Art of Prayer: An Orthodox Anthology,* ed. Timothy Ware (London: Faber and Faber, 1966), 110, cited in Henri Nouwen, *The Way of the Heart: Desert Spirituality and Contemporary Ministry* (Minneapolis: Seabury, 1981), 76.

37. D. W. Winnicott, "Playing: A Theoretical Statement," in *Playing and Reality* (New York: Basic Books, 1971), 41.

38. Johnson, *She Who Is.* For discussions of a monarchical image of God, see also Sallie McFague, *Models of God: Theology for an Ecological, Nuclear Age* (Minneapolis: Fortress Press,

1988); and Marcus Borg, *The God We Never Knew: Beyond Dogmatic Religion to a More Authentic Contemporary Faith* (San Francisco: HarperSanFrancisco, 1998), esp. ch. 3.

39. Augustine *Confessions* 10.6.

40. Julian of Norwich, *Showings,* trans. Edmund Colledge and James Welsh (New York: Paulist Press, 1988), 287. In the original medieval English, see Edmund Colledge and James Walsh, eds., *The Book of Showings to the Anchoress Julian of Norwich* (Toronto: Pontifical Institute of Medieval Studies, 1978), 566.

41. Julian, *Showings,* 288–89; in the original medieval English, see Colledge and Walsh, *The Book of Showings,* 571. Cf. Augustine: "You were more inward than my most inward part and higher than the highest element within me," *Confessions* 3.7.

42. LaCugna, *God for Us,* 383, also citing J. Zizioulas, *Being as Communion* (Crestwood, N.J.: St. Vladimir's Seminary Press, 1985). See also Chung on "God praxis, not just God talk," *Struggle to Be the Sun Again,* 100.

43. For a discussion of the Trinity in context of liberation, see Boff, *Holy Trinity, Perfect Community,* esp. xvi–xvii.

44. Winnicott, "Playing a Theoretical Statement," 41.

Index of Names

Index of Subjects

Abuse, 5, 6, 7, 14, 32, 45, 50, 51, 104, 105, 136, 141–45, 147, 149–50, 166, 168, 196n8–10, 202n77, 212n46, 221n12, 221n16, 223n31, 227n21, 230n54

Addiction, 7, 89, 94, 107, 221n12, 221n16, 230n65

Advocacy, 76, 101–2, 116, 124

Affect, 5, 6, 10, 23, 48–54, 56, 73, 110, 128, 138, 140, 143, 146, 153, 157, 159, 161–63, 167, 173–74, 176–80, 183, 187, 198n25–26, 200n64, 201n64, 213n50, 213n57, 213n59

African American, 61, 63–65, 69, 80, 203n51, 215n1, 216n3, 216n7, 217n10, 217n22, 222n22, 226n8
  community, 61; health, 216n3; pastoral care, 204n51, 217n10, 222n22; tradition, 80; women, 63, 65, 69, 84, 216n6, 217n10, 219n22

Aggression, 18, 196n12, 213n63

Alcohol, 88–90, 93–94, 110, 144, 220n11, 221n12, 221n16, 222n21

American Association of Pastoral Counselors (AAPC), 28, 156, 202n7, 226n8, 229n45

Anger, 62, 67, 71, 84, 89, 92, 126, 161, 173, 177

Antisocial, 19, 110, 112, 199n46, 224n53

Anxiety, 21, 29, 37, 51, 71, 88, 89, 90, 105, 132, 133, 148, 149, 151, 155, 176, 177, 179, 203n26, 204n42, 206n56

Assessment, 7, 8, 61, 66–73, 74, 76, 81–82, 95–98, 116–118, 131, 137–52, 217n11, 221n16, 222n20, 222n21, 225n69, 230n53, 230n64

Asymmetry, 59, 186

"Basic fault," 14, 198n23

Bible, 67, 69, 76, 78, 83, 124, 154, 210n18, 232n19

Biblical, 28, 40, 75, 77, 118, 122, 126, 210n18
  John, 103, 118–20, 122, 126, 193; Luke, 75, 100, 126–27, 128, 153; Mark, 153, 188; Matthew, 75, 100, 188; Psalms, 83, 100, 101, 154

Body, 37, 52, 53, 70, 97, 117, 120, 139, 184–86, 190, 208n75, 213n57, 213n62, 217n11, 221n15, 233n23

Body of Christ, 75, 126, 129

Borderline (diagnosis), 19, 159, 223n40, 228n33

Boundaries, xviii, 4, 7, 32, 50, 58, 60, 82, 104–5, 108, 110, 111, 126, 127, 128, 131, 139, 148, 149, 151, 152, 156, 158, 159, 164, 166, 169, 170, 171, 172, 175, 179, 186, 187, 196n10, 205n52, 206n55, 213n48, 215n83, 220n8, 222n30–31, 223n36, 223n38, 224n64, 225n80, 226n7, 227n19, 230n58, 230n64, 230n66, 230n71, 231n76

Boundary violation, 7, 104–5, 108, 152, 164, 166, 169, 170, 171, 172, 174, 222n30, 223n36, 224n64, 227n19, 230n58, 230n64, 230n66, 230n71, 231n76

Brain, 17, 51, 99, 213n57, 213n61–62

Burnout, 4, 32, 97, 127, 206n56, 221n17, 222n25

CAGE assessment, 221n16

Caregiver, vii, 5, 32, 33, 35, 36, 48, 61, 70, 77, 104, 122, 124–26, 128–30, 143, 165, 181, 189, 196n6, 106n54

Case study, viii–ix, 63, 74, 96, 105, 131, 135, 148, 155, 195n2, 208n71, 213n63, 216n6, 218n14
  method, 195n2

Chaplaincy, viii, 7, 29, 97, 128, 131, 137, 193, 219n2

Chaplain, 2, 8, 27, 62, 82, 89, 91, 94, 95, 97, 101–2, 196n6, 219n1–2, 221n17
  campus 89; hospital 62, 82, 95; role of, 101–2

Child abuse, 48, 50, 141, 147, 149, 196n8, 202n77, 212n46